ENGLAND IN 1835

The Development of Industrial Society Series

Frederick von Raumer

ENGLAND IN 1835

A Series of Letters
Written to Friends
in Germany during a Residence in
London and Excursions into the
Provinces

Volume 1

IRISH UNIVERSITY PRESS
Shannon   Ireland

First edition London 1836

This I U P reprint is a photolithographic facsimile of the first edition and is unabridged, retaining the original printer's imprint.

© *1971 Irish University Press Shannon Ireland*

All forms of micropublishing
© *Irish University Microforms Shannon Ireland*

ISBN 0 7165 1780 9 Three volumes
ISBN 0 7165 1781 7 Volume 1
ISBN 0 7165 1782 5 Volume 2
ISBN 0 7165 1783 3 Volume 3

T M MacGlinchey Publisher
Irish University Press Shannon Ireland

PRINTED IN THE REPUBLIC OF IRELAND BY
ROBERT HOGG PRINTER TO IRISH UNIVERSITY PRESS

The Development of Industrial Society Series

This series comprises reprints of contemporary documents and commentaries on the social, political and economic upheavals in nineteenth-century England.

England, as the first industrial nation, was also the first country to experience the tremendous social and cultural impact consequent on the alienation of people in industrialized countries from their rural ancestry. The Industrial Revolution which had begun to intensify in the mid-eighteenth century, spread swiftly from England to Europe and America. Its effects have been far-reaching: the growth of cities with their urgent social and physical problems; greater social mobility; mass education; increasingly complex administration requirements in both local and central government; the growth of democracy and the development of new theories in economics; agricultural reform and the transformation of a way of life.

While it would be pretentious to claim for a series such as this an in-depth coverage of all these aspects of the new society, the works selected range in content from *The Hungry Forties* (1904), a collection of letters by ordinary working people describing their living conditions and the effects of mechanization on their day-to-day lives, to such analytical studies as Leone Levi's *History of British Commerce* (1880) and *Wages and Earnings of the Working Classes* (1885); M. T. Sadler's *The Law of Population* (1830); John Wade's radical documentation of government corruption, *The Extraordinary Black Book* (1831); C. Edward Lester's trenchant social investigation, *The Glory and Shame of England* (1866); and many other influential books and pamphlets.

The editor's intention has been to make available important contemporary accounts, studies and records, written or compiled by men and women of integrity and scholarship whose reactions to the growth of a new kind of society are valid touchstones for today's reader. Each title (and the particular edition used) has been chosen on a twofold basis (1) its intrinsic worth as a record or commentary, and (2) its contribution to the development of an industrial society. It is hoped that this collection will help to increase our understanding of a people and an epoch.

The Editor
Irish University Press

RAUMER'S

ENGLAND IN 1835.

ENGLAND

IN

1835:

BEING

A SERIES OF LETTERS WRITTEN TO FRIENDS IN GERMANY,

DURING A

RESIDENCE IN LONDON AND EXCURSIONS
INTO THE PROVINCES:

BY

FREDERICK VON RAUMER,

PROFESSOR OF HISTORY AT THE UNIVERSITY OF BERLIN, AUTHOR OF THE
'HISTORY OF THE HOHENSTAUFEN;' OF THE 'HISTORY OF EUROPE
FROM THE END OF THE FIFTEENTH CENTURY;' OF 'ILLUS-
TRATIONS OF THE HISTORY OF THE SIXTEENTH AND
SEVENTEENTH CENTURIES,' &c. &c.

TRANSLATED FROM THE GERMAN,
By SARAH AUSTIN.

THREE VOLS.
VOLUME THE FIRST.

LONDON:
JOHN MURRAY, ALBEMARLE STREET.
MDCCCXXXVI.

LONDON:
PRINTED BY WILLIAM CLOWES AND SONS,
Stamford Street.

CONTENTS OF VOL. I.

LETTER I.

LETTER II.

LETTER III.

LETTER IV.

LETTER V.

LETTER VI.

LETTER VII.

LETTER VIII.

LETTER IX.

LETTER X.

LETTER XVI.

LETTER XVII.

LETTER XVIII.

LETTER XIX.

TRANSLATOR'S PREFACE.

As HERR VON RAUMER mentions in one of the following letters, that, when he did me the honour to request me to translate them, he gave me full powers to omit, abridge, and alter, it seems necessary that I should say whether I have used this permission, and to what extent.

At first it appeared to me expedient to omit a good deal; particularly the author's statements of the past history, and actual state, of certain English institutions, with which it seemed fair to presume English readers to be familiar. But, on looking nearer into the matter, I saw that his arguments and conclusions rested immediately on these statements; and that if I omitted the latter, I took upon myself the responsibility of the question, whether Herr v. Raumer's conclusions followed from his premises; and, if not, whether it was the statement that was incorrect, or the inference unsound. And this I did not feel myself justified in doing. I have therefore given them all.

I have omitted (as I have carefully noted in the several places) certain summaries of debates in Parliament. These debates are quite recent, and references are given by the author to Hansard's reports of them; so that those who desire it can easily refresh their memory.

I have also omitted one or two personal allusions. There is, however, little of this kind for the translator to do. Herr v. Raumer's objects were certainly far removed from the vulgar and discreditable one of collecting and retailing personal anecdotes; and I think the reader will perceive a general feeling of good will, respect, and gratitude towards England and Englishmen, which would naturally preserve him from all inclination to disparage or calumniate persons with whom he came in contact; as his high integrity would make him recoil from the idea of betraying confidence reposed in him.

I think it right to mention more particularly one instance in which I have used my discretionary power, because it may be liable to misinterpretation; though, as it is of a personal nature, I do so with extreme reluctance. The name of Mr. Bentham occurs not unfrequently in the work, as the supposed representative of the opinions of an existing party, and always accompanied with expressions of disapprobation or of contempt. I have constantly omitted it, when used in this manner, and have only inserted it in one place, where some remarks on Mr. Bentham's opinions occur. Allusions and insinuations, founded on what I believe to be an entire misapprehension of the character and sentiments of Mr. Bentham, were, as I thought, neither instructive nor convincing; and to me, who had much cause to know the warmth, singleness and kindness of heart of the venerable man of whom Herr v. Raumer has conceived such erroneous impressions, would have been, I confess, most painful to write. I am anxious, however, that this unfairness, if such it be, should be understood to be the effect of grateful and affectionate regard for the memory of a revered friend, and to have no relation to speculative systems of politics and ethics, which it is quite beyond my objects and my province to affect to judge.

With regard to the opinions generally contained in the work, it would be presumptuous in me to attempt either to advocate or to criticise them; nor should I have alluded to them had I not seen that the author's politeness has led him to express a wish that they might coincide with mine.

I am far from undervaluing any expression of Herr v. Raumer's respect; and there are many subjects, among those within my reach, on which I entirely agree with him; but I must protest against being made a party to the opinions of any author whatever. It is the peculiar and invaluable privilege of a translator, as such, to have no opinions; and this is precisely what renders the somewhat toilsome business of translating attractive to one who has a profound sense of the difficulty of forming mature and coherent opinions, and of the presumption of putting forth crude and incongruous ones; not to mention the more individual feeling of the unsuitableness of any prominent and independent station in the field of moral and political discussion, to a person naturally withdrawn from it.

The remark which I have just made as to the opinions of an author, also applies to his statements. In three volumes containing so large a variety of subjects, treated as they arose day by day under public discussion, even a native might be expected to commit occasional errors with regard to matters of fact. I have, however, abstained from verifying his statements, or from suggesting any corrections of assertions, as to the accuracy of which a doubt might occur to me: inasmuch as I wished to exhibit a faithful portraiture of the author's views, and of the amount of knowledge which he possessed on each subject, so as to enable an impartial estimate to be formed of the weight due to his opinions.

The Memoir of the Author, translated from the 'Conversations Lexicon,' I have prefixed, because the lives and writings of the eminent men of Germany are not in general familiar to English readers; because it would be worth while to insert it, if it were merely to show the transition of the man of business into the man of letters —so utterly unknown in this country; and because the history of Herr v. Raumer's political life affords the best commentary on his political opinions regarding England. They appear to be such as a loyal subject of Prussia, where reform has so long been the exclusive business of the government, would naturally fall into.

The extreme haste with which this work has

been translated is, I trust, sufficiently obvious to disarm all criticism. This plea is, in ordinary cases, quite inadmissible; but, in my own defence I must say, that when I acceded to Herr v. Raumer's request, I had no idea of the length of the book, nor of the extreme expedition with which it was to appear in Germany: two circumstances which have not only compelled me to write with the greatest rapidity, but to request Mr. Murray to put a considerable portion of the work into other hands. By this I am sure the author and the public will lose nothing; but it is fair to the gentleman who has translated the third volume, and to myself, to say that I have not so much as seen it; and that, as far as translation goes, it is an entirely distinct work.

It would be unreasonable to look at a work executed under such circumstances as in any degree a work of art, or amenable to the tribunals of art. Whatever defects may be visible in the style, they cannot be so obvious or so offensive to any eye as they are to mine.

Fortunately, the nature of the subjects of which Herr v. Raumer chiefly treats, renders *form* comparatively unimportant, and the *matter* is, to the best of my knowledge and belief, faithfully rendered.

As the greater part of the translation was done at a distance from works of reference on English affairs, the quotations and extracts have been re-translated from the German, which will account for their not appearing in the precise words of the original.

Disclaiming, as I do, all idea of affecting to sanction the opinions of such a man as Herr v. Raumer, I may yet venture to say that I have gone through my work with the satisfactory persuasion, that I was helping to give utterance to the sentiments of an honest, courageous, faithful, and enlightened friend to the highest interests of humanity. Of the fitness of the means he advocates I do not presume to judge; but it is permitted to every one to share his earnest and hopeful zeal for the end towards which his wishes and his labours are directed.

S. A.

London,
March 18, 1836.

MEMOIR

OF

PROFESSOR VON RAUMER.

(From the 'CONVERSATION'S LEXICON.')

FRIEDRICH LUDWIG GEORG VON RAUMER,
the eldest son of the Kammerdirector Georg
Friedrich von Raumer, born at Wörlitz,
near Dessau, on the 14th of May, 1781,
went in his twelfth year to the Joachims-
thal Gymnasium at Berlin, where his residence in the house of the Kammerpresident
von Gerlach exercised a beneficial influence
on his education. In his seventeenth year
Raumer entered the university, in order to
study law and economical science. After
three years' residence at Halle and Got-
tingen he passed a considerable time at
Dessau, in order to obtain a practical knowledge of rural economy. In 1801 he was

appointed Referendary in the Chamber of
the Kurmark*, and in the next year attended
the Oberpresident von Bassewitz to Eichs-
feld, recently annexed to Prussia, where he
obtained much experience in business, and
was appointed assessor. But notwithstanding these occupations, he never, from the
time of quitting the university, lost sight
of historical studies, and in 1803 he began
at Berlin to collect materials for his work
on the emperors of the house of Hohenstaufen. During the first French war
(1806—8), he was at the head of a de-
partment of the board for administering
the royal domains at Wusterhausen, near
Berlin; he nevertheless found time to make

---

* The Mark of Brandenburg was formerly divided into the
Kurmark, or the Electoral Mark; the *Altmark*, or the Old Mark;
and the *Neumark*, or the New Mark. The *Kammer*, or Chamber,
was a financial board, which had the management of the public
domains, and the quartering and provision of the troops; it also
exercised a superintendence over the police. The branches of
knowledge requisite for a member of one of these chambers were
termed *Cameralwissenschaften* (translated " economical science" in
the last page), and a man who devoted himself to them was
termed a *Cameralist*. The old triple division of the Mark of
Brandenburg has now been abolished, and the Chambers have
been supplanted by the *Regierungen*, or Administrative Boards:
(see the English translation of Cousin's Report on Instruction in
Prussia, Explanatory Notes, p. xxix.). The term *Cameralwissenschaften* is likewise now nearly abandoned, and has been supplanted by the more general term of *Staatswissenschaften*, or " political sciences."—*Translator.*

considerable advances in his historical labours, and for the first time gave lectures
on history. In 1809 he was appointed to
the situation of a councillor at Potsdam
under the newly organized government, and
in 1810 he was called to Berlin, where he
was employed in the office of the Minister
of Finance. At this period, Prince von
Hardenberg, the Chancellor of State, not
only intrusted him with the transaction of
important business, but received him into
his house, and admitted him to familiar
intercourse. However improving and advantageous this connexion might appear,
yet Raumer soon perceived that business
of such importance engrossed his entire
attention, and that he must either give up
this employment, or completely abandon
his historical career. Three years before,
he had almost resolved, on the recommendation of Johann von Müller, to become a
professor in a university of Southern Germany : this idea now recurred, and he himself drew the Cabinet order, by which the
king appointed him a professor at Breslau
in 1811. Here he lived devoted to science

and his friends, until, in 1815, a journey to
Venice served still more to convince him of
the necessity of undertaking a longer tour in
quest of historical information. At the recommendation of the ministry, and especially
of Prince v. Hardenberg, the king gave him
leave of absence, and furnished him with
the means of travelling. He was absent
from the summer of 1816 until the autumn
of 1817, and found in Germany, Switzerland, and Italy valuable materials for his
history of the Hohenstaufen. In 1819 he
was called to Berlin as professor of political science; but, with the exception of a
course on statistics and public law, delivered after the death of Professor Rühs,
he has chiefly confined himself to historical
lectures.

Within the last few years Herr von
Raumer has established fresh claims to the
attention and respect of the public, both
by his constant industry in the world of
letters, and, in that of politics, by the firmness and courage with which he has expressed his opinions in times of excitement,
and amid the agitations of party. His great

historical work, 'The History of the Hohenstaufen,' spite of the honest criticisms of
erudition, or the cavils of mortified pe-
dantry, had established his reputation for
ever in the field of science. It has already
become national property; as the various
reprints of the work, and the attempts made,
with greater or less success, to adapt Raumer's representations of this, the Heroic
Age of Germany, to the stage, sufficiently
prove. Since that time his historical inquiries, no longer concentrated upon one
large and well defined field, but diffused
over various interests—branching out into
different veins—like modern history itself,
have not so completely engrossed all his
mental faculties, as that story of the early
times of Germany; which in its beginning,
its catastrophe, and its single tragical issue,
seems to embrace the personal relations and
interests of one vast and varied human life.

As he had formerly abandoned a brilliant
political career, in order to devote his entire
strength to science, so when he had attained
this object, and had completed his great
work, he again turned his labours to the

living intercourse of the present. Raumer is one of a class of German *Gelehrten*
(men of letters and science), till lately very
few in number, who have been able to recon-
cile the most rigorous demands of science
with the cultivation of those lighter and more
graceful tastes which fit a man for society.

He has proved that it is possible for a
German *Gelehrter* to be also a man and
statesman, a political writer, and a lover
and a judge of Art, without detracting from
the profoundness of his learning, or impair-
ing his power of application. Although
this is a truth which daily becomes more
and more evident, and must at last succeed
in overturning the old aristocracy of pe-
dantry which ruled in Germany, yet a man
must be endowed with singular ardour and
vivacity and be placed in very favourable
circumstances, to be able to labour with
effect in such varied departments as Raumer has done.

The part he has taken in politics has
given rise to many misconstructions,—as
must happen when party rage can see
only party opinions. Raumer is a truly

free man, who opposes absolutism in every
shape ; but most strenuously when it assumes that of the despotism of exclusive
political creeds, given out as the only means
of political salvation. As the absolute
principle in government changed with the
disturbed times and the agitations of his
country, his opposition changed likewise.
He has remained perfectly steadfast and
consistent ; but the objects of his opposition
have altered with time. Never having
sworn implicit allegiance to any party ;
praised up to the skies one day by those who
persecuted him the next : he is no political
weathercock, but a truly independent man,
whose vote thrown into the scale gives it a
weight which, in Germany at least, no party
man can add to the cause he espouses.
Being a steady and zealous royalist upon
principle, and a faithful adherent of the
Prussian government, as the representative
of that progressive civilization which marked
its course up to the time of the congress of
Carlsbad, he opposed the boyish chimeras
of the disciples of Jahn, and thus incurred
the hatred of the liberals, who denounced

him as a feudalist, a papist, &c.   When, on
the other hand, the idea of legitimacy dege-
nerated from a useful fiction into an idolatry
destructive of all intellectual life and progress; when, amid the incense offered at the
foot of the throne and the altar, the spirit
of feudal aristocracy began to rise from
its long slumber, Raumer's sound and
acute understanding immediately perceived
whence the greatest danger was likely to
arise.   The historian raised a warning, the
Prussian patriot a strong, and, at last, an
indignant, voice.   He who had strenuously
laboured with Prince v. Hardenberg (whose
greatest merit was, that he rapidly detected
ability, and immediately employed it in the
service of the country) at the regeneration
of the Prussian monarchy could not but
protest, in the name of the principles which
had guided that great statesman, against
those now acted upon, which threatened to
destroy that glorious work.   His voice was
raised alone.   His former fellow-labourers
were grown old, or spiritless, or were ele-
vated to posts in which they found it convenient to be silent.   Raumer's name was

now hailed with acclamation by the liberals; they extolled him to the skies, and
exulted in the accession to their party, of a
man who was as far from sharing in their
dreams of freedom, as in the short-sighted
obstinacy which had driven him (apparently,
and for a moment) into their ranks.

There may, perhaps, come a time when
the latter will again turn from him with no
less indignation, than the old Prussian *em-
ployés*—who cannot understand how a servant of government can presume to exercise
his judgment on the acts of his superiors—
now regard him with alarm and horror.

If the much-talked-of *juste milieu* consists
in endless tacking between two opposite
principles, Raumer belongs rather to one
of the extremes, than to that; but if the
expression is taken to denote that free and
neutral ground on which a man, resting
upon the basis of justice, and untrammelled
by party views, combats for truth proved by
experience, careless whether his blows fall
to the right or the left,—then Raumer
unquestionably belongs to the *juste milieu;*
and it were to be wished that Germany pos-

sessed more such political independents.
His treatise on the Prussian Municipal
System * had opened a paper war, out of
which Raumer, in spite of many important
practical objections, came triumphant; inasmuch as Stein, then minister of state—the
creator of that system—avowed the principles of the work as his own.

The work which followed upon this, " On
the Historical Development of the Notions
of Law and Government†," an acute examination of all the theories of government
from the ancient to the most modern times,
has gained greatly in completeness and
practical interest in the latest edition.

Two journeys to Paris and the South of
France brought him intimately acquainted
with the elements of French political and
civil life (if, indeed, these can be separated).

In Paris he was a witness to the great
catastrophe of July. With prophetic spirit
he foretold it, in letters which are printed

* " Über die Preussiche Städteordnung." Leipzig, 1828.
† " Über die geschichtliche Entwickelung der Begriffe von
Recht, Staat, und Politik." Leipzig, 1826 and 1832.

precisely as they were written to his family*. It was no difficult matter indeed for the experienced historian who, with untroubled, though anxious eye, followed the obdurate policy of the Polignac ministry step by step, to predict the result. But the heightened effects of the approaching storm—the language of exasperation—the admirable descriptions—the calm glance, accustomed to watch the current of events—combined with the liveliest sympathy in all that was passing, and the most profound reflections on government—all expressed with perfect ease and frankness to his family and friends, stamp these letters with a peculiar value; and they will remain not only an historical document, but a singular proof that the qualities which best fit man for his purely human relations, are more nearly connected with those of the politician and statesman than is generally believed.

Another fruit of this journey is, the Letters from Paris, in Illustration of the History of the Sixteenth and Seventeenth Centuries †.

---

* Briefe aus Paris im Jahre 1830. 2 B^{de.} Leipzig, 1831.

† Briefe aus Paris zur Erläuterung der Geschichte des 16 und

The historical inquiries which led him to
France were destined to a new work, upon
which he has been employed for several
years, and which will extend to six volumes
—the History of Europe from the End of the
Fifteenth Century*—of which three volumes
have already appeared. This work is distinguished by accurate and profound re-
search which throws new light on many
historical problems; by a clear perception
and distinct grouping of events. In the
number of the Historical Annual † for 1831,
he published his History of the Downfall
of Poland ‡, which is also printed separately. On the merits of this work there
is but one opinion in Germany. In Prussia,
the timid could not understand how a man,
employed and paid by the government,
could declare in print, that that govern-

17 Jahrhunderts. 2 B^{de.} Leipzig, 1831. (Translated by Lord
F. Egerton.)

* Geschichte Europas seit dem Ende des 15 Jahrhunderts.
Leipzig, 1832-3. Since this was written two more volumes have
appeared. (A translation of this work is in preparation, and will
shortly be published.—*Translator.*)

† Historisches Taschenbuch, edited by Herr von Raumer since
1830.

‡ Polens Untergang. Zweite Aufl. Leipzig, 1832.

ment had acted unjustly. Not only is the historian free to say this, but it is his duty; besides, it is to be observed that Raumer had always expressed the warmest sympathy in the calamities of Poland. Raumer had long been at issue with the High Board of Censorship (Obercensurcollegium), of which he was a member, and whose timorous views he could not share. He regarded the tutelage under which the press had lately been placed, and the severity with which it was exercised, (as displayed, for example, in the prohibition of historical works which had not yet appeared, and of books which the present intellectual state of the Prussian people rendered perfectly innocuous,) as unworthy of the government, and foreign to the spirit of the nation. In his petition for leave to resign his office, he expressed himself most strongly against it. This document accidentally found its way into the Journals of Southern Germany *, and excited an extraordinary sensation.

* Herr v. Raumer refers to this in Letter XVI., vol. i. p. 169.—
Translator.

From that time Raumer has enjoyed the profound respect of every independent and unprejudiced man. He is now member of the Academy of Sciences. In the Academy of Singing he is regarded as the champion of classical music, and in the Court Theatre of Berlin, over which he has some control, as councillor, he has laboured with all his power to keep up the moral influence of that establishment as a school of art.

Herr v. Raumer is in the vigour of his age, and the world may yet hope much from knowledge, integrity, and activity like his.

Among his writings are ' Six Dialogues on War and Commerce' (1806, anonymous). 'The British System of Taxation,' &c.; Berlin, 1810. 'The Orations of Æschines and Demosthenes for the Crown ;' Berlin, 1811. ' CCI Emendationes ad Tabulas Genealogicas Arabum et Turcarum;' Heidelberg, 1811. 'Manual of Remarkable Passages from the Latin Historians of the Middle Ages;' Breslau, 1813.

' Journey to Venice;' Berlin, 1816 : 2 vols
' Lectures on Ancient History ;' Leipzig,
1821 : 2 vols., in which the affairs of the
East and of Greece are brought down to
281 B. C. 'History of the Hohenstaufen
and their Time ;' Leipzig, 1823—25 : 6
vols.*

* See in Quarterly Review, vol. li. p. 304, an able account of
this work, attributed to Mr. Milman.—*Translator.*

AUTHOR'S PREFACE.

I SUBMIT to the public these Letters, on the present state and circumstances of England, with great diffidence. For though, from my youth, English literature and English history have occupied a large share of my attention, and so long ago as the year 1810, I published a treatise on the British system of taxation*, it is beyond the powers of one man to attain to any complete or profound knowledge on all the momentous and complicated subjects which I have here ventured to touch upon.

If, however, during my stay in England, short as it was, I materially extended and rectified my former information, I have to thank the extraordinary hospitality, politeness, and readiness to serve, with which so many persons of different

* See Memoir, p. xxxii.

characters, parties and classes received, assisted, and instructed me.

I can say with truth that these marks of kindness were not bestowed on an ungrateful man— though, to avoid endless repetitions, I have erased many expressions of gratitude, many eulogies on individuals, many accounts of invitations, and other civilities.

In no other respect, however, have I altered the contents of the Letters; they are printed just as I wrote them from day to day. I have even suffered some repetitions and mistakes to stand, because they show how the first impression was gradually modified and softened.

If I had separated the long essays on Pauperism, Reform in Parliament, &c. from my own daily history, perhaps the former would have appeared too heavy, the latter too trifling. They now follow in the order in which they arose; and the index will afford every reader the facility of finding what is attractive, and of avoiding what is repulsive to him.

If, notwithstanding all the kind and valuable assistance I received in acquiring the in-

formation I sought, the book is not what it
might be and ought to be, the fault rests with
me—rather let me say with my head; for my
heart has no share in it.

I wrote under the influence of the deepest
and warmest feelings, and I shall esteem myself lavishly rewarded if I shall have succeeded
in removing any prejudices, or correcting any
errors concerning Great Britain; and in showing
that the bond of a common origin, and the
amity of fourteen centuries, which have bound
together Englishmen and Germans, are still in
force, and ought never to be broken.

Berlin, October 15, 1835.

ENGLAND IN 1835.

LETTER I.

Departure from Berlin—Magdeburg Cathedral—Progress of popular
singing—Düsseldorf—School of painting—Steam-experiment on
the Rhine.

Düsseldorf, Thursday morning, 6 o'clock,
March 19, 1835.

WE Germans say " A man's will is his heaven:" if
so, I must be on my way thither, since my will to
travel in England is about to be fulfilled. As yet,
however, I do not see paradise quite so clearly open
before me ; and had not fatigue sometimes put an
end to all reflection on the road, I should perhaps
have come to the conclusion that travelling is, on
many accounts, a mere madness. The longer we
live the more we find that heaven is by no means
to be expected from any single act, resolution, or
event; but if any gleam of it is to be enjoyed in
this world, it must be from a combination of a great
number of circumstances, pursuits, and occupations.

From this profound introduction I might make
an easy transition to various complaints, concerning
seats too narrow, and neighbours too wide—soup
nearly all water, and beef boiled to rags, &c.;
but as I am not fond of complaints, and may

perhaps be entitled to make them with greater
authority after I have been in England, I will
leave all these lesser miseries, and only add that the
weather was so windy and stormy, that it took away
all inclination to put one's head out of the coach.
My travelling companions, who were often changed,
were neither bad enough to complain of, nor good
enough to write about.

I took advantage of the time I had in Magdeburg
to visit the beautiful minster, and to enjoy the admirable singing of the soldiers. ' In this matter, at least,
our adorers of the good old times can hardly deny
the progress of the age: all they can do, therefore,
is to admire the strength of the individual will, and
the self-reliance, displayed in the ancient and meritorious practice of singing out of tune.

Here, too, and indeed throughout Germany, one is
struck with the great progress made in another art
—painting. The school of Düsseldorf will send to
the next exhibition pictures in the most varied styles;
among them excellent landscapes of Schirmer and
Lessing, and the Jeremiah of Bendemann, which is
conceived and executed in the spirit and style of
Michael Angelo. I almost dread that the English
should discover this new El Dorado of art, and carry
off its treasures to their remote island.

In the Elberfeld coach was an English manufacturer of machines, who lauded my English very
much. I thought how you sometimes praise the
German of Frenchmen and Englishmen, who don't
speak a word right; this recollection moderated my
satisfaction. The pocket dictionary is in perpetual
motion, like a steam-engine.

Yesterday I made part of an immense crowd

assembled to see one steam-boat drag four Dutch vessels against the deep and mighty current of the Rhine. The experiment was made in order to ascertain the relative force and expense of steam and of horses. Steam-boats, steam-carriages, iron railways, and custom-house unions, formed the main topics of conversation in all the diligences, and I took as lively a share in it as any of the mercantile men.

In an hour I shall set out for Rotterdam, where I shall arrive on the evening of the 20th, and shall perhaps embark for London on the 21st.

LETTER II.

Steam-boats and postwagen—Travelling companions—Nymwegen—Rotterdam — Voyage to London — Aspect of the Thames — Historical recollections—Characteristic buildings—Grandeur of London.

London, March 23, George Tavern, Lombard Street,
7 o'clock in the morning.

ON escaping from the diligence, I had infinite pleasure from my voyage on the Rhine, in a steam-boat—that first of all modes of travelling ever invented. The song 'Travel on foot,' may now be translated into 'Travel by steam.' Walking, standing, sitting, lying, sleeping, eating, drinking, reading, playing at cards, succeed each other in turn, with the greatest ease; whilst the strange monster of a machine labours unceasingly, and drives on towards its destined aim with matchless rapidity. Compare this with our prisons of postwagen, and their manifold miseries of creaking, rattling, stinking, cramped legs, tobacco-pipes, stoppages, greasings, wedging, &c., &c., and it cannot be denied that although Nagler has greatly improved our posting, no one would seat himself in a postwagen whilst the highly privileged steam-boat travels more quickly by its side.

As the surrounding country was not attractive, I examined the company. It was composed of a physician of Rotterdam, who had studied in Berlin, but of course knew nothing of me (although, for politeness' sake, he afterwards tried to introduce the subject); a so-called professor who cured stammering, but who spoke, or rather stammered out, all languages very badly; three ladies from Nürnberg going to Rotterdam, one of whom was called Sonntag; and a Prussian subaltern of the 16th regiment from Wesel. Towards evening we arrived at Nymwegen, which, like all the towns of the Netherlands, is considerable, and has a fresh and thriving air. I could not get into the Dutch theatre, because they would not take Prussian money, and I was too lazy and tired to go to a great distance to change it. The inn was poor enough. A common smoking-room, in which I got a cough; no snuffers to the tallow-candles, and nobody to clean the boots. I went to bed early, as the next morning we started at day-break.

A fine morning, and beautiful sunrise; passed Dordrecht; and on the 20th arrived at the great, increasing, bustling, and lively Rotterdam. Our inland towns seem dead and insignificant in comparison with such sea-ports. Mr. C., the Prussian consul, very obligingly conducted me all over the town, showed me the most remarkable buildings, and the statue of Erasmus, and gave me a great deal of information concerning commercial affairs. What a confusion both in politics and commerce does it cause, that Belgium and Holland have now for four years been forced into opposition, and that the communication between them can only be carried on through all sorts of tricks and evasions!

Innumerable maid-servants were employed in beating carpets, sprinkling the houses, and scouring the streets; in doing which they made so much dust and dirt, or, at any rate, dust and floods of water, that one could scarcely make one's way through it. In a reading-room to which Mr. C. took me, I saw in an English newspaper that my historical letters from Paris have been translated into English, which I accept as a good omen. The bill in the New Bath Hotel was, as compared with German, French, and Italian prices, very high.

On Saturday the 21st I embarked on board the steamer Liverpool, the fare of which is three pounds. Here I found one Englishman of education, the sailors, and a Prussian, a French, and a Neapolitan courier. You may think that I contributed to my utmost towards the confusion of tongues in this Babel. I got great applause by translating German, French, and Italian into English; not indeed quite so smoothly as a steam-boat, but with sundry jolts, botches, and halts, like an old yellow Saxon coach.

I ate with great moderation on board the steamer, from fear of sea-sickness. But behold, all my fears were this time unfounded. The sea was scarcely more rippled than the Havel at Potsdam. I not only stayed on deck to enjoy the sunset, but as night came on, I was not less delighted by the bright stars,

and the flickering lamps in the rigging of our vessel.
I slept very well in my berth, but was on deck again
before daybreak, that I might see the sunrise.   The
day before, the sea was like the most beautiful chrysophras interspersed with strings of pearls, caused
by the motion of the steamer; now it lay before me
still and solid—it looked as if one might skate on
the ice-coloured surface.   One of the Englishmen
said that he had crossed the sea forty times, but had
never before seen it so calm. I felt as little agitation
or inconvenience as if I had been lying on my sofa.

When I came on deck early on the 22nd, we had
already left the North Foreland and Margate behind
us; on one side lay the island of Sheppy with its
wooded hills, and shortly after the somewhat lower
coast of Essex came in sight.   Vessels of every kind
swarmed around us like sea-birds; · but when we
reached Gravesend, their number increased so much,
and the beauty of the nearer and richly-cultivated
shores became so much greater, that I was involun-
tarily overcome by wonder and emotion.   Recollections of the gradual upward course by which this
happy island had for eighteen centuries been advancing to a pitch of elevation unmatched in the history
of the world; of the deeds and the sufferings, the
exertions and the errors, the wars and the conquests,
of her kings, her barons, her churchmen, and her
people—all came crowding upon me.   I enjoyed the
delight of that high and generous enthusiasm which
the ordinary incidents of life cannot call forth, and
my whole journey seemed to me to be justified and
rewarded by this single hour.   But this was only
rendered possible by my having been for years at
home in England, and my having attuned the

strings of my head and heart for this Æolian touch
of external impressions, by solitary historic labour.
I was much moved by the sight of Tilbury Fort,
where, in 1588, the high-hearted Elizabeth assembled and encouraged her troops, and thus caused
the overthrow of Spain, and a new organization of
the world.

From Tilbury to Woolwich the banks of the
Thames are bare; from Woolwich to Greenwich
there are increasing signs of industry and cultivation; until, on arriving at the Docks, you are borne
along through absolute forests of ships. Compared
with this, anything of the kind that I have ever seen
at Havre, Bordeaux, or Marseilles, is like a single
room cut out of this immeasurable palace. It is
true that here, as in Paris, the buildings are, at first
sight, in no respect striking; but their very peculiarities show a definite practical aim which distin-
guishes them from ordinary buildings, and gives
them an interest of their own. If, however, the
predominancy of mere utility and convenience, to
the neglect of all considerations of beauty, be
objected to English architecture, this crowd of ships
is so far more striking and important a feature in
the view, that all those of the land appear insignificant.

Here one sees that London is the real capital of
the world; not Paris,—spite of the pretensions of
its journalists and coteries. Paris is more pre-emi-
nently the Town, Germany the Country, but London
alone is entitled to talk of being the World.

LETTER III.

Aspect of London—Vastness and quantity—Progress of Society—
Paris and London contrasted—Self-reflection—Berlin politicians.

London, Tuesday, March 24th, 1835.

           *   *   *

So much for domestic and economical affairs.

I cannot give you much information at present on other points, for to-day the delivery of my letters of introduction begins. As to the first impression made by the city, the houses, the shops, &c., I can tell you much, and of a very favourable kind. Extent, circumference, quantity, are certainly by no means the measure of value or of excellence (either in cities, or in art or science); but, in this instance, the *quantity*, which surpasses that of all other cities in Europe, or indeed in the world, is of itself in the highest degree remarkable and imposing. Add to this, that in, and with, the *quantity* of London, the *quality* also displays itself. Thus, for example, you perceive wealth growing out of the most varied and complicated activity, which demands and exercises both body and mind; you perceive the talent of acquiring and of enjoying; the security of property, widely diffused and deeply rooted amid these masses. Destruction and decline are indeed the lot of everything human; but oaks take root, grow, and endure somewhat differently from mushrooms. Does not Rome still stand, after thousands of years of decay?—was not her second life still more pregnant and powerful than her first? And what has not Paris withstood? whereas London has hardly known the touch of calamity.   When our Radicals and our Conservatives prophecy England's decline with such easy confidence, because they have no other measure than the false one they take from France, an Englishman, nay, even I, may say, *Stat mole suâ;* and may add the prayer, *Esto perpetua!*

There are fools in all parties, but the genuine Tory is right in opposing the destruction of the Christian Church; and the genuine Whig is right in affirming that it is not the mere reading of a liturgy which constitutes a Christian Church, but the careful training and instruction of youth.   God grant that these opposite lines may at length produce the true diagonals of the forces, the just mean motion!   I have no inclination to meddle with revolutions, but it is my hope and my faith, that mind is more than body, knowledge better than ignorance, civilization than barbarism, freedom than slavery. Would Britons change for the better by becoming Kalmucs and Bashkirs; by learning to acknowledge, not the Ruler of the Universe, but the knout, as their immediate sovereign and lord? People cant a great deal (even in England) about election by grace; but is it not the most profound and inexplicable of all mysteries—yet to be received with humility and gratitude—that man should be born endowed with all the powers and faculties of humanity; born a Briton or German, and not a Kamschatkadale; born in our often-calumniated days, and not under the Seleucidæ, the Roman Emperors, in the time of the migrations of nations, of the Mongolian devastations, of the Thirty years' war? Nobody has a greater horror than I of the excrescences of the French and other revolutions; yet the truth of what

I say is incontrovertible, in spite of all malcontents,
whether saints or sinners.

At the first glance Paris appears more brilliant,
elegant, and attractive than London; but, on the
other hand, that impression is to this, what the
substitute is to the reality; what the tastefully and
skilfully plated ware is to the noble metal in the ore.
These dingy walls bespeak far greater riches; perhaps, too, an indifference to all the small expedients
by which comparative poverty strives to diffuse an
air of competence and of elegance around it by dint
of care and ornament.   In like manner the noise and
bustle of the streets has a totally distinct character:
in London it is always the tumult and clamour of
business; in Paris, the obtrusiveness and petulance
of vanity; in Naples, the throng of idleness; in Berlin, at the utmost, the naughty boys: *suum cuique*.

*   *   *   *   *

It was too late last night to go to Covent Garden,
or Drury Lane, and I was not the least attracted
by ' Lestocq ' and the pantomime.   I was, therefore,
alone in my room till bed-time, and was almost con-
strained (contrary to my custom) to self-reflection.
When a man has once succeeded in catching the
right wind for his course on the sea of life, it seems
to me very useless to be continually shifting the
rudder, as some prescribe.   *Sursum corda* raises one
above those minutiæ with which many torment
themselves, and render it unnecessary to run into
the little creeks and harbours of superstitious devo-
tion or puritanical observance.   From my earliest
youth my eyes have been directed towards those
stars of history by whom I am enriched, transformed,
and enlightened, and who bear me along with them

in their brilliant path.   Am I nothing, because I do
not see it to be my vocation (as many historians do)
to play, in my own person, the part of a precise,
morose, detracting censor?   I deny it.   Or because
I imbibe life from those magnificent spirits, am I a
mere parasitic plant?   I deny that also.   I have
shared in the joys and the sorrows of those noble
hearts; there have been hours in which I have been
Alexander the Great, and Charles V., and William
of Orange, and a Hohenstaufen emperor and pope.
There have been moments, when, like Melusine, I
was transformed into Cambyses and Philip II. This
is a richer and more pregnant existence than can be
understood by those who condemn and despise it,
because they understand the maxim, " Know thy
self," in so narrow and paltry a sense.

*   *   *   *   *

What would become of many of our great men, if
they were refined in a furnace of the construction
and the heat of the British Parliament for twenty-
four hours?   The well-conned phrases, the doctrine
of the necessity of numerous lines of custom-houses
within the German territory, for preventing the
entrance of political errors; the declamations on the
beneficent effects of villenage; of the restoration of
the middle ages (not in their chivalrous glory, but
their rude tyranny), and the like, would fly up the
chimney in this temperature, in the first half hour.
Below, among the dross and ashes, would be found
a few ministers, &c., and many of our Radicals; who
having put themselves forward with delighted self-
conceit, would burn their fingers and learn discretion.

LETTER IV.

Party at the Duke of D——'s—General impressions—Beauty of
the Women—English compared with Roman Women—Absence
of orders and decorations—English language—Specimen of
German spelling by English officials.

London, Wednesday, March 25th, 1835.

Mrs. A—— had the goodness to invite me to come
to her at eleven o'clock in the evening, that she
might take me to the Duke of D——'s. This,
therefore, was my first English " rout." For any one
who knows the persons present, it must of course have
a very different degree of interest from that which
a stranger can feel. On the other hand, novelty
has an interest of its own ; and from this superficial
but natural point of view, I shall tell you what
struck me, though it is indeed but a repetition of
what I have often heard. The rooms and decorations vast and magnificent; but such as are suitable for a man of vast fortune to possess for his whole
life, without regard to little variations of fashion,
changes of taste, and such-like French prettinesses.
The space sufficient for the guests; but here, as
elsewhere, excessive heat and crowding in the
neighbourhood of the ball-room. Almost all the
men were dressed in black coats and pantaloons,
black or grey stockings, black or coloured waist-
coats, black or white cravats. Nothing remarkable, or different from our usages.

The women in general very simply and tastefully dressed; ornaments rich, but not overloaded,
neck and shoulders bare. Some with long pendant

locks, none *à la Chinoise,* or with forehead entirely
bare; most of them with curls on both sides, as we
see in their engravings. Hardly anything was danced
but waltzes, for which the crowd of spectators left
very little room.   And now—how stands it with
the main point—Beauty? The task of Paris, who,
with his three goddesses, won his fame at so easy a
rate, was a light one compared with that before me.
Although very few men in London wear spectacles
in company, I took heart, put on mine, and began
my investigation like an experienced and severe con-
noisseur and amateur, as I am. But when I thought
this was the most beautiful, came a second, then a
third, and put my judgment to shame.   In my whole
life, I never saw so many beautiful women and girls
assembled in one place, and I now understand
Tieck's preference of Englishwomen, better than I
did when I had seen only travellers. Yet, even in
this moment of observation, of admiration, of enthusiasm, I do not give up the Roman women.   A
certain resemblance runs through the two nations,
though there are marked differences both of form
and of expression. The Romans, as it seems to
me, neglect the *tournure* of the body, and the appearance of the feet; the English, on the other
hand, the finished statuesque form and carriage of
the neck and shoulders.

The men had unquestionably far less of the
beauty appropriate to their sex than the women:
this I observed to be the case in the canton of Berne,
while on the contrary, in Naples, the men are much
handsomer than the women. The company consisted
of persons most eminent for wealth and rank; dukes,
ambassadors, &c.   Among us, uniforms, crosses,

stars, orders, &c., would have swarmed in such a company; here nothing of the sort was to be seen : every man decorated or encumbered with such things was a foreigner. Our taste for seeking or conferring distinction by trumpery of this sort always reminds me of the instructive fable of the turning-lathe of Uckermark. At one o'clock, before the supper or collation began, I went home. Concerning individuals another time. You must be satisfied for the present with these hints; I have no time for longer details, I must hasten to the Museum.

The improvement in ear and tongue for English goes on slowly. But really the English ought not to be very indignant at our ignorance of their tongue, when, in the official paper, printed in four languages, for the information of foreigners, Germans are instructed to provide themselves with an *Unfunst zettel. Die Versäumung dieses macht sie entweder einer Geldbuße oder Gefängniss Strafe fähig.* This is letter for letter.

LETTER V.

Breakfast—Catholics in Prussia and in Ireland—Political crisis—State of the present Ministry, and dismissal of the last — Sir Robert Peel—Whigs and Tories—A Landscape Painter—Beauty an aristocratical privilege in England.

London, March 28th, 1835.

I BREAKFASTED yesterday with Mrs. A——. We fell upon Irish affairs. A gentleman said that the rule of Prussia over her Catholic subjects was tranquil and undisturbed, only because she was a military despotism. I replied that from the first existence of Prussia as a kingdom, to the present hour, not a single sword had been drawn against the Catholics; that, on the contrary, they had been conciliated by justice, charity, confidence, and a scrupulous equality in the treatment of them and of the Protestants. In Ireland, on the contrary, where this system had not been pursued, a large armed force had, for centuries, been absolutely indispensable to the preservation of the country.

In despotic states, he continued, it may be possible to make such concessions to the Catholics without danger, but in constitutional states it is not so: England is not Prussia.

I replied that the Prussians did not feel the despotism he talked of, and that no such complaints were heard among them as were constantly uttered by the Irish. I added that while I denied the despotism of Prussia, I could just as little admit the justice of the reproach he threw on constitutional governments; that I was convinced it was perfectly possible for them to grant the vast benefit of religious toleration, whenever they should come to a just view of the subject.

*   *   *   *   *

For some days to come I cannot reckon on seeing or speaking to any body. The political crisis occupies all minds. Next Monday the affair will probably be decided. It is certainly not difficult to blow up the present ministry, but very difficult to form a new one that will last. Peel stands alone, and a man of such distinguished talents cannot be displaced without a loss to the country. But his

colleagues, who, as they pretend, are now anxious
to effect those measures which all their lives they
have stigmatized as destructive, are neither entitled
to be trusted, nor to be considered as statesmen in
any high sense of the word. On the other hand, the
moderate Whigs can reckon on no large or permanent majority, in case the Tories and Radicals should
combine against them. The number of the Radicals
of bad character in Parliament is very small; the
others ask for no more than we Prussians are so
happy as already to possess. The danger, "the
crisis," has been brought on by the manner in which
the king dismissed the Melbourne ministry, which,
as far as form is concerned, it would be difficult to
justify.

It was impossible that ministry could last; part
of it was already gone. Instead of proceeding
from these undeniable facts to demonstrate the necessity of some change, and to take means to effect
it in the most conciliatory way, the dismissal was
given (without any sudden obvious cause) so abruptly, that some of the ministers first heard of
it in the street; and this was done without the
rational precaution of first recalling Peel, and thus
avoiding Wellington's formless and needless *inter-
ministerium.* This has naturally exasperated the
Whigs, and Peel is compelled to ally himself with
the high Tories. He cannot now obtain the co-
operation of men like Althorp, Russell, Spring
Rice, and Thomson, and he stands with his plans
of reform, by no means in a *" juste milieu,"* but
with all his good intentions, and his great endowments, in a *" fausse position."* The thing cannot go
on thus. With this daily uncertainty of a majority

it is impossible to govern; and unimportant questions (such, for instance, as that concerning the London University) lead to partial defeats which lower the consideration of the ministry, and increase the audacity of its opponents. If Sir Robert Peel were well quit of his "tail," far more and better things might be hoped from him. With other allies, and other troops, he might begin a more glorious and successful campaign.

The stratagem which was employed to show the complete difference of the present Irish Tithe Bill from the former could deceive no unprejudiced person. This isolated measure will not tranquillize Ireland; the evil must be thoroughly remedied; and it is obvious to every man in what that consists. The Irish were originally oppressed and maltreated mainly because they were Tories; and now that the modern Whigs are willing to repair the injuries of their ancestors, the English Tories justify the injustice of their former adversaries, and regard it as the Palladium of religion and of the state. What changes and what confusion!—in words, names, opinions and facts!

People wonder that the Whigs have never long held their post at the helm, but have always been driven out by the Tories. This seems to me natural, and even inevitable. The former have always been the exciters and the executors of great changes, and in certain crises have undertaken the task of daring physicians; but their practice is less suited to the ordinary course of affairs; in quiet times people return to their old diet. Had the Tories always done the right thing at the right time, the Whigs would never have come into power. But they carelessly let the clock run down, and then the Whigs stepped in and wound it up. When they had done this they were driven out again. The idol of the ultra-Tories is the *vis inertiæ;* that of the ultra-Whigs, the *perpetuum mobile:* but motion to be true and accurate requires the centripetal as well as the centrifugal force ; and if this is true of matter, how much more so of the varied and intricate movements of moral life ! Our abstract statesmen, who affect so much importance with a few scraps of Haller and Sièyes, are mere quacks, who, knowing neither the diversity of diseases nor the nature of remedies, think they can cure everything with a universal medicine. In such abstractions, strangely inter-mingled with mere personalities, the French now too often deal; in England, everything assumes a more concrete form, and is therefore more tranquil and moderate. The struggle concerning present in-terests may be carried on in a mean and petty tone ; but the way, the matter, the means, and the end, are clear and obvious. Abstractions are like clouds, which assume a hundred different forms, and which men may run after for ever without catching anything real.

*   *   *   *   *

The day before yesterday I went to see the works of a celebrated English landscape painter. There is certainly a great deal to admire in them ; yet, ac-cording to my judgment, this artist is too much a *nebulist,* and does not sufficiently combine distinct-ness of outline with his lights and mists.

*   *   *   *   *

My admiration of the ladies I saw at the duke's was not exaggerated : on the other hand, those

whom I daily meet in the streets,' adorned or un-
adorned, are surpassed by the women I have seen
in other cities. Is beauty, then, in this country, a
privilege of the highest aristocracy? If so, the
ladies, even the most fervent Tories, will consent
to part with the " rotten boroughs" rather than with
that.

LETTER VI.

Whig Ministry—Causes of its formation and dismissal—Manner of
dismissal—Its effects—Points at issue between Tories and Whigs
—Lord ——— ——Prussian Church policy—Irish Catholics genuine
Conservatives— O'Connell — Causes of his power — Tithes in
Ireland—Attempts at reform—Private and public property—Mr.
Stanley's motion—London and Paris news.

London, Monday, March 30.

THE motion of Lord John Russell, to-day, on the
Irish Church, is so important that naturally enough
my morning thoughts are of a political colour.

The death of George IV.—the French days of
July—the desire to be more popular than his brother
—the declaration of Wellington against all reform—
these, and other causes, induced William IV. to form
a Whig ministry. It is, however, affirmed that the
majority of the powerful and the rich will continue to
be conservative so long as, for political reasons, the
law of inheritance is so extremely favourable to the
elder son. It is mere blind partizanship to deny
that reforms were necessary, or that some have been
accomplished with ability by the Whig ministry.
Let us put aside parliamentary reform as doubtful

and contested; other reforms of the greatest importance, which are now applauded even by their former opponents,—such, for instance, as negro emancipation,—are either effected, or under consideration. Among these I may mention the affairs of India, of the Bank, and some financial and legal reforms.

The first shock to the Whig ministry was the king's refusal (in my opinion a very well-grounded one) to create a considerable number of peers with a view to carry the Reform Bill. Wellington and Peel, to whom he applied to form a ministry, could not accomplish this without a dissolution of parliament, which was not then thought expedient; accordingly, the Whig ministry was recalled, and the Reform Bill, as you know, carried. Meanwhile, the king was hissed in public, which greatly diminished his zeal for, and his faith in, popularity, and lowered the consideration of the Whigs, whose power was based upon it. Next followed the resignation of Lords Grey and Stanley; the quarrel between Lords Brougham and Durham; and, lastly, the death of Lord Spencer. Add to this, that Tories and Radicals combined against the Whigs, as formerly (in a contrary sense) the extremes of the French Chamber against the Martignac ministry. It was necessary to modify the ministry, or to dismiss it. Coalitions are always attended with great difficulties; the latter course was therefore preferred. But for more than a century no King of England has resorted to it, except when the ministry has been repeatedly left in a minority. To this rule the King resolved to form an exception.

On occasion of Wellington's former unsuccess-
ful attempt to form a ministry, during the debates
on the Reform Bill, he and Peel had affirmed
that the majority in the Commons was on the side
of the Whigs only because they had the King's
name with them; that as soon as the King should
declare himself against them, and consent to a
dissolution of the Lower House, there would be
no difficulty in obtaining a decided majority in
favour of a Tory administration. It was also
alleged that the King attached extreme importance
to the maintenance of the Protestant Church without the slightest change, and that this was wholly
incompatible with the continuance of the Whigs in
office. All this was turned to account by the Tories,
and after Lord Spencer's death was urged with redoubled vehemence, and accompanied with efforts
and promises of all sorts. "The King's name is a
tower of strength," was their watch-word; and that,
doubtless, is generally the right watch-word.

Granting, however, that this course was just, useful, or even necessary, yet passion, precipitation, or
other causes, led to great mistakes in the form; and
as Wellington formerly threw out the Tories by his
unqualified declaration against reform, so, as it
seems, he has a second time placed them in the
most unfortunate position. When Lords Brougham
and Durham were at variance, Lords Grey and
Althorp had resigned, and the Irish members were
discontented, the necessity for change was, as I
have said, manifest; and Lord Melbourne was the
last person who could deny it. According to the
assertions of many, as to Peel's inclination towards
reform, he, perhaps, might have succeeded to Lord

Althorp ; or, if it were impossible to act in concert,
the Whigs must have seen their own weakness, and
resigned.   But instead of prudent negotiation, dexterous conciliation of opinions, soothing of tempers
and passions, came the sudden dismissal of the
ministry in a manner in which it is not usual or
decorous to dismiss livery servants.   Hence, irritation, coalition of parties before opposed, and elections of a very different complexion from what had
been anticipated; hence, also, Peel's isolated position ;   hence his unpopular colleagues, who with
incredible audacity have called themselves friends of
reform, though it would have been much more to
their honour to have continued to resist, as they
have always resisted, reform as dangerous and destructive ; hence, also, many other and obscurer
effects; hence Peel's plan of beginning with the
English Church as the easier task, and afterwards
proceeding to the Irish.   Now, he is compelled to
look the grand evil in the face at once, and to investigate and decide on the grand principle which is
to govern the whole line of policy.

The old Tory party (the new cannot yet be cha-
racterized) considered the entire property of the
Church, not only as unconditionally private property, but even all the existing divisions of it,
(such, for example, as the celebrated income of the
Bishop of Durham,) as the inalienable property of
him and his successors to all futurity : the Whigs,
on the other hand, maintain that it is allowable to
take from the too-much to add to the too-little.
The Tories affirm that Church and School are so
utterly distinct and severed, that the superfluous
wealth of the former must not be applied to the

wants of the latter; while the Whigs seek to show the contrary, and regard Church and School as one great and indissoluble whole. The Tories call it unjust and sinful ever, on any pretext, to expend the money of the Church or of the State on the Catholic church, and think it sufficiently favoured in being permitted to exist; while a portion of the Whigs do not entirely forget that the revenues of their church were derived from Catholic sources, and that, since the emancipation, the hostility of former days ought not to be kept alive. These and similar questions are now to be decided.

Lord ——— had made some inquiries as to the line of policy which had been pursued in Prussia with respect to the two churches, and had been referred to me. This was the occasion of my visit to him yesterday. From the engraving of him, I expected to see a tall, thin man, instead of which I found a small man, with a refined and intelligent, though not an imposing air. I told him what is well known to you all, and added that I could see no other means of establishing peace and unity, but toleration, mildness, and equity. Extirpation, banishment, and forcible conversion, are the three great means which were formerly employed to arrive at this end. Who is there that has the courage now explicitly to recommend any one of them? And what avail all the shifts and evasions by which men try to disguise, or to conceal, intolerance and selfishness? The much-abused Holy Alliance talks far better sense on this subject than Sir Edward Knatchbull and the Bishop of Exeter.

Let me return to Ireland. It remained catholic and royalist, in great measure, because the hated

English were protestant and republican; it was as conservative as even the Duke of Wellington could desire. For that reason was it so cruelly treated by the republican and puritanical tyrant Cromwell; and private as well as ecclesiastical property were confiscated with scandalous injustice, not even on alleged theological grounds, but on political pretexts. Charles II. did nothing for the redress of these iniquitous acts; and the success of William III., so advantageous to the liberties of Europe, laid Ireland alone—tory, conservative Ireland—in chains. For a century the struggle endured; slowly and reluctantly did England concede something to the claims of nature and of justice, while every step she set in this course was denounced by many as a dangerous innovation—as the destruction of State, Church, and Religion. At every step it was said that far too much had already been conceded. Too much? What, then, can explain the existence of such a man as O'Connell? Whence the possibility of the position occupied—of the influence exercised by O'Connell?—a demagogue of a shape and magnitude such as history never yet beheld. With the most powerful government in the world as his antagonist, a single man has become the counsellor, the trust, the ruler of a people; the poor and hungry voluntarily give to their advocate a salary larger than the King of England can afford to pay his ministers. That, reply some, is merely a consequence of the frenzy and the revolutionary tendency of our days. Is this a satisfactory answer? What, then, are the causes of this frenzy, and of this tendency? Has there been no irritation to account for the fever and delirium now so bitterly complained

of? Wisdom, and justice, and moderation, alone
can heal it; arbitrary, violent conduct certainly will
not. Treat the Irish Catholics as the Prussian
Catholics are treated, and O'Connell's revolutionary
fire, which you pretend is so vast and unquench-
able, is in that same moment extinct; instead of
flame, you will find but ashes, and the turbulent
declaimer will be reduced to order and to peace.

In all Demagogism there lies somewhat irregular, lawless, and indeed incompatible with law;
and therefore it is one of the first and most important duties of all governments to check such
deviations of the public mind, and to reduce them
to the path of law and order. But means conceived
in so narrow and one-sided a spirit,—so impotent,
nay, so destructive,—as those which, from the time
of Elizabeth to the present day, have uniformly
been applied to this evil in Ireland, must of necessity
raise up O'Neils and O'Connells. You know my
admiration for Elizabeth; but do you think that
because I admire her, I cannot understand O'Neil?
—because I honour Wellington, must I see in
O'Connell an incarnate fiend? By no means;
matters like these have two sides; so was it as long
ago as the days of the Gracchi and of the Consul
Opimius.

"Jene machen Partei! Welch unerlaubtes Beginnen!
Aber unsere Partei, freilich versteht sich von selbst."*

Let us take as an illustration the question of
tithes in Ireland. I shall put aside all party writings, and only notice what has been adduced and
admitted in parliament. Originally all tithes be-

* Those people are making a party! What an unjustifiable attempt!
But *our* party—oh! that, indeed, of course.

longed to the catholic church. They came into
other hands in Ireland, not, as I have already remarked, because the body of the people became
protestant and agreed upon the change, but because
Protestants conquered the country, and churchmen
and laymen of the conquering party seized and
appropriated the tithes. The Catholics, who remained faithful to the religion they had always
professed, thus lost the means of supporting their
church; they were forced to pay tithes to the very
small number of converts to the protestant faith, or
to the more numerous immigrant Protestants, military settlers, &c. Matters, therefore, stand on a
perfectly different footing in Ireland, and in those
countries where the inhabitants have become protestant, and have transferred the churches and the
church property to the new religion.

But this grievance of tithes necessarily assumed
a most aggravated form in Ireland; since, to the
general and natural disinclination to pay catholic
dues to Protestants, was added positive want of
means to pay at all. According to the letter of the
law, indeed, all taxes appear to stand on equal
ground, and imply an equal obligation; but both
science and experience daily prove more clearly, that
literal justice is here the greatest injustice in practice. A tithe levied on the gross product is especially fatal to agricultural improvement; inasmuch
as the tithe-owner participates in the profit, without
any share in the outlay or risk; and a superficial
arithmetical view of the matter is made a cover for
palpable injustice, so that the fraction $\frac{1}{10}$ might be
changed into $\frac{1}{4}$.

In this state of things discontent and resistance

grew to such a pitch, that, as long ago as the year
1822, the experiment of tithe compositions was
made*. It had, however, very little success; partly
because the bishops opposed it; partly because
other zealous friends feared injury to the Church;
partly, because many landowners resisted it, on the
ground that the calculation had been founded on
the entire superficial extent of soil, consequently
that grazing land was included, and the burden
thereby enormously increased.

In August, 1831, fresh complaints were laid
before Parliament. The tithes, it was said, often
amounted to more than the rent; and not only the
cattle, but the very beds of those who were unable
to pay, were seized and sold. All contracts and
moduses for the collection of the tithe in any other
manner, are liable to be declared void. It was
affirmed to be absolutely necessary to fix some term
of years during which the church should not be
permitted to agitate demands of a higher rate of
tithe. Claims of this sort often slept for fifteen or
sixteen years, and were all at once enforced, although
the tithe-payer was wholly unable to satisfy them.
As a pretext for this cruel proceeding, it was alleged
that the cost of levying accumulated masses of
tithe was less than that of collecting small sums.
For obvious reasons this practice, which was perpe-
tuated in England, was, in the year 1816, limited to
six years for Ireland, and was afterwards shortened
by a year.

Tithe, it is said, is a tax on land: to remit it is
neither more nor less than to make the proprietor a

* Hansard's Parliamentary Debates, ix. 239.

present, at the expense of the owner of the estate
which grants the remission.

On this I must remark, first, that every change in
a system of taxation implies, more or less, a present
bounty to some—a loss to others ; but this has never
been esteemed a sufficient reason for preserving to
all eternity every defective form of taxation.

2ndly. That nobody has asked such a thing
as an unconditional remission on merely abstract
grounds.

3rdly. That tithes are not a fixed tax on land
which can be conveniently calculated in making an
agreement with a new purchaser or tenant.

4thly. That their operation in Ireland is very different, and more oppressive than would be inferred
from general views of the subject ; for they are not
paid by the landlord, nor even by the immediate
tenant, but by the numerous sub-tenants. Hence the
portions of tithe are so small, that the cost of levying often exceeds the value. The form of payment
and the inspection of the tithe-payer far exceeds in
expense the value of the tithe. If (to take an
instance which was adduced in Parliament) the tithe
amounted to one shilling and eightpence, the tithe-
payer must drive his cattle six times to the place of
inspection, which, independently of all loss of time
and labour, costs him each time two shillings and
sixpence fees ; and this takes place a seventh time
on account of the so called vestry cess, or tax for the
church. According to this, the tithe is a tax which
costs the payer about fourteen times as much as it
brings to the receiver.

The picture drawn by Mr. Stanley, a well-known
friend of the protestant Church in Ireland, in his

place in parliament (December 15th, 1831*), is, if possible, still darker. " As soon," he affirms, " as the tithe collector, with his escort of police and military, is seen coming along a road to collect arrears of tithe, signals are given on every side, and all the cattle are driven away with the greatest speed. If he is lucky enough to find a cow, nobody will bid for it,—it is knocked down to him. But nobody will sell him fodder—nobody will let a cow so bought enter his stall—nobody will buy it. Even if, with great expense and delay, he sends it to England, he finds the dealers there informed of the matter, and resolved to buy no cattle distrained for tithe."

If the clergy have recourse to process of law, this, according to Mr. Stanley, often costs ten times as much as their demand, and, at last, the persons condemned to pay are wholly unable to do so. Good will and attachment are transformed into hatred, and hate and distress lead to crime: any happy, harmonious intercourse between the clergyman and his parishioners is totally out of the question.

Within three years there were 30,000 decrees issued against persons owing arrears of tithe, and only 2923l. 10s. 10d. collected in consequence; 4684 persons had each less than 1s. to pay. The entire arrear of tithe amounted to 115l. 6s. 4d.†

Sir Robert Peel said, that ecclesiastical property and private property stood on the same grounds, and must be equally protected by law. This maxim is true, and not true. Unquestionably the basis of all society is security of property; and any attempt to destroy this foundation of human prosperity and civilization is mad and wicked. On the other hand,

* Hansard, ix. 266.　　　　† Ibid. xviii. 1053.

reverence for private property may go so far as to be utterly incompatible with the idea of State, or of legislation for the common-weal. Moreover, private property and state or church property are *not* the same; the latter is granted or transferred only under certain conditions, and in consideration of the performance of certain duties.

Lastly, the State does, in fact, daily meddle with private property; increases or diminishes it, changes its distribution, &c. (as for example, by taxation, and by laws of inheritance). After such vast changes in all trades and occupations, is it not a strange thing that the maintenance of the whole Church should now, as formerly, be imposed on the landowner, and merchants, manufacturers, and fundholders be exempted?

In Ireland, however, as I have said, the landowner does not generally pay the tithe; and the opinion that the under-tenant deducts the amount of the tithe from his rent is erroneous. The press of miserable beings, who have neither bread nor home, is there so great, that they outbid each other, and regard a mere temporary shelter as a gain. If they are driven out of their little farms in any great numbers on account of their arrears, this merely increases the misery and the danger. The most advantageous thing that such an outcast can do, says a well-informed witness*, is to commit some crime which may get him into prison!

The main source of the evil, however, does not consist in the tithes alone, but in the total want of small landed proprietors,—in the excessive dependence of the poor on the rich,—in the excessive disparity

* Quarterly Review, xiv. 514.

between them.   How the laws aggravate, instead of
diminishing, this evil, I shall describe another time.
The levying the tithe on the proprietor, instead
of on the tenant, would indeed change the injurious
relation in which the clergyman stands to the latter,
but would bring upon the poor man only a more
rapid execution of the laws from his temporal lord.
It was a mistake to anticipate any adequate remedy
from this measure.

While these affairs were discussed at great length,
without arriving at any conclusion, there arose, in
November, 1831, a universal resistance to tithes in
Ireland.   With the aid of an extremely expensive
and overpowering military force, and of the most
rigorous measures employed during two months,
scarcely a tenth of the tithe had, according to Mr.
Stanley, been collected*.   " If (said Sir Robert
Peel) prescription affords no protection to the
Church, neither will it to the lay-proprietor†; and
if the conspiracy against tithes is suffered to prevail,
there remains no security for property or for life‡."
This observation certainly admitted one side of the
existing evil; viz. the help which the non-payers had
sought and found in themselves; but it did not in
the slightest degree touch the causes of this de-
plorable fact; and referred to antiquity as to a reason for suffering a state of things to endure, which,
against the steadfast and express will of six millions
of people, ought not to have been maintained for a
single day.

Still more one-sided and irrational was the assertion of Lord Eldon §, that the plan of Lord Stanley

* Hansard, xi. 137   † Ibid. 169.
‡ Ibid. xi. 421.   § Ibid. x. 1297.

and the government to abolish tithes, and give a
compensation for them out of the land or the rent,
was radically destructive.

The Archbishop of Dublin* remarked, with justice, that the tithe-system hitherto pursued could be
maintained only by the sword, and at the expense of
a civil war. The Archbishop of Canterbury and the
Bishop of London also declared, that it must be
altered, not only for the reasons already stated, but
because the clergy did not receive the half of the
tithes that were levied; that, indeed, many of them
were in such distress, that the government must
advance them money to preserve them from absolute starvation†.

How just were the observations of Mr. Wyse !
The moment, said he, that public opinion reaches
such a degree of force and unanimity as it now displays, a new state of things commences, and the
law is virtually abrogated, though it may continue
to exist in name. The sooner parliament confirms
the decision of the people the better. A wise government will observe and understand the signs of
the times, and take upon itself the direction of opinion; if it does not, it will be compelled to follow
where it ought to lead.

And again; the right point of time is already
lost ; and what, at a former period, would perhaps
have tranquillized the people of Ireland, would
now be regarded as superficial and unsatisfactory.
All the defects of the tithe system which I have
touched upon would have been sufficiently obvious,
had they existed between protestant payers and
receivers ; but, in Ireland, the Catholics have to

* Hansard, 1277.   † Ibid. 1122.

pay for protestant worship. The former affirm, that such a system is imposed on them by unjust force, and that no prescription can convert a wrong into a right. Scotland struggled for fifty years against a hated Church, and at length conquered; so also, in Ireland, will hatred against the present order of things endure so long as one spark of the sentiment of justice lives in the breasts of Irishmen. What would the Presbyterians, or the members of the Church of England say, if, while their own clergy were left to want, they were compelled to maintain a costly catholic church? And were there any real need of a protestant church of such magnitude? But the Catholics have to pay tithes to protestant clergymen who have no flocks. These ecclesiastical sinecures, with large revenues, are absolutely intolerable; while protestant curates, who perform the duty, often receive extremely little, and the catholic clergy nothing at all. On affixing the legacy stamp, it appeared that an Archbishop of Dublin left 150,000*l.*; an Archbishop of Tuam, 250,000*l.*; an Archbishop of Cashel, 400,000*l.** Does this show an equitable distribution of ecclesiastical revenues? Protestant churches, frequented by ten or twelve parishioners, are built with funds extracted from Catholics, while the numerous catholic population is crowded into a small chapel, or compelled, by want of room, to kneel on the earth before the door.

In one case, there are 66,634 Catholics to 259 Protestants, for each of whom, on an average, the former pay 30*l.* 17*s.* 9¾*d.*: in another, 120,000 Catholics pay, for 76 Protestants, 157*l.* 17*s.* 10*d.* each.

And these are the institutions which are called

---

* Hansard, xiv. 360-390.

sacred and inviolable! This is regarded as a wise distribution and employment of the property of the church! Blackstone, Burn, and other writers, show, that of the tithes a quarter belongs to the bishop, a fourth to the church, a fourth to the preacher or incumbent, a fourth to the poor. Nobody, however, thinks of any such division*. For every contribution levied on the subject, something is done or given in return; the Catholics alone, who are too poor to pay their own pastors and maintain their own churches, are to pay those who render them nothing in return, and who have not even the tyrant's plea— necessity. This is a phenomenon of which the world cannot furnish another example. In no age or country has such a demand been made by Catholics upon Protestants, or by Protestants upon Catholics.

This, and other arguments, induced the Ministry, in July, 1832, to submit, through the mouth of Mr. Stanley, a plan by which all tithes taken on an average of seven years should be commuted for a fixed tax, and should in future be collected and paid by the landlords†. This proposition, which passed the House of Lords, certainly contained, or at least aimed at, material improvements, but left the very important questions of the partition of the church revenues, the extremely small proportion of Protestants, the application of surplus funds, the claims of schools, and the participation of Catholics in them, entirely untouched. A Bill which was brought into the House of Commons, in 1834, was so altered, that Stanley retired from the administration, and the Lords threw out the Bill.

* Hansard, x. 70.   † Ibid. xiv. 95, 1413.

VI.]   IRISH TITHES.   **35**

Scarcely a member of the Upper House is now to be found who denies that this was a mistake. It wantonly postponed all reforms to an indefinite distance: it engendered fresh discontent in Ireland, and necessarily brought on the grand question which Peel is now trying to evade, but which Lord John Russell and his party are determined to bring to a decision; since it is impossible that measures of detail can acquire a consistent and rational character till the principles on which all are founded, and to which all refer, are established. Of these plans of the year 1834, and the debates upon them, I shall speak hereafter. You will already find this letter too long and dry, and will have enough to do to read it through.

But intelligence from England must of necessity have a different tone and character from that from France. There is less of the amusing and the piquant, but more of the instructive and the profound. Paris affords fireworks, which sparkle and amuse for a moment; but here the coal-fire of industry and thought burns steadily the livelong day. Whether there be not a still better light, and purer flame in Germany, or whether such be not possible, is a question I do not undertake to answer now.

All the several branches of legislation must certainly be materially affected and modified by the reform of parliament; I must, therefore, write you a long letter on that subject, since the details scattered in newspapers generally afford no comprehensive view; and principles and facts are placed in a false light, or wholly forgotten. Enough, or too much, for to-day.

LETTER VII.

Mr. Babbage's Calculating Machine—Philosophy and Mathematics
—Dinner party, its length and luxury— Climate — Museum—
Rhubarb tart—Vastness of London—Its metropolitan and com-
mercial character—Comparison with other capitals—Squares—
Parks—Regent's Park.

London, March 31, 1835.

IT seems to me expedient to keep my journal of
daily occurrences separate from the political circumstances and events of Britain, and to write any remarks on the latter separately.

On Sunday, then, the 29th of March, I was at Lord
R——'s, then at Hr. v. B——'s, and then at Charles
Babbage's.   The latter showed me and another
gentleman his calculating machine. I very soon perceived that an hour's explanation in a language with
which I was little familiar would not make a mathe-
matician of me : yet thus much I understood, that
the machine accomplished such extraordinary and
marvellous things by the mere motion of its relative
parts, that most certainly Mr. Babbage would have
been burned for a conjurer a few centuries ago.   In
his well known work you will find more on this subject. It was necessary to show, both mathematically
and popularly, how the possibility of such a machine,
and the necessity of its results followed, from the
very nature of mathematics. The relations and
working of mere quantities are, as it seems to me,
subject to such natural and inflexible laws, that the
mind may go to rest as soon as it has discovered
and applied those laws.   When that is done, there

really remains nothing more for the intellect to do; the remaining work may be committed to a machine. This necessarily leads to the conclusion enounced by Plato, that mathematics are essentially inferior to philosophy.   Raymond Lully's attempt to invent a kind of *philosophical* calculating machine is ingenious enough; but he could not catch thoughts in mathematical nets, or move them by mathematical machinery.

When C— M— gave me a letter to his relation, L— M—, he added, if you wish to save your money, you must not follow his advice.   I thought of this yesterday, when he said to me, that I ought to go into the boxes and not into the pit, and that they cost no more.   I accepted his invitation to dinner, which was not over till midnight.   If I am to infer from my own humble dinner the expense of this, it certainly cost more pounds per head than that does shillings.   In the first place, the furniture of the rooms was antique; hangings and furniture resplendent with silk and gold; the dinner service of silver, a silver hot plate under every plate, change of knives and silver forks with every dish, and of these dishes, as well as of the wines, a countless succession; servants in full livery, and all in white kid gloves.   Though I passed on all the strong wines, and drank but few of the healths or toasts, I yet drank too much.   This was almost inevitable, from the want of any drinks for quenching thirst, and the high seasoning of the dishes, which are almost as burning as the wines.   Several times, when all the plates were removed, I thought the business was at an end, but in a minute the table was full again.   At length we came to the rinsing the mouth; but instead of rising after this operation, it was only succeeded by new varieties of sweet dishes. Again the table was cleared, and a large silver basin was placed before one of the gentlemen. He poured a bottle of water into it, dipped in a corner of his napkin, and pushed the basin to me. It was filled with rose water, and was a new and very refreshing luxury to me. At length we arose; but the ladies only left the room, and passed their time in amusement or in ennui, while the gentlemen sat down again and did not rejoin the ladies of an hour. Cards were now introduced; but I made my escape, mindful of the coming day, and got home about midnight.

Till yesterday, the atmosphere was damp, foggy, and icy cold—of course unpleasant in the highest degree; now the wind has changed, and it is become milder. The Museum alone is as cold as ever; and thus, as in Paris, there is every possible facility for catching cold. I take, however, great precautions, and am a very industrious eater of rhubarb-tart. The first time this was offered me I was alarmed; but it is not made of the root of the Asiatic, but of the stalk of the English rhubarb, and tastes very like apple-tart—indeed apples are not unfrequently mixed with it.

This town is really immeasurable; and though perhaps there is no one point so beautiful and so rich as the Pont des Arts in Paris, or the exit from the Linden in Berlin; yet, on the other hand, fresh masses and rows of houses, palaces, shops, &c., continually arise before you. The number of coaches and equipages far exceeds all that can be seen in other cities; and you are led to think something extraordinary is going on in this or that street, whereas it is only the daily customary routine. That so many human beings can live together in such a space, carry on their occupations, and procure food, seems, in spite of all explanations, a miracle, and indicates a pitch of civilization compared to which the *latifundia* are at best but grazing-grounds and sheep-walks. All the continental capitals are capitals of one country only; London is the capital of Great Britain, and of so many other countries beside; and it is, at the same time, the greatest commercial city in the world. In this union of metropolitan and commercial city lies its peculiar character—its exhaustless principle of life and increase. Madrid, Paris, Rome, Vienna, Berlin, &c., are capitals, and act only as such; they are not, from their very position, power, and industry, also essentially commercial cities. Petersburg has some resemblance with London, but is far from being equally favoured by climate and situation.

A great and peculiar beauty of London is the number of the squares. They are not, as in Berlin, given up to hucksters and soldiers, or to horse-breakers and grooms; but, leaving the broad streets for such uses, they are inclosed with elegant iron railings, and the fine green turf in the inside (already beautiful) is intersected with gravel walks, and adorned with trees, flowers, and shrubs.

These squares, however, are far surpassed by the parks. Regent's Park, with its surrounding terraces and mansions, is alone of great extent and magnificence, and none but a frozen stockfish could really put in practice the *nil admirari* while looking at it.

LETTER VIII.

Irish Church—Lord Althorp's motion—Debates upon it—Grievances
of the Catholics—Kildare Street Society—Mr. Stanley's motion—
Opposition to it—Its success—Duties of a Statesman—Tory
doctrines—Church property—Violence of parties—Necessity of
concession—Irish Union—Improvement in Irish commerce—
Irish poverty—Middlemen—Poor Laws for Ireland—State and
prospects of Ireland.

London, Thursday, April 2, 1835.

I HAVE already written you a long letter about Irish
tithes; allow me to say somewhat more on this
point, and on the Irish Church. It may enable you
to understand what you read in the newspapers.

As long ago as the year 1830, this question was
warmly agitated in Parliament, and the excitement
was so great, that Mr. Stanley declared that the
attempt to ascertain the proportion the Catholics
bore to the Protestants of Ireland would only revive
and strengthen religious hatred.

The following views and facts were, however,
brought forward. The Catholics, it was said, are
willing and able to maintain *one* church, but not
two; they require a different partition and application of church property. And why should an
absentee rector receive 1500*l.* or 2000*l.* a-year, and
the protestant curate only 70*l.**? In one parish,
which may serve as an example, there are five
thousand Catholics, and twenty Protestants, of whom
fifteen are absent on the coast service. Nevertheless, the five thousand pay tithes to the rector,

* Hansard, vi. 778, 1307 ; iv. 572.

though he never beheld his parish or his five parishioners*.

Supported by such facts as these, Lord Althorp, on the 12th February, 1833, produced a plan for the reform of the Irish Church. He said that the accounts of the revenues of this church were exaggerated. The net incomes

of the bishops, were about .	£130,000
of the 1400 livings, . .	600,000
of the chapters, . . .	23,000
in round numbers . .	£800,000.

This statement has been again assumed by Lord John Russell as the basis of his proposed reforms. He added, however, that during the last century the ecclesiastical revenues had risen more than tenfold, while the number of the Protestants, and the burdens and duties of the clergy, had decreased. And yet the divisions of these augmented revenues was so unequal, that two hundred livings yield less than 200*l.* a-year, whilst the income of the Bishop of Derry was calculated at 22,000*l.*

Lord Althorp proposed to abolish the so-called first fruits, and to make certain deductions. That, 1st, Benefices which yielded from

200*l.* to 500*l.* a-year should give up	5 per cent.
500*l.* to 800*l.* „ „ „	7 per cent.
800*l.* to 1200*l.* „ „ „	10 per cent.
above 1200*l.* „ „ „	15 per cent.

2nd, Bishoprics which yielded under

4000*l.* „ „ „ „	5 per cent.
6000*l.* „ „ „ „	7 per cent.
10,000*l.* „ „ „ „	10 per cent.
above 10,000*l.* „ „ „	15 per cent.

* Hansard, vii. 22; xv. 561.

A board or commission composed of members of the church should divide and apply the revenue arising from these sources, for the good of the church. Even after these deductions, the income of the Bishop of Derry would, on a moderate calculation, amount to 50,000 Thaler*, and that of the Archbishop of Armagh to 70,000.

This proposition was further enlarged upon in the House of Lords by Lord Grey. The aim of it, he said, was to abolish a burdensome tax; to make a more equal distribution of the revenues; to provide for the building of churches, and a more advantageous cultivation of church lands; and to diminish the number of the bishops.

There are about 11,000 benefices in England, and 1306 in Ireland; in England, 26 bishops and archbishops; in Ireland, 22; in England, a population of 8,000,000 belonging to the national church; in Ireland, 1,000,000. If the number of Irish bishops were reduced to ten, each of them would still not have a fourth as many clergymen and parishioners under his care as an English bishop; indeed, the diocese of Lincoln alone contains as many as 1273 livings. According to a law of Henry VIII., every beneficed clergyman is bound to maintain a school, or in some way to provide for its establishment; a subscription of forty shillings has, however, been considered by the clergy as a satisfactory fulfilment of this law.

Every project for the reform of these and similar abuses was met by the determined resistance of Lords Londonderry and Winchilsea, Sir Robert Inglis, and other high Tories. They contended that such reforms were contrary to the King's oath,

* A Prussian Thaler (dollar) is about equal to three shillings.— *Trans.*

and to all sound principles; that they would bring
incalculable misfortunes upon Ireland and upon
England, upon Church and religion, and would
increase the power and influence of the Pope.

The Bishop of London and the Archbishop of
Dublin spoke in favour of the measure. They
maintained that the Irish Church was in the utmost
peril, if some means were not taken to reform its
abuses. Even the Duke of Wellington admitted
the expediency of the proposed plan; upon which
the Duke of Newcastle reproached him* with post-
poning principle and right to expediency. On this
the Bishop of London remarked, with great justice,
that it was a mistake in certain Lords to overlook
the consequences of their decision on this practical
experiment; that, indeed, the very question at issue
was—what was right? and that the existing system
could not be unconditionally approved, seeing that
their object and their duty was to discover and to
establish a new system.

The Duke of Cumberland's unmeaning reference
to the coronation oath was strongly contrasted with
the good sense of the last-mentioned speech. If
this oath really expresses absolute and eternal immutability, all one can say is, that the first thing to
alter is, so gross an absurdity. But, in fact, it pro-
hibits only partial alterations unsanctioned by Parliament. The words, the king shall maintain to
the bishops and clergy all such rights and privileges
' as by law do or shall appertain to them,' point, as
the Duke of Sussex truly observed, to legal changes,
and leave the possibility of such open.

Several alterations had already taken place in the

* Hansard, xix. 970.

Irish Church. Thus, for instance, with regard to the so-called vestry-dues, which were levied mainly for the purpose of church repairs. The assessment was made by a few Protestants, who compelled the Catholics to pay it; and if any litigation arose, the costs fell on the parish—that is to say, on the Catholics*. The churches, often badly built by jobbers, did not stand above forty or fifty years; and thus fresh burdens were continually imposed.

Although these propositions were carried (July 30, 1833)†, they have as yet had little effect on the state of the protestant church; but since nothing was done for the education of the people, or for the catholic church, the main evil remained untouched, and must necessarily become more flagrant with every succeeding year.

The reproach has unjustly been cast upon the Catholics, that, contrary to the hopes so often excited, they are not satisfied with any concession granted them, but are continually making fresh demands. But these concessions have always been merely matters of detail, and have left a host of evils untouched; which naturally excited double attention and inflicted double pain, when the hoped-for cure was found to have been but partial and imperfect.

The emancipation, for instance, in consequence of which rich Catholics could be returned to parliament, did nothing for the poor; improvements in the protestant livings only exhibited the wretched and unprovided state of the catholic church in a more striking light; and grants for protestant schools irritated the excluded Catholics, who are

* Hansard, vi. 768.   † Ibid. xx. 126.

now sensible to the want and the value of better
education.

I shall make this more clear to you by the aid of
some facts concerning the Kildare Street Society,
for the education of the Irish poor. Government had
granted a sum in aid of the contributions of this
society, which professed to receive children without any distinction of sects. It was indeed impossible to deny that catholic children were admitted;
but it is equally certain that two-thirds of the
schools existed, in practice, for the benefit of Protestants alone. Only one-third were attended by
Catholics, while five-sixths of the population of the
whole country is Catholic. The causes of this
strange disproportion were sought partly in the indifference of the Catholics to instruction; partly in a
prohibition of the Pope to attend these schools, at
which many Catholics took alarm. But the grand
question still remained unanswered. Whence came
this aversion of the Catholics? and what determined
the Pope to this hostile declaration? The answer
was this; that the Protestants were indeed willing to
receive Catholics into their schools, but on condition
that they read the whole Bible without comment;
in short, that they held it to be their right and their
duty to educate catholic children as Protestants.
This proceeding excited the distrust and hostility of
the Catholics, who naturally chose to have them educated as Catholics, or to provide for their education
themselves, as they best could.* It remained with
the government either to put a stop to this system,
or to make a separate grant for the Catholics. In
spite of the injurious language of many who called

* Hansard, Series III., i., 975; iii., 402, 1293; iv., 1259.

such a concession, a favouring of idolatry, the protestant and the catholic archbishops of Dublin united to make a selection of passages from scripture, suited to the education of children of both persuasions; and added to these, some truly Christian admonitions to love and unity. This, however, was violently attacked in certain protestant polemical journals*, as a profane mutilation of the sacred scriptures; and even some Tory peers, though loud in their complaints of agitation, joined in this fanatical cry.

At length government took the affair in hand, and on the 9th of September, 1831, Mr. Stanley brought forward a plan†, in pursuance of which all secular instruction of the children of both persuasions was to be common; while the reading of the Bible, and religious instruction, was to occupy separate hours. Government was to grant 30,000*l.* a year for the execution of this plan.

Nothing could appear more rational, simple, and natural; yet this again gave rise to a violent outcry on the side of the over zealous Protestants; it was " a withholding of the Bible‡." Only three bishops voted for the measure, two archbishops and thirteen bishops against it§. The Archbishop of Armagh said, that to adopt such a system would be to renounce the principles of Protestantism, and to render the Bible inaccessible. Lord Roden exclaimed, "That is an *infamous* system of education from which the unmutilated word of God is excluded. Ministers want to rob the people of the Bible‖."

It is evident that this was a silly and a malicious calumny. Nobody had thought of depriving the

---

* Hansard, Series III., x., 869, 886.   † Ibid. vi., 1249.
‡ Ibid. x., 262.   § Ibid. xi., 648.   ‖ Ibid. viii., 1271; xiv., 682.

people, i.e., the adult population, of the Bible; on the contrary, if Protestants and Catholics could not agree on any common religious instruction, each party was at full liberty to adopt its own system, at separate hours; and to read the Bible with its own children, entire or in part, with or without commentary.

On this occasion the Duke of Wellington observed, that a system which entirely severed Catholics from Protestants would be best adapted to the situation of Ireland. To this it might be replied, that where Catholics and Protestants live at a distance from each other, such a system is easily put in practice; but that where they live intermingled, some conciliatory plan must be devised; and that this becomes more obviously necessary in a country where the revenues do not suffice for one school;—how much less for two?

In spite of all the violent excitement, the abuse and the misrepresentation, to which this plan gave rise*, it gradually became more and more popular; and in six months the number of schools and of scholars increased more, than, on the Kildare Street system, in six years.

It is manifest, however, that with such extremely slender means, nothing like an adequate system of education in its various stages could be carried into effect for a whole nation; and thus we continually come back to the grand question concerning the partition and employment of the property of the Protestant Church, and the duty of the State to provide for the Catholic churches and schools.

---

* Hansard, Series III., xi., 637; xiii., 1182; xiv., 357.

April 3rd.

The ministers have drawn upon themselves another defeat. I must stay here long, and learn much, before I shall be able to comprehend their line of conduct. It is the part of a statesman to lead, and not to be led; to gain and to govern the confidence and the opinions of men by positive action, and not to defend himself behind mere negations, and suffer himself to be driven even from this defensive position, inch by inch.

If I set aside long and irrelevant declamation, and sum up impartially what the Tories propound, it amounts briefly to this. We are the Positive,—the upholders, and what we uphold and desire to retain, is the just, the dignified, and the salutary; our opponents are the Negative,—the pullers down, the destructives. Those who require that this destruction should originate with us, require something absurd and infamous; even defeat is more honourable to us, and more satisfactory to our own consciences, than victory can be to our enemies.

This, however, involves a *petitio principii;* it is obvious that the Whigs could easily retort, and have indeed retorted. It is impossible to arrive at any certain results, without full and accurate investigation; to endeavour to check inquiry into the state of Ireland, or to limit it to a single point, is like defending an untenable fortress.

Nobody can more utterly disapprove the confiscation of church property under shallow pretexts, or with a view to cover wasteful public expenditure, than I do; nor will I here presume to decide on the question of the alleged excess or inequality in the incomes of the Protestant clergy of Ireland; but that things *as they are* are in a state neither healthy nor justifiable, it seems to me utterly impossible for any man sincerely to doubt.

But, unhappily, party spirit is more intense and one-sided on this subject, than the world has a right to expect from the practised intelligence and good sense of England. I heard, for instance, a distinguished Tory clergyman say, that the abrogation of the results and the acquisitions of centuries, the sacrifices of Protestantism to Catholicism, by the House of Commons, was received with " devilish shouts." It was, he added, a grief and a shame that a few Scotch and Irish members, as ignorant as they are fanatical, should overpower the intelligent majority, and be able to destroy the Protestant Church of England and Ireland, which was never more admirable than now. Indeed it was evident that Lord John Russell openly aimed at the overthrow of the British Constitution, and the introduction of the American.

If the opposite opinions and sentiments are equally full of violence and exaggeration, where is that true and healthful mean, in which alone the pulse and power of life is to be found ?

Were it unnatural if some one, admitting these assertions of the Tories, but following them out still further, asked,—Can that be a good form of government, "a free and happy constitution," in which it depends every evening on chance and caprice, on the presence or absence, the good or ill-will, of a few members, how and by whom the vast internal and external affairs of Great Britain shall be conducted ? Certainly no administration can permanently go on

under this uncertainty ; it must have a secure preponderancy, and be, not governed, but informed
and corrected, by the opposition.

It is to be hoped that England will regain this
position. So long, however, as the ministry regards the abolition of sinecures for younger sons
as sacrilege ; so long as it does nothing, or next
to nothing, for the Catholics ; so long as it protects
unprofitable industry, and forgets the commerce of
Europe, it can hardly be expected to attain to that
security. It knows not what is the sort of education demanded by the present times ; and by such a
course of policy it will no more succeed in restrain-
ing and directing the present appetite for novelty,
than our ——, who, compared with English conservatives, are only *imitatorum pecus*. My remarks,
be it observed, on the defects and the dangers of
constitutional forms, are not at all meant to favour
the absolutism of a Camarilla, in which the affairs
of the nation are discussed, if not decided, by cham-
berlains and valets, ruined landlords and bankrupt
projectors, bigoted old women or profligate young
ones.

What will be done now about the Irish question ?
asked some one. It will be thrown out in the
Lords, replied B. P., a dignified clergyman ; or the
King, if an address be presented to him to that
effect, will admonish the Commons,—and then see
if they will venture farther. These two expedients
which the speaker seemed to anticipate as triumphs,
appeared to me pregnant with dangers, and symp-
toms of a violent disease. I am much more inclined
to believe that King and Lords must absolutely

cede what is reasonable, if they would not provoke unreasonable demands.

It was observed with great justice by Lord John Russell, that the mischievous cry for the repeal of the Union can be effectually silenced, only by concessions to Ireland. The Irish agitators put this forward as a bugbear, in order to force the English nation into granting to fear, what they will not grant to justice. If, said one, (with a show of reason,) we had an Irish parliament, our church affairs would long ago have been settled, whereas the English majority is invariably against us.

That many Englishmen describe the Irish and Scotch Members as ignorant and absurd, is the consequence of their one-sided, not to say their conceited, habits of mind. The Scotch and Irish must be counted as in all respects equal, or it is vain to expect that they can be satisfied with a union which is, in fact, but a subjection.

In Scotland, however, the results of the union of 1706 have long been so secured to the nation, that the dissolution of it is never so much as thought of; although many grievances, in regard to the quantity and the quality of political rights, existed till the passing of the Reform Bill. Of that another time.

As to Ireland, I must remark, that people are apt to forget, in their indignation against the existing evils, that things were infinitely worse *before* the union.

Mr. Wilson said in Parliament,* "Before the Union, the grossest abuses of the legislative power prevailed on every hand; monopolies of every kind

* December 11th, 1830, Hansard, i. 1006.

existed to the greatest extent ; venal patronage was
suffered, and every interest of the people was utterly
disregarded.   I will not revert to the barbarous
penal code by which bigoted Protestants have
so long ruled, and thought to convert, fanatical Catholics.   I shall confine myself to the one point of
the commercial relations of the two countries.   Till
1779 Ireland was treated in this respect completely
as a foreign country.   It was not till the December
of that year that three important restrictions were
removed.

1. The export of wool and woollen manufactures
to the European continent, and

2. The export of glass wares, and the import of
glass elsewhere than in England, were permitted.

3. The trade with the British Colonies in America
and the West Indies was thrown open.

In the year 1785 eleven of the true principles of
a fair and equitable commercial system were submitted by the Irish Parliament ; but in spite of Pitt's
recommendation, they were so altered and disfigured,
that the Irish would not accept them in their new
form.   Thus the evil went on till the Union of the
1st of January, 1801 ; when it was established, that
all grants, premiums, and encouragements to trade
should for the future be alike in both countries ; that
all produce and manufactures should be freely transported from the one to the other, and should pay
only such duties as were necessary to equalize certain taxes on consumption.

I subjoin a few but striking proofs of the improvement in agriculture and in manufactures in
Ireland since the Union.   The consumption was, of

Cotton,

1777, 429,000 lbs.	1826, 4,378,000 lbs.

Sugar,

1793, 184,000 cwts.	1832, 342,000 cwts.

Tea,

1777, 808,000 lbs.	1830, 3,887,000 lbs.

Coals,

1800, 364,000 tons.	1830, 940,000 tons.

Exported,

Linen,

1800, 36,000 yards	1826, 51,000 yards.

Oxen,

$180\frac{1}{10}$, 19,000	$182\frac{2}{8}$, 57,000

Sheep,

—— 10,000	—— 62,000

Pigs,

—— 9,800	—— 73,000*

Corn,

1810, 61,000 qrs.	1826, 375,000 qrs.	1830, 525,000 qrs.

If then Ireland has made such great, such unquestionable advances in the foregoing respects,
whence, asks every one in amazement, these complaints of the abject misery, the perpetual disquiet,
the countless crimes and disorders? None of the
single answers so often given afford any sufficient
solution: the causes are evidently manifold. I will
only suggest a few.

All this increasing wealth and prosperity affects,
in fact, only the landowners and the clergy—it does
not reach the mass of small farmers and under-
tenants, who outbid each other. While herds of
cattle cross over to England, and the granaries are
filled with corn, the poor have neither meat nor
bread; the Union, as well as the increasing prosperity of the country, only afford the rich double
inducements, and double facilities, for leaving their

---

* Browning's 'Political Condition of Great Britain,' p. 365. Hansard, xvii., 525.

country, and spending their lightly won incomes in England and other foreign lands. Poverty, neglected education, indifference to all civil institutions, hatred to ancient and modern oppressors, selfishness, rapacity—such are among the causes which have led to the countless terrific crimes, for the prevention or the suppression of which severe laws were, with great reason, enacted in the year 1832.

In the province of Leinster alone there were, in one year, 163 cases of homicide, 387 of robbery, 1823 of burglary, 194 of arson.*

Whatever there might be to allege against the high and the rich,—against bad taxes or bad laws,—nothing good could come of such diabolical acts as these. It was, however, necessary that the most accurate inquiry into the causes of these fearful phenomena, and the most vigorous efforts to remove those causes, should go hand in hand with severe penalties. With this view, in August, 1831, Mr. Sadler brought forward a motion for introducing poor-laws into Ireland. He alleged that the monstrous confiscations of former times had transferred a vast portion of the soil to foreigners; who are, and must be expected to be absentees. All business, therefore, — all intercourse with the tenants, — is in the hands of middlemen, who almost invariably (like the Fattori in Italy) oppress and grind the people, without pity or remorse†. Generally speaking, the people are industrious, contented with little, anxious for work, and more laborious than slaves, while they live the life of condemned criminals. The English poor are infinitely better off than the Irish, and the absence of all compulsory

* Hansard, xv., 1215; iv., 1097.   † Ibid. vi., 786.

provision for the latter has had no effect in increasing voluntary contributions. Absentees who yearly receive eighty or ninety thousand pounds, subscribe, in the most pressing emergencies, eighty or ninety.

In reply to this and similar statements, it was said, that it would be highly injudicious to introduce poor-laws into Ireland at the very moment when they were declared to be the greatest calamity of England; that the question, whether a compulsory provision for the poor ought to exist was extremely difficult and intricate, and depended on the various considerations of labour, wages, capital, rent, value of land, &c.; that the utmost caution ought to be used, not to excite hopes and claims which it might be found impossible to realize. Even O'Connell maintained that the introduction of English poor-laws into Ireland would only increase the evil, and aggravate the hatred between rich and poor. Mr. Sadler's motion thus fell to the ground.

It seems to me that in this case, as in many others, an impartial observer sees error in both extremes. The one tends to agrarian laws, to equal partition of property, or to fantastic St. Simonian theories; the other to heartless selfishness and self-isolation: whereas every society ought to oppose and to correct the severance of a portion of its members; whether of the helpless, through the neglect of others, or of the selfish, from want of sympathies.

Spontaneous benevolence and Christian wisdom can and ought to do much for the poor; but where these are not sufficient, government has a right to interpose for the mitigation of actual misery. It is a mistake, as I shall show hereafter, to reject all poor-laws on account of England's unfavourable experience. The evils arose out of the false extension given to the word *poor*, and the perversion and misapplication of originally good laws.

Legislation has often, and particularly in Ireland, done more for the object than the subject; more for the establishment and the maintenance of property, than for persons; far more (by taxes, corn-laws, &c.) for the rich, than for the poor. Here lies the main root of the numerous offshoots and ramifications of the revolutionary spirit. Mere moral admonitions have small effect, when the high are deficient in Christian charity, and the low in Christian humility.

Another circumstance to be considered is, the very different condition of the people in England and in Ireland. In the former, the average rate of wages is about from eight to sixteen shillings a week; in the latter, from five to eight: hence emigrations of the Irish to England are inevitable, until either all intercourse between the two countries is interdicted, or their condition is in some degree assimilated.

Such are the facts which drew from Mr. Wyse the exclamation, "Ireland possesses a population full of intelligence, and more numerous than that of nineteen of the states of Europe; a soil more fruitful than that of England; the richest mines and fisheries. She is, besides, a connecting link between two hemispheres. Such has God made Ireland; but what has she been made by man? Gifted with every physical blessing, she is a prey to every moral curse; the rich are absent, the poor are unemployed; Irish beggary, Irish misery, have cost England countless sums, and, with the course hitherto pursued, and the measures hitherto employed, the end is as remote as ever*."

Much has been done, or attempted, since these words were pronounced; and the recent votes of Parliament afford good hope that more still will be done. One of the greatest grievances was that of the grand juries, which regulated the payment of the police, the maintenance of prisons, hospitals, bridges, roads, &c.; appointed the contractors and other officers, and passed the accounts. All these local burthens, which were continually on the increase, fell on the farmer, the last under-tenant, and were assessed according to the superficial extent of soil, without any reference to its goodness or badness; a principle as unjust as the mode of taxing according to the seed-corn, introduced among us at the time of the French domination. The persons who made the assessments, and disbursed the funds accruing from them, were not the payers, and of course their proceedings were subject to no controul. It was impossible for the tenant to know beforehand what would be imposed upon him†; and the competition for farms I have so often mentioned, was too hot to admit of careful and provident calculation. Another evil was, that the grand juries were so entirely occupied with these financial affairs, that they had no time for their duties connected with criminal law. Thus, it is affirmed, 244 persons decided, in three or four days, above 5369 trials or actions; each trial, on an average, occupying five minutes.

* Hansard, iii., 1210 et seq.; i., 910.
† Since 1810 the gross amount has risen from 607,000l. to 940,000l. Hansard, vii., 838 ; xv., 955.

Since the year 1815 numerous committees have been appointed for inquiring into the state of Ireland, and have elicited very important facts. Mr. Stanley's judicious plans, proposed in September, 1831, and February, 1833, went to this: the civil and criminal business was for the most part divided; seventy old laws were repealed; the projects concerning local taxes were discussed before magistrates, with the aid of persons competent to the matter; the jurors were appointed in a better manner; contracts for public works put up to open competition; and the assessments laid upon the landowners.

LETTER IX.

London Shops—Hackney Carriages, Omnibuses—Clubs—Wealth and Magnificence of the Church of England—London and Southwark Bridges—Thames—English value for Time—Political Spirit of Prussia—Dinner at Lord M———'s.

London, April 4, 1835.

YESTERDAY I delivered letters in various parts of the town. The more I become acquainted with it, the more I am struck with its vastness and variety, its activity and wealth. The shops do not seem to me to surpass those of Paris in elegance and taste; but the prodigious quantities of goods which lie there make them appear, what they are—storehouses for the world.

The inscriptions and bills in shop-windows sometimes allude to the measures of government. Thus, a tea-dealer assures his customers that he will never have anything to do with "the miserable stuff called free-trade tea."

I have already spoken of the various sorts of carriages. The coaches with two horses are exactly like ours, and have no peculiar character, as the one-horse cabriolets have. In Vienna, there is nothing of the kind; and as to our droschkes, I need not describe their virtues or their defects. In Naples, there are small two-wheeled carriages, but quite open. The driver sits sidewards at the feet of the gentleman or lady, and drives leaning all the while to the right. In Paris, the driver sits in the cabriolet, by the side of the person he is driving. Here, the latter sits alone in the carriage, and the driver has a very narrow seat on the right hand, stuck on to the main body like a swallow's nest. Now, prove all, and hold to that which is best—or to the droschke.

In the great omnibuses six or seven persons sit sideways opposite to each other, and the entrance is from behind. They have names of all sorts, from 'Emperor,' 'Nelson,' and such lofty titles, to the names of the proprietors or of animals. Every ride, long or short, costs sixpence, or five silver groschen. The carriages are, however, much longer than those in Berlin, and the profits much greater. It is to be hoped they will soon be imitated among us.

*   *   *   *   *

I have been introduced, with the greatest and readiest civility, into three clubs—the Athenæum, the Travellers', and the Clarence. I find in them society, books, journals, and dinners; in short, all possible provision for body and mind.

*   *   *   *   *

Yesterday I dined with the Archbishop of C., an amiable, well-bred, and well-informed man. His conduct has been marked by uniform moderation; and though he has naturally endeavoured, to the utmost of his power, to uphold the Church, he has tried to remedy its defects. The difference between the high and magnificent church of England and her humbler sister of Germany was clearly to be seen even in this single dinner; the silver spoons, knives, forks, plates, dishes, and covers would alone have absorbed the whole stipend of any of our pastors. It was, according to the rigid presbyterian standard, too much; but little, when compared with the splendours of our old electoral archbishops and bishops. However, one rule is not good for all; and if the infinite disparity of fortunes among the laity is not only permitted but approved, degrees may be allowed among the clergy. A poor church is not the best, merely in virtue of its poverty; and where all the sons of the wealthy and the well-born shun the clerical profession because it offers no external inducement or consideration, defects, though of a different character, will arise.

London, April 5, 1835.

Yesterday I worked at the British Museum, then delivered a few letters, and saw, for the first time, the London and Southwark bridges. The latter is less traversed than the former, partly, perhaps, because there is a small toll. Both bridges are boldly and yet solidly built; broad, handsome, and imposing. The view down the Thames, from

London bridge, is peculiarly striking. What a
forest of ships, and what ceaseless activity! Compared with this, Paris is nothing, with its two or
three Seine boats. On the other hand, here is,
unfortunately, a total want of the beautiful quays
which border the Seine, and are the chief ornament of Paris. Rome and Vienna are equally without this great advantage; and Berlin possesses it
only partially.

*   *   *   *   *

No where is time more precious than here; the
value the English set upon it is conspicuous in
everything. There can be no stronger contrast
than their principles and their practice concerning
the employment of time, and the celebrated *dolce
far niente* of the Italians. Their whole history and
character may be derived or inferred from this
national peculiarity.

During my Berlin home-sickness, ——, to whom
I was introduced by ——, called on me. A well-
informed, clever man; but so much a citizen of
England, that Prussia and his native city, Berlin,
appear to him petty, and in all respects behind-
hand. I know how much of this is true, and how
much false; and, in spite of all my discretion, I
could not forbear saying that all trees did not grow
with the same bark, neither was it desirable that
they should; but that each *was* a tree nevertheless,
and had a bark of its own. I added, that it would
not be difficult to discover the dark sides of England,
nor to hold them up to view.

The assertion that Prussia has no political education, has only a partial and conditional meaning; for
all real education must eventually have a political sig-

nificancy, and a political influence; and if that of
Prussia is not conducted by means of parliamentary
debates and newspaper articles, on the other hand,
many parts of England are wholly without the first
elements of instruction. When events demanded
it, there was no more lack of political perspicacity,
vigour, and enthusiasm in Prussia than in England,
although they arose under other circumstances and
other conditions. I dissent, however, entirely from
the notion that it is incumbent on every man to
busy himself perpetually with politics, and to bestow
the greater part of his thoughts and energies on
public business. This French excitement seems to
me just as much a disease, as the apathy which is
displayed in some passages of the history of Germany. Where politics exercise an immoderate influence over the present, all other subjects of human
thought and action, however noble and refined, are
apt to fall into neglect. Nor do politics, in a high
and large sense, consist in the events or opinions of
the day; but in that statesmanlike science which
can only grow out of a profound acquaintance with
the past as well as present condition of mankind.
The old complaint, that history and science lose
their interest to men excited by the business and
the passions of the day, may be repeated with great
truth, even in London.

But I must return to my journal. I dined on
Sunday the 5th at Lord M——'s, the Under Secretary of Foreign Affairs. He is very well informed,
and has written a good history of the Spanish
succession war. His person reminds me much of
Niebuhr. Lady M—— sang some English songs
with great expression; but if I do not always under-

stand the words without the music, how much less
when concealed under musical tones. Lord M——
speaks German; Miss G——, whom I should have
rather taken for a handsome Italian than for an
English woman, speaks it still more fluently.

LETTER X.

State and Prospects of the Ministry—Cost of Elections—Sentiment
of an English Minister—Letter of Lord Holdernesse, on the
Ministry of 1757—Resignation of the Ministry—Sir Robert Peel
—Religious Tolerance—Power of Words—Idolatry of Forms.

London, April 5th, 1835.

I HAVE some hesitation about writing to you on the
political events of the day, since the newspapers give
you sufficient intelligence of all that *has* actually
occurred, and any conjectures or discussions on possibilities are useless; before my letter can reach
Berlin, one contingency is become a certainty, and
the other is of no farther interest.

On the other hand, these affairs are, just now, so
important, and so entirely engross the public mind,
that it would seem an absurd affectation to abstain
from all mention of them.

Since Sir Robert Peel's final declaration concerning Irish affairs, matters stand in a very curious
position in Parliament. The former of the two
alternatives proposed by the spiritual Lord mentioned in my last, " that a bill would be sent up to
the House of Lords, and there be thrown out,"
cannot, after that declaration of Peel's, be carried

into effect: for he has not made his staying in or going out of office dependent on *this* event; nor has he declared himself ready to adopt a modified form of the proposal of the committee, and thus to place the final decision in the hands of the Lords. He will prefer a second time to try (if the committee pronounces in favour of the measure) to maintain a majority by unconditional rejection; and, if this does not succeed, to resign. Hence it is very doubtful whether Lord John Russell and his party will adopt the other alternative—that of presenting an address to the King. He might certainly—in so far as he would be borne out by a majority—declare that the conflict and the " fair trial " were at an end. The Opposition wished for such a conflict, and there were three fields on which battle might be given;—1st. Foreign policy; 2nd. Finance; 3rd. Church affairs.

The first topic was entirely avoided, because a thorough change in European policy was not proposed, nor possible, and, indeed, would have been in contradiction to the principles of the Whigs.

As little could the Opposition accede to the motion of the Marquis of Chandos for the repeal of the malt-tax; since, during its ministerial reign, it had opposed and defeated this very measure. Sp——'s correspondent is wrong, therefore, in considering, as I see he does, the majority for ministers on this question as a test of decisive superiority. It proves nothing,—but that the Whigs will not vote against their old professed opinions; nor could they, if the present ministry had been thrown out on this question, have carried through a new system of finance. It was, therefore, with perfect justice, as well as sagacity, that the Opposition gave battle on the field of the Church; and especially the Church of Ireland, where abuses are the most rife and salient, and the ministry must necessarily have greater difficulties to encounter than on any other subject.

How, then, is all this to end?

Several issues are possible. In the first place, the people show, by their petitions, such an attachment to the ministry, that, in spite of all I have said above, Peel may be enabled, by their confidence, to continue at the helm. But then the approving petitions will soon be met by hostile ones; and, contrary to all constitutional forms and principles, more importance is sometimes attached to petitions of this kind, — though perhaps procured by disgraceful means,—than to that grand petition which is constitutionally enounced by the majority of parliament.

In the second place, the ministry, according to Peel's declaration, may tender its resignation to the king. If the latter accepts it, he is placed in the extremely disagreeable necessity of recalling to his councils the ministers he so abruptly dismissed. The powerful Tories are disappointed; and the irritated conquerors will endeavour to ensure the permanency of their power, by measures going far beyond the limits of former demands.

Or, thirdly, the now united parties will fall asunder, and will prepare the way for a fresh violent change, which will again throw the power into the hands of the Tories. If, on the other hand, the king does not accept the offered resignation, it is hardly possible to conceive of any consecutive course of government consistent with such an equal balance of opposite parties; therefore this supposition tacitly involves that of a dissolution of parliament. It is possible that the Opposition may lose votes by a new election; but it is also possible that they may gain. Such rapidly repeated *appels au peuple* excite the passions anew at every time, place an excessive and ever-fluctuating preponderancy in the hands of the masses, occasion monstrous expense, accustom the people to disgraceful modes of getting money, and have uniformly been unfavourable to kingly power. I am too much of an '*Historiker*' not to recollect with anxiety the numerous precipitate dissolutions under Charles I.

General ———, father of Lady ———, sacrificed his whole yearly income (20,000*l.*) at the last election, and is ready, if necessary, to make similar exertions again. You see how passionately the state of things is taken up—how decisive it is considered.

A member of the ministry, a very instructed man, and one of mild temper on other subjects, said to me, "We will grant the Catholics everything, but we will have nothing to do with them; above all, we will not live with them." This *granting*, however, amounts, at last, only to this—that they will allow the poor Irish (on condition of maintaining the rich Protestant Church) to give their own money for the support of their own clergy and churches. The latter part of his expression implies a feeling of antipathy amounting to hate, which is more injurious and exasperating than the extortion of money; and which, God be praised, has either totally disappeared, or sunk into perfect impotence in Germany.

April 7th, 1835.

As was to be foreseen, the Opposition, after having gained ground by Peel's declaration, has taken up an advanced position, and now requires that the new principle of the application of church revenues be adopted as the basis of the Tithe Bill. On this point their victory is not doubtful, after what has taken place. *This* battle the ministry will certainly lose in a few days. It does not at all follow, however, that the superiority will be decided in the same manner on other questions. The state of things now is extremely like that which existed at the end of the year 1757. I read yesterday, in Mitchell's papers, an accurate description of the latter, by Lord Holdernesse, then Under Secretary of State. He complains bitterly of disunion within, feebleness without, uncertainty and vacillation as to all propositions and all measures. Ministers, he says, have a small majority in parliament one day, the next they are in a minority : it is perfectly impossible to govern a country under such circumstances. —In short, the most hopeless strain of lamentation. And what happened? In a few weeks the leaders coalesced. The Duke of Newcastle and the elder Pitt were reconciled, and stood at the head ; plans were pursued in concert, and executed with the greatest promptitude ; and king, people, and minister, says Lord Holdernesse, are now more united and contented than perhaps they ever were before.

God grant a similar consummation now !

April 9th, 1835.

Yesterday evening, after a long agony, the ministry expired. That a Tory ministry, in the old sense of the word, could not subsist, I never for a moment doubted. The only question was this,— how far the Tories were willing to go in the path newly opened to them? The church question has demonstrated that the maintenance of the hostile principles and attitude of the religious parties appears to them a more sacred and imperative duty than their reconciliation. The peculiar form of expression which certain men have given to the Christian doctrine,—or rather, the differences created by different confessions, — are, in their view, the primary object; the fountain-head of that doctrine, the Gospel, the secondary one. Still more important in their eyes is that external constitution of the church which secures to them such large revenues. They regard the property of the Irish church as our nobles used to regard the sinecures in the cathedral chapters.

Peel's attitude was that of a very skilful champion of an untenable cause. His colleagues did not venture forth into day-light; probably from a fear of inconvenient parallels with their former speeches denouncing all reforms. Peel had to prop the tottering palace of aristocratical church establishments; single-handed, he had to defend it, and to beat back all its assailants; he was compelled to fight on disadvantageous ground. From the moment that he could not, or would not, induce his timorous or bigoted allies to take up a new position, from that moment his overthrow was certain.

My historical and theological researches have tended to produce the most intimate conviction in my mind that every kind of fanaticism is pernicious; that charity and patience are more efficient teachers than force and exclusiveness; that all Christian sects arise from the same well-spring of mercy and redemption; and that some diversities of opinion may and ought to be tolerated. Greater diversities have indeed been tolerated in England than in most other countries, and hence the contradiction of ecclesiastical monopoly is the more flagrant and untenable.

I regard the triumph of the tolerant principle, therefore, as a great, substantial, and permanent gain; even although errors of detail, or some acts of individual wrong, should be inseparable from it. Errors and wrongs were committed in the seventeenth century; but the principle of the right of private judgment in matters of religion, which the Independents asserted, has, God be praised, never been lost!

The prediction that the king would dismiss the ministry on the grounds I have mentioned, without any parliamentary necessity, has not in this case been fulfilled; the well-grounded practice which has subsisted for more than a century must now be reverted to. Nature has provided crises enough for the political, as well as for the human body; in neither case ought we to seek to multiply them. It is true the Tories regarded this as a means of averting a worse evil; as people inoculate the cow-pox to escape the more dangerous disease. Here, however, the natural catastrophe was not to be averted by the artificial one; the former might have supervened with double violence, and perhaps the cure will now be safer and more complete.

The Crown, as many lament, has again lost ground to the already excessive power of the people —

not without blame to its counsellors. But the real loss is that which threatens the aristocracy; the King is more likely to maintain the supremacy of his station, than the Tories the enjoyment of their privileges, and of their old immediate or mediate possessions—*i. e.* their ecclesiastical benefices and secular sinecures.

It is the trick of every aristocracy to represent itself as identical with the throne: thus the abolition of the beer monopoly was pronounced by the loyal among us to be the ruin of the authority and dignity of his Majesty the King. It is also the trick of democrats to represent themselves as identical with the people; and designedly to confound or intermix their personal interests with the interests of the mass. A true statesman will be on his guard against both these delusions, and take care to hold them in check, and render them innocuous.

What battles of words about words!—how often is an unmeaning or a dyslogistic word accepted as decisive of a question! One day I had briefly explained to an Irish Catholic member of Parliament the state of religious parties in Prussia. He replied, " Your *despot,* then, has *forced* upon you very useful institutions." The words *"despot"* and *"forced"* made me wince; and in spite of all my caution I could not entirely " close the hedge of my teeth " (as Homer says). I said, " Yes; if a kind father is to be called a *despot,* and the love and gratitude of children to be deemed *forced.*"

If ten votes in Parliament had given legal perpetuity to all the atrocities which have been practised against the Irish ever since the year 1650, would that have been no " despotism?"—and would the observance of a certain *form* have rendered the question of the *matter* superfluous? I repeat, how can men practise this idolatry of forms and formulæ, and be so enslaved to them that they either cannot understand anything which deviates from their darling usages, or peremptorily deny its very existence?

But we, in our turn, cherish errors which are perhaps not less in degree, though different in kind.

LETTER XI.

Philharmonic Concert—Comparison of London and Paris Music— Mr. Hallam—Sir F. Palgrave—Mr. Cooper.

London, April 7, 1835.

Yesterday evening, Mr. M———— took me to the Philharmonic concert. I ought to be doubly grateful to him, since it is very difficult to get tickets for this exclusive assembly. The room is large, lighted with ten chandeliers, and the roof is arched. Between the windows (which in the evening are mirrors) are Corinthian pilasters. There are no other decorations worth mentioning. At one end of the room is a sort of royal box supported by pillars; at the other the orchestra, which rises very abruptly. The centre is filled with benches, and three rows run along each side, as in our Academy of Singing.

The first thing was a symphony of Maurer, which bore marks of industry and originality, but was too long, and entirely in the modern, overloaded chromatic style.

Next, the tenor song out of Haydn's 'Orfeo,' remarkable for its simplicity, more especially when contrasted with the symphony. Mr. Parry's voice is soft and agreeable, but he wants force and animation.

Aria, out of the 'Donna del Lago,' sung by Mdle. Brambilla, *Elena, o tu ch' io chiamo.* Often as I have heard Rossiniades, I cannot help wondering afresh every time at the music which this audacious composer sets to the words before him. It is quite impossible to guess the melodies from the words, or to infer the words from the melodies. Mdle. Brambilla, a mezzo-soprano, sang the *colorature* so well and so piano, that one could make nothing distinct out of such sweet quavering, and then dropped fortissimo to the lowest notes of her voice,— to the admiration of the audience; but, in my opinion, in a manner neither feminine nor sublime, but simply coarse and mannish. It is not necessary for me to enlarge upon this manner, which Pisaroni, though with far different powers and skill, brought into fashion.

Overture to 'Leonore'—the old one, which is inferior to the new.

Second Act. — Mozart's Symphony 'Jupiter.' I immediately concluded that, under this name, the symphony in C sharp must be meant; and I was not mistaken : without question the most brilliant thing of the evening.

Scena out of Spohr's 'Pietro di Albano,' sung by Mrs. Bishop. If the modern Italians do not trouble themselves about the *general* meaning of the text of an air, on the other hand the modern Germans are in danger of falling into the opposite fault, of laboriously running after the expression of each single word. Mrs. Bishop is but a second-rate singer; very inferior to Mad. Grünbaum, as Mdlle. Brambilla is to Mdlle. Hahnel.

Mori had studied Beethoven's violin concerto and played it accurately; but it seemed to me to want the necessary inspiration. He is certainly inferior to the great French and German masters.

In one of Mozart's quintetts, Mr. Wilman played the clarionet with great sweetness of tone and beauty of style.

A terzetto from ' Cosi fan tutte,' and the overture to Weber's ' Euryanthe,' were to follow. But as I have often heard the former in greater perfection than I could have heard it here, you will not blame me for going away. As it was, I did not get to bed till midnight.

If I may venture, after one concert, to compare London with Paris, the result, on the whole, is this. The mass of instruments may be equal; but the effect is better in the Salle at Paris, and the French performers on the stringed and wind instruments seem to me more thorough artists than the English. In London, you hear distinctly that the music is produced by many; whereas in Paris it appears as if the whole were the work of one mind and one hand. Like the half shadows and the flickering lights on a landscape, so I often thought I perceived uncertainties and tremblings of tone, though the main stream flowed on its regular course. In Paris, my expectations, as to instrumental music, were far exceeded: here, they are in a degree disappointed, because I had heard people assert that it is doubtful which capital has the pre-eminence. In both, vocal music seems quite subordinate.

*   *   *   *   *

That Mr. Hallam is a very distinguished writer everybody knows. I have to add, that he is a no less agreeable man. He had the kindness to invite Sir F. Palgrave and Mr. Cooper to meet me. The former is the author of an excellent history of England at an early period; the latter has arranged a great mass of historical documents, of which he has given a learned and accurate report in two volumes, and has superintended the printing of much important matter. Both these gentlemen testified the greatest readiness to serve me; so that, both scientifically and socially, I am in danger of falling into an *embarras de richesses*.

The number of letters of introduction has been raised to a hundred and twelve by your last large packet. I deliver them gradually: many have no effect, while others produce unexpected results. The best are those which are connected with an interest in my labours.

S——'s caution, "That one must go everywhere in a carriage, or one passes for nobody," is either an old fable, or an antiquated truth. Judging by the descriptions and the warnings that one often hears in Germany, or receives on the road, one must needs believe that most Englishmen are fools themselves, or take foreigners to be so. This is mere absurd talk. They are, in all respects, as reasonable as other reasonable men in Europe; and whatever their peculiarities or their prejudices on this point may be, they do not manifest them. So, too,

in their dress; there is nothing at all remarkable;
and even the great talk about their extravagant
supply of clean linen is groundless. I see what
I have seen everywhere else, all possible gradations of fine and coarse linen; and, indeed, the
frequent use of cotton would greatly shock our
female critics. The French and Germans are not
a whit worse provided with clean linen; the only
difference is, that in London clean linen is soon
dirty, and therefore must be very frequently changed.
For the same reason hands and face must be oftener
washed than elsewhere. If I go out clean, and
return in an hour, I am certain to see a dozen
black spots on my face.

Just as absurd are the cautions one receives, as if
one were in danger of being, if not maltreated, at
least insulted and laughed at, in the streets. I have
purposely asked information of all kinds of people
of every class, from the most elegant-looking down
to coalheavers and errand-boys; and, in every instance, it was given with a readiness, fulness, and
accuracy, such as it is difficult for a foreigner to find
in any other country. Some even accompanied me,
without asking for, or thinking of, any pecuniary reward; and, on one occasion, a man who had told me
left, by mistake, instead of right, ran after me to
correct his error.

The grand question of using or not using a
carriage thus falls entirely to the ground. In
the first place, the incessant noise of carriages of
all sorts renders it impossible that the people you
go to see should know how their visiters come. And
am I to imagine that the Archbishop of Canterbury,
the Speaker of the House of Commons, and Lord

Holland, are persons likely to take me for a rich
man, because I am jolted to their doors in a hackney-
coach, or to think me the worse company because I
come on foot ? And so I do here as I do elsewhere :
if the distance is not too great, and the weather is
good, I walk ; if I lose too much time in walking, or
the weather is bad, I ride.

April 9th, 1835.

Yesterday I breakfasted at Mr. H——'s. He is
distinguished, both as a lawyer, and as the translator
of Goethe's 'Faust.' There I met Mr. L——, the
translator of Müller's ' Dorians,' and a young German jurist, Zachariæ, who is principally occupied with
researches on the subject of Byzantine law. The
conversation turned mainly on German literature,
especially on the second part of ' Faust,' which has
few admirers here.

From the Museum I went to walk, and then
stayed at home till Mr. M—— called me to go to a
great dinner of a society for the relief of decayed
actors. It has subsisted for eighteen years, and
enjoys considerable patronage. The King sub-
scribes 105*l.*, the Duchess of Kent 25*l.*, the Duke of
Devonshire 105*l.*, the Duke of Bedford 50*l.*, the
Duchess of St. Alban's 50*l.*, and so on.

The room was large, and the company was seated
at several tables : it consisted only of men. In
the galleries, however, there were some ladies, who
looked down upon the feast. The tables were so
narrow, and so crowded with dishes, that it appeared as if the eating must have lasted for many
hours ; but, no sooner was the signal for the attack
given, than a furious charge was made ;—one took

soup, another fish, another flesh, and so on. A universal slaughter of the viands was thus effected in a very short space of time, and singing and speaking began. The object and condition of the society were stated by the chairman; the patronage of the Princess Victoria was mentioned, and excited great applause; a sacred canon was sung, and was followed by ' God save the King,' &c.; and, lastly, Mori played on the violin better than he had done at the Philharmonic Concert. Moscheles also played, but I did not stay to hear his performance. All this was accompanied and interrupted by marks of approbation expressed by voices, sticks, feet, knives, forks, glasses, &c., in such a fashion, that our *fortissimo* would be a mere gentle murmur to it.

I could tell you a great deal more about the dinner, but all these particulars lost their interest with me in comparison with one thought. In this very same hour the ministry was dissolved; and this dissolution was not (as it so often is in France) a mere concern of *cotéries* and *tracasséries*, but had a real substantive meaning, and tended to real and efficient changes. What a deal of wit, good and bad —what angry passions—what hope and fear—what praise and blame—would have foamed over, like *champagne mousseux*, in such an hour, in Paris ! Here, not a trace of the kind. The first toast to the King (not as with us, with three times three, but with nine times nine, and as *sforzato* as possible); then to the Queen, the Royal Family, — all with the greatest applause,—so, likewise, ' God save the King.' It seemed as if all that was passing without were but a light ripple on the surface of the waters. The weal of England, her riches, her laws, her freedom, seemed moored to some immoveable anchor in the securest and serenest depths of ocean, whence neither winds nor waves can ever tear them loose. The clouds which flit along the face of heaven, and so often seem, to us timid spectators, to portend a coming storm, may here be regarded as but the passing fleeces of a summer sky; or rather as the proof and the earnest of an equable and safe state of the atmosphere.

In short, there was something to my mind in the whole proceeding—both what was done, and what was left undone—so wholly peculiar, so above all measure exciting, that in my sympathy with England, (and have not years of my life been given to this country?) I could hardly refrain from tears; and I earnestly prayed to God that this star might not be quenched, but that He would be pleased to purify and enlighten it, and to remove from it all the spots which partially obscure its brightness.

LETTER XII.

Sir Robert Peel—House of Lords—Situation of the Catholic Clergy—English and German Protestantism—Historical Sketch of the Church of England—Motions and Debates on Church Reform—Church Revenues—Dissenters—English Tithes—Tithe Reforms—Voluntary System—Necessity for Reform.

Thursday, April 8th, 1835.

PARLIAMENT will most probably not be dissolved. Peel, Wellington, and Lyndhurst are said to have decidedly dissuaded so perilous a step. I feel great regret for the former: he has fought the battle of his party with every conceivable effort of mind and body; he has sacrificed himself to it, nor did he quit the field till he was driven from every post; and, now, many of the high Tories are the loudest in his condemnation. They say, "That the interests of the aristocracy should not have been intrusted to a cotton-spinner; that he wants resolution and courage; and, instead of dissolving parliament, and boldly pursuing his course, he has beaten a retreat, and poorly quitted the field."

The English nobility is richer and more powerful than the French of the year 1789; but if the more zealous of them persist in this career of opposition (which goes even into such matters as the marriage of Dissenters, and the graduation of students), they will lose ground from day to day, and a far more absolute change in their social and political position than has overtaken the French most surely awaits them. In former times, land was the only source of wealth, and the possession of it necessarily conferred dignity and privileges; but this is wholly altered, and the old modes of thinking and acting must be accommodated to the change.

The formation of a new ministry appears to me attended with great difficulties. As a single party, the Tories are the most numerous; therefore, whenever their antagonists are disunited,—whenever the Tories vote with those whose principles are opposite to their own,—the middle or moderate party are left in a minority, and a fresh change of ministry must take place; which, however, would again end in no other result than a repetition of the present state of things. But grant that a new ministry retains a majority in the Commons, if the moderate Tories join the moderate Whigs, nothing is gained in the Lords. If, for example, they throw out the proposed laws concerning Ireland, the only consequence will be, that the Irish Protestant Church will be inevitably ruined by the non-payment of tithes; and the Lords can hardly assume a perpetual conflict with the Lower House as their leading principle. If the King were to create a number of peers, *une fournée,* in order to ensure the adoption, by the Upper House, of Bills passed by the Lower, this is in opposition to all true political wisdom; and will more completely destroy the peculiar character, and the salutary influence, of the Lords, than any individual concessions of their own can do.

However ill all this may look, when considered in a general and abstract point of view, I hold fast to the hope that a mediation is possible, and, as in the year 1757, will be effected.

Stanley, more irritable than Peel, has for the present closed the entrance to office against himself.

But if it is once decided that a provision must be made out of the funds of the State or the Church for the Catholics, and that the School is the second half of the Church, those who now oppose this as a principle, may do as they did in the case of the Reform Bill, accept, and act upon it as law. But it is very difficult, as we see, to win confidence, and to avoid the reproach of time-serving.

How injurious the influence of the existing state of things has been on the Catholic Church is but too evident. Without any assured ecclesiastical revenues, without endowments, the Catholic clergy are driven to have recourse to the voluntary contributions of their flocks and to surplice fees; and hence

so much selfishness, so much indecorum, so much
encouragement of profitable superstition, and other
things so utterly unchristian, that Protestants lie
under the most urgent duty to remove the causes of
temptation to such evil. It is not clearly ascertained whether, after a more equal distribution of
the Protestant Church property, much would remain
for the Catholics; and, indeed, the *immediate* trans-
fer of the surplus, be it what it might, would only
enhance the mutual hatred of the other religious
sects. Better forms and means must be found for
carrying into effect the principle of toleration, when
once it has triumphed.

Whenever the question of the Irish Church is disposed of, public attention will turn to the English
Church, which likewise stands in need of material
reforms. Setting entirely aside the aspect under
which the question presents itself to a Catholic, or
a Presbyterian, it is certain that, within the circle
of episcopalian conformity, many defects have crept
in which must be remedied, unless the whole Establishment be abandoned to destruction.

The Reformation, which, in many countries, over-
threw at once the monarchical power of the Pope,
and the aristocratical power of the bishops, in England did not extend to the latter. Their office was,
indeed, held to be necessary, and of divine right;
and thus a truly Episcopalian Church arose here,
while in other countries bishop became little more
than an insignificant title.

Before I proceed to the events of the last few
years, you must allow me to retrace the state and the
institutions of the English Church generally during
the eighteenth century. Among other things, you

will clearly perceive how widely English Protestantism differs from German Protestantism.

The King is head of the Church; convokes or dismisses synods, confirms laws relating to the Church, and nominates bishops. He cannot, however, perform any of the functions of a bishop in his own person. In former times the King received, immediately, various dues from the clergy: these have gradually fallen into disuse, together with most of the privileges of the latter, in so far as they related to *things*. Among their *personal* privileges, I may mention, that clergymen are not liable to serve on juries; that they cannot be arrested while performing divine service, &c.

The Archbishop of Canterbury is Primate of all England: in his diocese are twenty-one bishops; in that of the Archbishop of York four. The Bishops of London, Durham, and Winchester, take precedence of all others; the rest follow according to seniority. The Archbishop is chosen by a chapter of the cathedral, after the royal permission has been obtained. This is accompanied by a royal recommendation,—a *commendamus*—which, in practice, never encounters any opposition. The clergy receive all their temporal possessions from the hand of the King.

The Archbishop has, besides his own diocese, the supreme control over all the churches and bishops within his archbishopric. He convokes the latter (but not without the King's permission), hears appeals in various spiritual matters, consecrates bishops, superintends all spiritual affairs, even to the filling vacant bishoprics, grants dispensations, in cases where they are compatible with law and morality, and so forth.

The bishop is subject to the same temporal laws as the archbishop, has his court of justice and his representative there, especially during his absence in parliament. He inducts the clergy into the temporal and spiritual possession of their livings, &c.

The dean and the chapter form the bishop's council, and assist him in the direction of affairs connected with public worship. Since the time of Henry VIII., the dean has been appointed by the King. The chapter is in some cases appointed by the King; in others by the bishop; in others, again, its members are elected by the body itself. The archdeacon has jurisdiction immediately subordinate to the bishop, either over the whole diocese, or a part of it. He is usually nominated by the bishop, and he himself appoints his own spiritual court. The office of rural dean, or deacon, is fallen into disuse : the multiplication of superintendents was thought too great. This increased the importance of the priests (*persona,* parson, *personam seu vicem ecclesiæ gerit,*) and vicars,—and here we come to the matter now so warmly discussed—of appropriation. In so far as many churches were gradually appropriated to monasteries, abbeys, &c., the latter took upon themselves the service of them, and, in return, received all the revenues : they were the real parsons, and those whom they appointed were merely vicars. Such appropriations might be terminated in various ways ;—by the voluntary appointment of an independent priest—by the dissolution of the corporation to which such churches were attached, and so on. But, above all, at the suppression of the monasteries, the right of appointing such vicars devolved on the King, or on the persons to whom he was pleased to

delegate it. Although many arrangements have
been gradually introduced for the advantage of
these vicars* (often miserably provided for, and capri-
ciously treated), the appropriator, or rector, still receives the greater part of the revenues; and this is
certainly a far less defensible application of church
property than that which the Whigs are now endeavouring to effect for the education of the people.

In order to become parson or vicar, four conditions are necessary:—1. Consecration, or holy
orders; 2. Presentation; 3. Institution; 4. Induction. No man can become a priest till he is twenty-
three years of age. The presentation depends on the
patron: of this more hereafter. The bishop, however, can refuse the nominee on various grounds; as,
for instance, in old times, when the patron lay under
excommunication; or if the presentee himself appeared ineligible; whether the objections lay to his
person (if, for example, he were a bastard, an alien, or
a minor,) or to his faith, his knowledge or his morals.

General accusations,— such as that he was an
hereticus inveteratus,—were not, however, sufficient:
accurate and weighty proofs must be given. The
contested facts, whether of a spiritual or temporal
nature, are referred to a jury. If the facts are
proved, the jury has again to decide on the temporal loss sustained; but the spiritual is referred to
an ecclesiastical court. In some cases an appeal is
made to the archbishop.

Institution regards only the spiritual rights, and
rests with the bishop.

* The reader will have observed that H. von Raumer uses vicar
(vicarius) in its original and proper sense, as it is still used everywhere but in England.—*Translator.*

Induction regards the temporal property, and is often performed by persons authorized by the bishop.

The curates form the lowest class of ecclesiastical persons, and have no established right to the posts they occupy.

The right of patronage is called *appendant*, when it is attached to property in land; *in gross*, when it relates to a person. It is *presentative*, when a patron presents the candidate to the bishop; *collative*, when the bishop himself is the patron. If a patron makes no use of his right of presentation for six months, it lapses to the bishop; and, after an equal term, to the archbishop; and finally to the king. Questions as to the right of presentation are decided either by a jury composed of six clergymen and six laymen, under the presidency of the chancellor of the diocese, and with appeal to the higher ecclesiastical courts; or, oftener, by a temporal court, in so far as the question involves property.

This slight sketch of the ancient and general laws and usages of the Church of England will enable you to understand better the questions and objections agitated in our own days. It has been alleged ;—

1st. That the English Church is too rich. But a more accurate inquiry seems much rather to show that the enormous spoliation under Henry VIII. took from it a great deal too much; and that the Nemesis consequent upon this misdeed is, the inability of the Church to fulfil its strict duties of providing for poor clergymen, and for the education of the people.

2nd. It has been urged that the ecclesiastical revenues are improperly divided; that many have

too little, and some too much. We shall see that
the partition is certainly very unequal; nevertheless,
an unconditional equalization would be as unjust
and as impolitic in this case as in every other; nor,
further, are the sums which could be differently
apportioned by any means sufficient, without fresh
resources, to supply the wants, or remedy the evils
complained of.

3rd. The most vehement objections are those
directed against the system of tithes and that of
pluralities; they are also the best founded.

I must add a few facts on this head. According
to Lord Althorp's calculation*, the incomes in England were—

Bishops	£158,000
Deans and chapters . .	236,000
Clergy	3,000,000
In round numbers .	£3,500,000

This, on an average, gives to 11,500 livings a
yearly income of about 250*l.* This calculation is,
however, corrected in another place by the admission, that the actually resident, active clergy in
England receive only about 185*l.* yearly on an
average; while the Scotch Church, so much poorer
on the whole, from the difference of its Presbyterian
system, allows for each 275*l.*† On the other hand
that there are livings in England which bring in
6000*l.* yearly.

Let us see, in order to come nearer to the truth,
what the two principal journals of the two great
parties advance on these points. The ' Quarterly

* April 18th, 1833. Hansard, xvii., 274.　　† Ibid., ii., 479.

Review'* says there are 10,533 benefices in England.
Of these 4361 give, yearly, less than 150*l.*; 1350
less than 70*l.*; and some less than 12*l.* At 4809
livings no clergyman can reside, because the houses
are in so dilapidated a state; 2626 have no houses.
Certainly, from this follows the necessity of uniting
several livings; but not less the necessity of meeting
the evil which has arisen from Henry VIII.'s spoliation, or from later errors.

The ' Edinburgh Review†' says there are in
England—

3000 livings, which give yearly under £100					
1970	„	„	„	„	70
689	„	„	„	„	50
248	„	„	„	„	40
69	„	„	„	„	30

Lord Brougham asserted in parliament‡ that a
short time ago there were livings, the yearly income
of which was from 5*l.* to 8*l.*; and that there were
from 800 to 1000 livings with a yearly income of
less than 60*l.*

That a mere alteration in the division of the
actual gross revenue of the English Church is not
sufficient to produce a suitable income for all the
clergy is easily shown. For, in the first place, a
total abolition of the episcopal, and an introduction
of the presbyterian system, is out of the question;
and, secondly, legislation can reach only a part of
the church livings. For, according to a calculation,

The Crown has, in its gift, only .	990 livings
The two universities . . .	760 „
The bishops and chapters . .	2280 „
Lay patrons	7300 „

* Hansard, xlviii., 562.   † Ibid., lvi., 205.
‡ July 29th, 1831. Hansard, v., 517.

Granting that the universities (which have refused to give up so much as the monopoly of granting degrees) could, as well as the bishops and
chapters, be compelled to submit to general laws
for the division of church revenues; yet the 7300
(with all their advantages, or disadvantages) would
remain untouched, as being private property or
endowment; and herewith the great evil of pluralities stands in the closest connexion. 4416 clergymen live where their duty demands; 6080 are not in
their places,—are non-residents; 2100 clergymen
hold several livings at the same time*; and it is
sufficient to pass one day in the year at a living to
constitute a clergyman resident.

In 1831 the Archbishop of Canterbury proposed
some measures for the remedy of this abuse. His
project was to reduce the number of pluralities to
700; to establish rigorous rules against the giving
several livings to one person; not to unite two
parishes if they were more than thirty miles apart
(instead of forty-five, as at present); to compel
every pluralist to live at least six months in the
year in the largest parish, &c.

Unquestionably these were improvements, yet
only the smaller half of the evil would have been
redressed by them; they would have left many very
objectionable unions of lucrative livings; nor does
the neighbourhood of two afford any reasonable
ground for the continuance of this abuse. There
could be no deficiency of eligible clergymen; since
it was maintained, on the other hand, that more
learning, zeal, and assiduity were now to be found
among them than at any former period†.

* Hansard, x., 1103; vii., 22; vi., 854.
† Quarterly Review, xlii., 234. Hansard, x., 1107; xi., 316.

However true this last assertion may be, the bishops are, on account of their aristocratical views, not popular. Many of them are connected by birth with the aristocracy. It is, therefore, by no means impossible that (as in France) the lower clergy will sever itself from the higher, and will lean more and more to democratical opinions. The overthrow of the Church would, however, give a lamentable preponderance to those gloomy and fanatical sects which are the enemies of art and science. May they rather mutually instruct, refine, and purify each other! The whole conduct of the Church towards the Dissenters has had the inevitable consequence of driving them into bitter and inflexible hostility. For example:—So late as the year 1831 marriages performed by their own clergy were illegal, and the children of such marriages bastards. So late as the twelfth year of George III. a Catholic priest who married a Catholic and a Protestant was liable to the punishment of death; and later, to a fine of 500l.

In June, 1833*, Mr. Perrin proposed to put the Catholic on the same footing with the Dissenting clergy; but even the most recent laws are very far from placing either the one or the other on a level with the clergy, or even the laity, of the established Church.

London, 9th April.

The political and clerical high-Tories of the old sort are, as a numerous and powerful party, no longer in existence: they have conceded, or they must concede, innumerable points to which they

* Hansard, vi., 1030; xviii., 1239.

formerly offered unqualified opposition. And other important changes await them; such, for instance, as those which must be made in the English tithe system. In spite of all I have written on Irish tithes, there are some facts which I must mention.

The 'Quarterly Review*,' which is generally the champion of the old order of things, expressed itself in substance to this effect:—

" Changes, with regard to the revenues of the church, may be necessary, and a better distribution may be desirable : they ought not, however, to import any confiscation or securalization, which, as the French revolution proves, always lead to mischievous consequences. A rich church is preferable to a poor one, and a bishop often spends his large income far better than a peer or a merchant. The equalization of all clergymen gives a democratic tendency to the church; and where the pay of all is low, none take orders except persons of inferior rank. The clergyman, however, ought to be a focus of civilization; and ought not to be behind the layman of his parish. With regard to the tithes, against which so much has been said, a commutation of them into a fixed money payment would not only make any increase in the amount impossible, but would in time lead to a reduction of it. A commutation of tithes for land brings too much land into mortmain, and in times of danger facilitates the confiscation of church property : the best measure would perhaps be a commutation into a *corn-rent*, which might at certain intervals be valued and fixed according to the market prices."

In the debate on this question in the House of

* Vol. xlii., p. 110, and the following.

Peers, the Bishop of London said * that tithes were held by the same tenure as other property, and that it was just that they should rise *pari passu* with other property.

This proposition is true, and it is false. The Church is perfectly right in wishing to secure her property and her revenues; and it is the bounden duty of the State,—whatever be the relation in which they stand to each other,—to protect her. But whether she govern herself, or be governed by the civil power, the immutability of her system of levying contributions can just as little be assumed as a paramount and salutary principle, as the immutability of any secular system of taxation. No tax imposed by government rises or falls immediately with the rise or fall in the income of the tax-payer (except the income-tax, which, on that very account, is so hard to levy); on the contrary, the fixedness of the tax affords security to property, and facilitates the calculations of prudent men. That tithes levied on the gross amount of produce can, or ought, to rise or fall in exact proportion to that, is an error which has been confuted again and again. On the other hand, a settlement with the tithe-payer, on his annual *net* income, would lead to interminable disputes.

I must give you two or three proofs and examples of the abuses connected with this principle. The claims of the Church are never obsolete; she can enforce any claims, which the opposite party cannot prove to have been set aside before the year 1180. Thus any titheable property, though it may not have paid for centuries, is subject to new de-

* Dec. 14th, 1830. Hansard, i., 1111.

mands at any time; and every *modus*, every agreement as to the manner and the rate of payment, is void, whenever it pleases the clergymen to declare it so.

Thus, for example, in many parts of England, a lamb had, from time immemorial, been reckoned at 10*d.*; but a clergyman lately demanded that it should be rated at 1*l.* 7*s.* 6*d.*, in consequence of which his income was increased 200*l.* a-year by this article alone. A farmer wished to take a cow and calf to market; the receiver of tithes forbade this till the calf had attained a titheable age, and could live without its mother. Another refused to receive a tenth of the milk daily; he insisted on having all the milk from all the cows every tenth day. In one case, the strictest account was demanded of the eggs, how many were laid, how many put to hatch, or stolen by the weasel. A tithe of five cabbages and three heads of celery gave occasion to a great law-suit. Another matter of six pounds value was determined in the ecclesiastical courts at a cost of 180*l.*

From the circumstance of the tithe being levied on the gross income, and so many other things (for example, the poor-rates) charged on the rent, it has often happened that when the rent amounted to 100*l.*, the tithe amounted to 80*l.* Generally speaking, this has risen enormously with the improvements in agriculture : and yet no new livings have been created where they were obviously wanted; no better division of burdens and claims effected; no schools established; in short, no attempt at a return to the old true principles of the application of tithes. In the course of one life the gross amount of tithes has often been trebled; yet nothing more was done for the security, honour, or efficacy of the Church, with this vast increase, than with the original third.

Observe, too, that the system of the corn-laws also augmented the value of tithes. In a district where the tithes amounted to 6000*l*., various persons, holding no ecclesiastical offices, shared among them £4900

The absent rector received . . . 1000

The curate, who performed the whole duty 100

And this crying abuse actually passes with many men for something sacred and inviolable—essential to the very existence of tithes—nay, of the Church itself !

Lord Caernarvon said[*], that if every clergyman were compelled to reside on his own living, the useful body of curates would be utterly destroyed ! What a confusion of ideas ! Why then pay the absent so profusely, and these useful labourers so miserably ? Why then not convert either the one or the other into the real and actual pastors and curates of souls ?

On the 13th of July, 1831, the Archbishop of Canterbury brought forward a plan for a " commutation" of tithes[†]. He described the system hitherto pursued as unfavourable to agriculture; a " composition" for a time as uncertain and fluctuating; and was of opinion that a complete change should be introduced as soon as three-fourths of the parishioners were unanimous for it. Heretofore, the slightest opposition on the part of the rector was sufficient to obstruct any reforms, and a composition was rendered void by the death of every successive rector. In future, any change which had been regu-

* Hansard, ii., 239.　　　　† Ibid., iv., 1363.

larly agreed to by the incumbent should be binding on his successor or successors for seven years, if the rate of payment was determined in corn ; for fourteen, if in money.

An entire abolition of tithes he pronounced to be unjust and inexpedient : for,—

Firstly, Compensation in land, or an application of the public money, were both subject to great difficulties and objections :

Secondly, It were to be feared that the clergy and the landlords might be led, by selfish and narrow considerations, to unite for the future detriment of the Church :

Thirdly, The clergy would, by this means, easily fall into absolute dependance on the laity, and would lose their right (a right continually strengthening with time) to a tenth of *all* profits from land.

A second plan, proposed by Lord Dacre*, was withdrawn. The fierce opposition which the foregoing lesser changes encountered seemed to render it hopeless to attempt more. This proposal was for a redemption of tithe by a fixed duty on corn. The landowner was to be indemnified for the cost of improvements by a proportionate reduction in the rate of his tithes.

On the 18th of April, 1833†, a third plan was submitted to Parliament by the Government. According to this, every tithe-owner and every tithe-payer should have a right to agree upon an *entire* redemption of tithe by a fixed corn-rate; which rate, however, should rise and fall according to the standard of prices. Every clergyman was to have the assent of his bishop and patron ; every farmer that of his

* Hansard, iv., 1386.   † Ibid., xvii., 273.

landlord. Each party was to name a valuer or appraiser, who was to take the value of the tithes on an average of seven years, and to be empowered to vary the redemption money from five to ten per cent., according to circumstances. If the valuers could not agree on certain points, an arbitrator was to be called in.

To this plan, as well as to the others, numerous objections were raised. It was alleged, for instance, that the mean profits upon which the estimate was made would be far too high in case the corn-laws were repealed; that the generous tithe-owner would then be a loser—the rapacious, a gainer; that if the poor-rate were to be levied in proportion, according to the existing mode, there would often be nothing left for the tithe-owner, &c.

So that although a vast deal has been said and written on this subject, everything, in fact, is yet to do.

There can be no doubt (as other countries sufficiently demonstrate) that means are to be found of securing the property of the Church, without clinging to the mode in which the Jews paid their Levites as the sole, immutable, and eternal model. It is also indisputable that Church and School ought to be established on the securest foundations; and that nothing could be more absurd and mischievous than to make either of them absolutely dependant on voluntary contributions, on fees, or on private resources or private caprices of any kind. Either or both might thus be left to the chances of a zeal transient in its duration, and changeable in its nature; or to the mercy of the indifference and the rapacity which might contemplate their destruction as a source of gain.

A fresh partition of those revenues which are in any degree superfluous and disposable ought to be accompanied with an accurate estimation of the extent and the weight of clerical duties.

In short, it is clear that those whose affections are the most faithful,—whose intentions the most pure, —towards the Church of England, must of necessity be the most active and zealous labourers for the removal of existing abuses;—the least inclined to foster, by whatever means, defects which are pregnant with destruction. If they are negligent and lukewarm in this holy work, or if their efforts are counteracted, the beneficent parts of her institutions will gradually fall more and more into the shade, till at length really Radical schemes (in the bad sense of the word) for her destruction will be not only proposed, but effected. What is now often called "radical," by no means deserves this term of reproach; far rather is it "radical" to degrade the Church, and the property consecrated to the highest and holiest purposes, into instruments for the gratification of certain aristocratical ends.

The arguments used by many of the high Tories —that no time can obliterate the claims of the Church; or that, at least, those claims extend back to the year 1180—might, if carried out, be brought to prove that the spoliations of Henry VIII., and the confiscations of the seventeenth century, are all invalid; and that the nobles are bound to disgorge their illegally-acquired church property, with all the accumulated profits they have derived from it. This, indeed, would be ecclesiastically radical, and yet perfectly in accordance with the logic upon which many speeches in Parliament are based.

As yet, the whole struggle—the whole difficulty—exclusively regards the *external* Church, and the property belonging to it; the question concerning the spiritual part and its dogmas is left in the background; and many are indifferent to the latter, while their zeal is over-fervent about the former.

I must confess, however, that I cannot feel any great fear that the plunder of the Church and the destruction of Christianity are so near at hand as some would have us believe.

LETTER XIII.

Newspapers—The Times—The Standard—Athenæum Club House—Dinner at H——— House—Squares—Domestic Architecture and Furniture — Hyde Park and Kensington Gardens—Dinner with Turkish Ambassador—Specimen of General Seydlitz' French—Museum—Chapter-house, Westminster—Sir F. Palgrave—Doomsday Book—Germanic Institutions of England—Rich materials for History possessed by England—Regent's Park—Zoological Gardens.

Friday, April 10th, 1835.

To-day is my deceased father's birthday. Yesterday was Charles's. Would not one give all the travels and all the cities in Europe, to see the loved and lost, once more together in one spot? And who would bear to be robbed of this consoling hope and promise, although it be beyond the reach of mere intelligence?

If time and strength do not suffice to see a few living persons in London, how, if all the immortal dead from the time of Moses and of Homer were gathered together in one place? In what way, or by what organs, could the feeble contracted thing,

VOL. I.

whom we call man, hold that nearer intercourse he would aspire after, with the all great and honoured of past ages—to say nothing of the obscurer masses of relations, and friends, and acquaintances? Here must be other means and other powers than steam-boats or steam-carriages. But you want news from London, and not hypotheses of another world.

The 'Times' is violently attacked, and not without reason; unless, indeed, we accept its versatility as the true sign of the times, and find its justification in its consistency with its name. But the stiff-necked pertinacity with which some other papers, for instance the 'Standard,' repeat the same things for ever and ever, without taking the slightest note of totally altered circumstances, is no proof of greater intellectual strength.

From Mr. ——— I went for the first time to the Athenæum—a magnificent building, furnished with all sorts of newspapers and periodicals. The admission costs twenty guineas, and the yearly subscription six. Foreigners who are introduced pay nothing.

I dined yesterday at Lord H———'s with the Marquis of Lansdowne, Messrs. Hallam, Cooper, and some other remarkable persons. My frozen ears and lips gradually thaw, so that I do not stand by quite so stupidly, without either hearing or speaking. I learn more, consequently, though this cannot be done with facility, and *en passant*, as in Paris. In that city, for instance, there would have been no talk of anything but the state of parties, the new ministry, &c. Yesterday, on the contrary, these topics were only slightly touched upon, and the conversation flowed on freely in various channels, with-

out being contracted or absorbed by politics. Lady
H——— appeared well informed on literary subjects.
Lord H——— unites a very agreeable tone of conversation with varied attainments. As a gastronomic
novelty, I must remark, for your information or imitation, that oysters were handed round before the
soup.

Sunday, April 12th, 1835.

In the course of delivering letters, which I do by
way of necessary exercise, I went for the first time
through Torrington, Woburn, Gordon, Tavistock,
Russell, and Bloomsbury squares, and discovered,
with fresh astonishment, a whole city of the most
beautiful streets, squares, and gardens. But the
greater part of the new buildings, although they present a wide and stately front adorned with pillars and
other decorations, are divided into many comparatively small and narrow houses. Most of the houses
have but three windows, and each house is inhabited
by only one family, who are more usually tenants than
proprietors of it. The English like better to dis-
perse themselves through three stories, than to in-
habit a large suite of apartments, and endure strange
occupants above and below them. Hence persons
even in moderate circumstances, at Berlin, seem,
when they throw open their rooms, to have larger
and better habitations than here, where the dining-
room is usually below, the sitting-room on the first,
and the bed-room on the second floor. On the
other hand, the hall and staircase of these houses
are far more elegant than in ours. The stairs and
floors are usually covered with handsome carpets,
and even my lodging is not without this luxury.

The Berlin houses have a more cheerful aspect from their gay and various colours. But if people attempted to wash or colour the houses here, they would very soon be blackened again.

Monday, April 13th, 1835.

I went yesterday, on a most beautiful morning, down Oxford Street, and through Hyde Park, to Kensington, to breakfast with Mr. S. The distance is about the same as from my house in Berlin, to Charlottenburg. The young green was shooting up on every side in spite of the chilly mornings and evenings; the turf already wears its English hue. There is no prohibition against treading upon it, as with us, which shows how confidently an after-growth is reckoned upon : on the contrary, children play about, and enormously fat sheep graze at will. Hyde Park is little more than a large meadow. The finest trees are in Kensington Gardens. There is no trace of that elegance of detail which delights one so much in the Tuileries and the Luxembourg; but on the other hand, the extent is far greater, and the general effect far more rural and natural. It is rather to be compared with our Thiergarten, or with the road from Dessau to Wörtitz. The portion of the royal family which appears to be most popular, lives at Kensington; namely, the Duke of Sussex, the Duchess of Kent, and the Princess Victoria.

I dined yesterday at Mr. ——, with the Turkish ambassador, who told us the history of his life. He lost his father very early, and was carefully brought up by his mother, who prevented him from contracting a premature marriage. He became interpreter, general, and ambassador. He maintained, and not without some grounds, that in some respects there is more individual freedom in Turkey than in England, where the tyranny of countless laws is more oppressive than the tyranny of one man's will. But certainly a general conclusion drawn from such particulars would be very fallacious. He also affirmed that polygamy occurred among the Turks only as an exception, and was necessarily confined to a few rich men.

Among the graver spoils of my labours, I now and then stumble on a "curiosum;" for example, some French letters from General Seydlitz to Mitchell, which prove that the Berliners spelt French still worse in his time than they do now. Guess, now, the meaning of these words: *suven, fain, laitre, trete, orian?*

I send the following extract as a specimen:—
"Aveuque le plesier le plus sensieble je Recu lagreable nuvelle don son Excelence a bien me voulu honore touchant sa scante, je souhaite De tout mon Ceour que elle trouve l Ars de Monsieur Cotenius et les effet des l Os dinge des ces louanges."

Tuesday, April 14th, 1835.

I left Berlin a month ago to-day. I can scarcely believe that the time has not been longer; I have seen, heard, and learned so much in this short period. Hardly any part of my life has been so rich in new thoughts and new sensations, or, at any rate, it ranks with those in which I first saw Paris, Rome, Naples, or Switzerland. When I gave up the career of active life, with all the advantages which it promised me, it was with the view of devoting myself to science;

—which I have done; but it was by no means my intention to remain immoveably fixed in one place, giving lectures. My science—history—requires a more much varied and abundant life. And I am convinced that both men and events appear to me in a different and a juster light, than if I had always sat in my chimney corner, and had lived exclusively in one circle. These thoughts often pass through my mind in justification of my stay here, and you will not think it unnatural that I should give utterance to them.

Yesterday's harvest at the Museum was a failure: I got nothing but dust; besides which I could stay there but a couple of hours, for at ten o'clock I went to Sir Francis Palgrave at the Chapter-house, Westminster. There I found an immense number of old chronicles and rotuli, or rolls of paper in the shape of large Swiss cheeses. Much as Sir F. Palgrave has done, the greater part of these are still unexamined and unknown. I saw the original of the curious Doomsday-book; Henry VIII.'s will with his own signature, (at least there is no stamp,) and many other most interesting things. Unfortunately these archives only extend down to the time of Henry VIII., concerning whom, however, there is a long series of very curious documents. The results of Sir F. Palgrave's late researches exhibit the old German principles and customs, particularly those of a judicial nature, in quite a new light. Perhaps no country is so rich in materials for a continued and perfect history of law, as England. The Saxon law was not by any means entirely superseded by the Norman; it was not so much altered by William I., nor did he introduce so com-

plete a feudal system, as is generally imagined. Indeed, the coincidence of the Norman law with the
English appears so complete, that it suggests fresh
riddles concerning the origin of those sea-wanderers,
and concerning Normandy, which will, perhaps, lead
to the solution of all the questions relating to them.

At three o'clock, Mr. T., with whom I made acquaintance at M.'s, called me for a walk. We went
to see the great Regent's Park, which exhibits all
the beauties of a large English garden, and is surrounded with handsome palace-like façades divided
into houses. There is an immense collection of
animals of all kinds, from the elephant and the rhino-
ceros to rats and mice. The dens and cages are distributed over a large garden, tastefully laid out and
well kept, and each is differently arranged and ornamented. It is only in the neighbourhood of such a city
as London that such an establishment could be maintained by voluntary subscriptions and contributions.

LETTER XIV.

New Ministry—False maxims concerning the English Constitution—
Relations of Lords and Commons—Tories and Radicals—Party
inconsistencies—Hereditary Peerage—Peers of Life—Example of
Rome—Ecclesiastical Aristocracy—Decline of Aristocracy—Duke
of S——Domestic finance—Eating-house—Dinner of Artisans—
Drury Lane Theatre; Oratorio—Performance of the Messiah at
Berlin and London compared—Modern Italian Singing and Music
—Dinner—Comparative Prices of London, Paris, and Berlin—Tea
Trade with China.

London, April 14th, 1835.

To-day it is expected that the new ministry will be
formed. It may fairly be presumed, after recent
experience, that the Tories of the old school (to

which, however, Peel does not belong) will never again come into power; for their sway would involve a repeal of the Reform Bill, and a return to the old elective system; a thing not to be thought of, and about as likely as the restoration of the Slave-trade.

The theoretical and abstract manner of considering the English constitution must be abandoned. From this are derived maxims like the following, which have been repeated countless times: The King has the sole right of declaring war; and has the free and absolute choice of his ministers: The House of Lords has the right of confirming or of rejecting all bills proceeding from the Lower House: The King can create as many Peers as he pleases. The House of Commons can vote taxes, *or withhold them.*

All these dicta, and many of the same kind, cannot be denied; they are constitutionally established; and yet a literal adherence to them would leave the State without life or motion. It would end in the impractical French division of powers, which is, in fact, the extinction of all power. The King cannot, in fact, declare war unless the Commons vote money to carry it on; he may nominate ministers, but they cannot stand (as experience shows) if they have not a majority in Parliament; the Lords can maintain no long continued struggle with the Commons, without being worsted in the end; the king cannot create *fournées* of Peers à la Française, without destroying the whole character and weight of the Upper House; the Commons cannot flatly refuse the supplies, but must try to attain their end without resorting to this violent extremity; and so forth.

The life of England, therefore, does not reside

in these dry bones of the body politic. The springs
are far more complicated, the rules and conditions far
more numerous; and when these thousand accessary
conditions and incidents are wanting, the transplant-
ation of a bare political osteology is mere folly. It is
certain that the Reform Bill also has introduced
changes which are not expressed in the mere letter,
or are very obscurely hinted at: for example, formerly,
(and this is an essential point,) the House of Lords
virtually governed the House of Commons as pos-
sessors of the rotten boroughs. The latter is now
rendered more independent; when the close and
self-electing corporations are re-organized, the aristocracy will lose many more votes. The preponderancy has thus been transferred from the Upper
to the Lower House; and if more violent contrari-
eties manifest themselves, other means must be devised, other tactics employed, than those of simple
negation.

Supposing, for example, the bill concerning the
Irish Church, together with the new clause on the
application of the surplus fund to schools, pass the
House of Commons and be thrown out on the second reading in the Lords,—the latter will only have
exercised their unquestionable right; but what
would be the probable consequence? a complete
and universal refusal to pay tithes throughout Ireland, and misery and starvation for the Protestant
clergy. The next spring would only present the
same evil in an aggravated form; and a Tory ministry would hardly be able to obtain a victory then,
on the field where it had suffered defeat now.

He who cannot mediate is not fit to rule. It is
most justly observed by Burke, that " the disposition

to maintain, and the skill to improve, are the two elements, the union of which forms the great statesman." Hence it follows, that neither high Tories nor Radicals are statesmen, and that neither can permanently govern. The former see no value but in the past; the latter, in the present, or in their own ideal future. This is a false division, a rending asunder of parts which intimately cohere in real life; an attempt to maintain, or to change, absolutely and without qualification. The commands, the will, nay, the simple wish, of a father influences his children and his children's children; a total disregard of them is a proof of heartlessness and presumption. But this pious and salutary reverence degenerates into foolish superstition, when it seeks to bind the existing generation in such fetters as would utterly incapacitate it from producing, in its turn, any thing valuable, as a bequest to its successors. It is no proof of reverence for forefathers, to hold to their institutions, when all the circumstances which suggested those institutions have changed; it is rather a most irreverent assumption, that, if they were alive, they would cling with obstinate idolatry to unsuitable and inexpedient courses. The appeals .made by the high Tories to their departed ancestors, and by the Radicals to their unborn posterity, are often not only one-sided, but a mere convenient pretext for accomplishing party purposes.

The apparent consistency of party men is often pregnant with the greatest inconsistencies. Those, for instance, who want to alienate all church property, and to leave all religious establishments to voluntary contributions, forget that this (independent of all other results) has already led in Ireland to a sort of poll-tax, which, if presented under another form, they would be the first to oppose.   Those who were the most violent in their opposition to the centralization of the uncertain and unconnected regulations for the poor, have been no less vehement in their defence of the excessive centralization of the administration of justice.

To return to the affairs of the day.   In case the Lords throw out the Irish Bill, the superficial enemies of an upper house will perhaps not, as yet, gain a majority ; but the question, whether the hereditary peerage should not be qualified with an admixture of peers for life will doubtless be agitated with redoubled vehemence.   If all power ultimately rests on three elements, birth, wealth, and talent, the utility, indeed the necessity of the first element in governments of a certain form, *and with reference to hereditary monarchy*, remain unshaken; the example of the United States of America, with their president, is entirely irrelevant.   The circumstances of that new and remote country are wholly peculiar, and so recent, that one generation may probably see them totally altered.

The principle of *hereditary* monarchy, and the immense importance to society of the clearest possible laws of succession, have been fully recognized of late years ; and any departure from them has been regarded, even by the change-loving French, as an exception which necessity alone can justify.   This persuasion is, however, far from being equally strong or general, with regard to hereditary nobility.   On the contrary, theories are at variance, and practice is unfavourable, to hereditary privileges.   These

are no longer recommended except as means to
great political ends; scarcely indeed does any
nobleman attempt to justify the unequal distribution
of property among his children, or the exclusive
right to employments, dignities, or exemptions, on
any other ground.

Of the three above-mentioned bases of power,
birth has certainly lost extremely in importance, and
stands in greater need than ever of the support of
wealth. But as this, in England, is often possessed
in an equal, and instruction in a superior, degree, by
the mercantile class, the loss the hereditary nobility
has sustained on the side of birth cannot be compensated by any gain on that of wealth. Their power
has declined and is declining. The result of the
long struggle between the patricians and plebeians
of Rome was their perfect equality; and incontes-
tably this is the tendency of modern Europe.

Will not the result of this levelling, this annihi-
lation of various organs, be fatal to the variety and
the beauty of social life? Perhaps it will be, as in
Athens, a swift destruction. Perhaps something
new and peculiar, something adapted to the times,
will shape itself out; as, in Rome, the nobles and
the citizens blended into one great aristocracy—the
senate. In this, steadiness and mobility were combined; whereas, in the Roman patricians, the nobility of Venice, Berne, &c., the hereditary element
was exclusively predominant. The English peerage
is not so sharply severed from the other classes as
these aristocracies, inasmuch as it is accessible to
new persons and families; but whether this will long
suffice as a counterpoise to the wealth and the talent
of the lower house, may be doubted. A judicious

employment of their fortunes for purposes of general utility, and the most laborious cultivation of mind, is therefore now become the imperative duty and the strongest interest of every peer : both will do no more than keep them on a level with the commonalty.

But as little as in the sixteenth century the Pope had the good sense to place himself at the head of the Reformation, and the prudence to direct the current, so little does the aristocracy of our days seem disposed to act this part with regard to political reforms: and because rulers do not understand how to bend and to mould, the people come at last to breaking and destroying. The hereditary rights of the aristocracy, it is argued, are precisely what afford security for its permanence, steadiness and independence ; if these, either from levity or malignity, are thrown into the vortex, constancy, moderation, and order are lost. This argument deserves infinite attention. But we must remember that not only were these privileges, as I just observed, regarded with more veneration formerly than now ; but that a multitude of other conditions, aids, and props, were connected with them, some of which no longer exist, others are equally in the possession of the *tiers état*. If, then, the reverence for birth cannot be restored ; if the aggregate wealth of the nobility is less than that of the other classes, the question remains, whether their strength might not be increased by the addition of talent and knowledge.

And here we come to the question, whether it were not expedient to associate, for life, to the hereditary peers, certain distinguished men, who might help, as in the Roman Senate, to support the optimates against the plebeians. But if (contrary to the Roman prac-

tice) children and grandchildren were thus introduced
to power, what was strength in the beginning, would
perhaps be weakness in the end; and the means
taken to command authority and reverence might
lead to contempt and degradation. There is another example of an aristocracy besides that of
Rome—one of boundless power—which holds its
privileges for life alone; that of the Church. Opposed to the mental activity of Europe, how long
would an hereditary caste of priests have retained
their power and influence? But arguments against
an hereditary priesthood are now turned, by analogy,
against an hereditary peerage.

All this does not affect to be an exhaustive view
of the subject. I only start from the undeniable fact
that, compared with former times, the power of the
House of Lords has declined, and that of the Commons increased. But if the existence and influence
of the Upper House is regarded by all moderate
and reasonable men as beneficial and even necessary,
this two-fold truth leads inevitably to the question,
how the lost balance is to be restored. The rotten
boroughs were not only materially, but politically,
decayed; instead of holding to crumbling ruins, it
would have been wiser to discover and to apply
means of propping and repairing the edifice. It is
impossible to go on in the old road; a new path
must be opened for the Upper House, if it is to keep
pace with the Lower.

To throw all the blame on the Reform Bill, Lord
John Russell, or his party, is just as rational as it
would have been for the Catholics of the sixteenth
century to forget, or to deny, their own character
and position, or the state of the world, and to re-

proach Luther and his adherents as the sole authors
of that stupendous change.   When all the previous
conditions of change are already in existence ; when
all remedies are either contemned or worn out; when
the Archimedean point of motion is given, the motion is inevitable,—it must come ; and the only remaining problem is, to understand its peculiar laws,
and to turn it into safe channels and to salutary uses.

But if the aristocratical prudence of persistency is
dangerous and mistaken, not less shallow is the wisdom of most of the republicans of our days, who find
in an assembly representing the people, *with reference
to numbers alone,* the full solution of the problem of
government; the full compensation for all those
various forms which the whole history of the world
displays.   God be praised, these cannot be permanently destroyed by such barren and dull expedients !   There are, it is true, excrescences and
deformities in the richest organization, but a worm
is not better than a man because it has fewer
organs, members, and nerves : and has this political
scheme, and all that was expected from it, outlived
so much as the diseases of its infancy ?   My conclusion, therefore, is, that the ultra-aristocrats, and
ultra-democrats, are equally irrational, and equally
dangerous.   God grant the ministry now to be
formed, strength, moderation and wisdom, to master
so many difficulties !

Wednesday, April 15*th,* 1835.

The countenance of the Duke of S——, spite of
his feeble sight, has an expression of the greatest
good humour, cheerfulness, and *bonhommie*, and his
conversation confirmed the impression made by his

appearance. As the gentlemen present did not understand German, English was spoken, and, happily for me, so distinctly by the Duke, that I hardly lost a word. He inquired particularly into my scientific views and pursuits, and promised me his best services, particularly with the State Paper-Office.

The Duke conversed on the affairs of the church and the universities, the change of ministry, and the Tories, who had learned nothing, misunderstood the times, and called out the strength of the Radicals by fruitless and injudicious opposition. But you know his opinions, and I have an insuperable objection to write down what might appear like gossip, or might give rise to it. No greater contrast in all principles and purposes can possibly be formed than that which exists between the Duke of C—— and the Duke of S——. The latter speaks with fluency and acuteness; so that during two hours and a half, the thread of interesting conversation was never broken, and time passed with wonderful rapidity. I looked at his large and well-arranged library. Among the most remarkable contents of it, is a collection of bibles, in all languages, which can hardly be surpassed in Europe.

Thursday, April 16th.

I found yesterday, in an instructive letter of Lord Burleigh's to his son, a *literal* confirmation of my old doctrine of domestic finance; namely, that one ought never to devote more than two-thirds of one's income to the *ordinary* expenses of life, for that the *extraordinary* will be certain to absorb the other third.

*　　*　　*　　*　　*　　*

*   *   *   *   *   *

All this occupied so much time, that the hour drew near when I was to go to Drury Lane to hear " a sacred oratorio ;" in other words, a miscellaneous concert. The house where I was accustomed to dine lay in a totally different direction; I accordingly took the way towards Drury Lane, in the hope of finding eating-houses in abundance in the course of my long walk. But this Parisian hope was delusive ; far and near no eating-house appeared; till at length, for my consolation, I saw the word " soup " at a window. Where soup is to be found in England, thought I, other eatables certainly exist; another delusion. The moment I entered, it was evident that I had fallen upon a company of a rather different quality from that which attracts the stranger to the elegant Traveller's club. But my hunger was great, time short, and curiosity excited. I wished to see how the lowest class of London artisans dine. Many things in the external appearance reminded me of the Roman Osterie, and yet they were different. No table-cloth; yet not, as in Rome, the bare wood, but an oil-cloth; pewter spoons, and two-pronged forks; tin saltcellar and pepper-box. The tables not placed along the wall, as if for a social meal, but separated in the farther corners, to prevent strife, whether by words or blows. I asked for several kinds of English dishes; but I was told, that there was nothing to be had but the fore-mentioned soup. As I had said A, I must needs say B, and content myself with the humblest possible dinner. I received a large portion of black Laconian broth, in which pepper played a conspicuous part; and in this broth a number of pieces of something like meat, which transported me from foggy London to Sorrento, with its *frutti di mare*. With this was a large piece of wheaten bread, and two gigantic potatoes, the cubic contents of which were about equal to those of eight or ten Berlin ones. Having eaten these, I was perfectly satisfied, and paid three pence, twelve of which are equal to ten silver groschen.

Next, to Drury Lane; where, on my repeatedly asking where I could buy a ticket for the pit, I received various, to me unintelligible, answers; such as that no tickets were sold; that there were none; did I want one at half-price? and so on. I thought the fault must be with my bad English; but then the words were so simple, and I had tutored my tongue and lips with the utmost care. At last I fell into the *queue* of the pit, which is not, as in Paris, enclosed within a zigzag passage, in order to lessen the pressure. The English stood quietly and at their ease till, at half-past seven, the doors opened, and then there was such a rush (" *choc* ") that some ladies began to scream. As soon, however, as we were through the narrow entrance, we went on commodiously enough : and now the fore-mentioned mystery was cleared up. For three shillings and a half (1 thaler 5 sgr.) you receive no ticket, but a copper check, which you immediately give again. Instead of *bureaus* for the sale of tickets, checks, counter-checks, *controle*, and so on, here the whole business is done by two men in half an hour's time; and done just as effectually as by all our expensive machinery of men and *bureaus*.

I had time enough before the concert began to look about the house. The stage is not so wide, nor the whole so large as the Opera-house in Berlin; but there are five tiers of boxes or seats one above another. There are only two rows of stalls or enclosed seats, the remaining benches belong to the pit. They rise much more abruptly than in most houses, so that one can see better over one's neighbour's head than with us. For the same reason there are no boxes level with the pit, except near the stage. On the other hand, a new division of benches is made directly opposite to the stage, under the ceiling, so that what is lost below may be said to be gained above; thus it is that five tiers of people are seated one above the other.

There are boxes close to the proscenium, and pillars two and two like those in the Berlin Opera-house; they are, however, ill-proportioned, and look as if they were made of tin. The principal colour of the boxes is red, and the fronts ornamented with white and gold. The pillars between the boxes are as slender as those in our theatres. There are some boxes for lovers of retirement, but no royal box. The pit is entirely filled with benches, only every other one of which has a back. Contrary to the custom in Paris, ladies sit in the pit.

At length we came to the performance, which was recommended to the public with some strokes of Italian rhetoric, in a large bill; it ran as follows:—
" *Unprecedented attraction for this night only. A grand selection of Ancient and Modern Music, presenting a combination of the most eminent talent ever introduced in one evening in the national theatres.*"
This sounds very like a mere puff. It was not so, however; in the first place, for three shillings and sixpence you had about as much again for your money as in Berlin. The concert began soon after

seven o'clock, and I was not at home till midnight. Do not think the time long if I take you through the whole concert (without the music.)

Part I.— Selection from the Messiah; Overture. The orchestra stronger than in the Academy of Singing—not so strong as at our Opera. The adagio softer, more *cantando* than in Berlin, and in my opinion, were it but for contrast sake, so much the better. The old Handelian score was, with few exceptions, used without the added accompaniments, which was very interesting to me. The music has, if not a stronger, yet a more calm, I might say a holier effect, without this higher seasoning, and with only the stringed instruments.

2. ' Comfort ye,' and ' Every Valley,' sung by Mr. Hobbs; a soft cultivated tenor, but not remarkable for power or tone.

3. Chorus, ' And the glory of the Lord.' The bass and tenor, in comparison with ours, very strong; the alto and soprano, on the contrary, *much* weaker : but there were more male alto singers than with us. The treble consisted of ten girls and ten boys; it was therefore weak, even in comparison with the proportions usual here; how much more so, compared with ours! The absence or the paucity of female voices gave to the choruses generally a certain hardness and coldness; otherwise they went correctly, and with animation and force. The bass was peculiarly excellent.

5. ' O Thou that tellest,' sung by Miss Cawse; with no expression, but a powerful and equable voice, and a much chaster style than that of Mdlle. Brambilla.

5. ' The people that walked in darkness,' sung

with appropriate expression by Mr. Seguin, a very fine powerful bass. The wind instruments came in only at one part towards the end.

6. ' For unto us,' was encored.

7. ' Rejoice greatly,' sung by Mdme. Stockhausen; her voice has not the grandeur and fullness requisite for Handel's sacred music; but it is pure, sweet, and bears marks of a good school.

8. ' Why do the Heathen?' well sung by Mr. Seguin.

9. ' But thou didst not leave,' Mdme .Stockhausen.

10. ' Hallelujah,' executed with power and effect.

A duet was now to follow by Grisi and Rubini, instead of which the latter came on alone, and the orchestra began to play the symphony to ' Il mio tesoro,' from ' Don Juan.' But such a noise arose, such a cry of ' Grisi, Grisi,' that, after long hesitation, Rubini retired. After some pause the director appeared and announced that Mdlle. Grisi was not yet come, and begged the audience to hear Rubini in the meanwhile. He sang his song, and not only once but twice, with the greatest applause. His voice is an uncommonly powerful tenor, or rather barytone, with a falsetto. None of our singers equal him in power and facility, but his application of the modern Italian manner to Mozart seemed to me thoroughly inappropriate.

Part II.—Selection from Haydn's ' Creation.'

11. Introduction, ' Chaos,' very well executed, with the requisite light and shade.

12 to 21. Various airs and choruses.

In the second act, Ivanhoff sang an air from Rossini's ' Otello.' A beautiful voice, but the unnatural and impure style of the modern Italian school

pushed to the utmost : violent shouting, alternated
in the same bar, with an effeminate and almost in-
audible whisper : light and shade blotched on in
hard and unartistlike contrast ; no sustained style,
but a superficial striving after effect. But this is
what the musical multitude like.

Part III.—Miscellaneous.

23. Overture to ' William Tell.' This noisy,
incoherent *pasticcio* was *encored*, at least the latter
half, that Handel and Mozart might not be too much
flattered by the distinction.

The Impresario now appeared again, and announced with many expressions of distress, that
Tamburini was ill, and some omissions were therefore necessary.

Seven pieces followed out of Rossini's and Mer-
cadante's operas, and a favourite Swiss song. The
singers were Miss Cawse, Mdme. Stockhausen,
Mdlle. Grisi, Messrs. Rubini, Ivanhoff, Seguin, and
Lablache. Grisi has a fine rich voice, with good
lower, and well-managed upper, notes ; great execution, great power, and (as far as it is possible with
such music) appropriate expression. She certainly
is one of the greatest living singers, yet (so far as
the recollection of one performance serves me to
decide) I prefer Malibran. Whether she is a dramatic singer, I hope to have opportunities of judging. Lablache has the most powerful bass voice I
ever heard in my life, and gave Rossini's ' Largo al
factotum ' in a manner which it is impossible to
surpass.

Whatever admiration, however, this singular production may deserve, the hearing of seven pieces
out of seven Italian operas convinced me that there

is a great similarity and poverty in the means employed, the ornaments always the same, the melodies undramatic and continually recurring. What variety, what distinct and appropriate individuality, on the other hand, in one of Mozart's operas !

Thus, then, I heard thirty, or, with the encores, about thirty-five pieces, (recitatives not included,) for thirty-five *silver groschen;* certainly not dear, though it would have shown a better feeling of art to divide the performance into two. The applause was generally so loud and lasted so long, that German singers may well think their countrymen apathetic in the comparison: I can now understand Devrient's saying, " You have fishes' blood." But German composers certainly bore off the palm in this London concert. I came home well pleased, for what I had heard was very curious, and much of it very admirable.

Friday, April 17*th,* 1835.

My design of having a quiet day, yesterday, was favoured by the heavens. The cold was accompanied by the thickest, dampest fog, and both together produced such a fall of snow and rain, that I could only take my most necessary walks at intervals; to the Museum, the Athenæum, and to dinner. In Wardour-street, I had, for a thaler, gravy-soup, beef-steak, sea-kail, (an excellent vegetable, approaching to asparagus, indeed better than any I have seen here,) salmon, rice pudding, bread, and half a pint of ale. This dinner is dearer than what may be had at some restaurants at Paris, but cheaper, on the whole, than in Berlin. The weather yesterday made it necessary to drink stronger wine, so in the evening, while I sat at home studying the English poor-laws, I regaled myself with a sort of punch, made of hot water, sherry, and sugar, which is better than that made with rum and lemons. But I cannot accustom myself to tea. A-propos of tea, I must tell you some facts which I found in the ' Westminster Review,' April, 1835.

Since the monopoly of the China trade has been taken from the East India Company, it is expected that the price will fall and the demand increase. It is estimated that the annual consumption is, in Great Britain and Ireland, 40 millions of pounds.

Russia	6½	,,
Holland	3	,,
Germany	2	,,
France, only	250,000 lbs.	
United States	10 millions of pounds.	
British America	1	,,
—— India	1	,,
—— Australia	250,000 lbs.	

which, adding half a million for the rest of Europe, will give a total of sixty-five millions of pounds. What a change in industry, trade, social habits, and enjoyments, when we reflect that two hundred years ago tea was unknown ! Whether health has been improved by it may be doubted, inasmuch as it has diminished the consumption of beer ; but at all events a tea party is necessarily something very different from a beer party, or a brandy party.

The value of these sixty-five millions of pounds, in China, is equal to about twenty-eight millions of thalers. What a source of revenue to that country, and what folly to fear that. out of love for the East India Company, it will reject the free traders,

and prohibit the export. The attempts to grow tea
in Brazil, Java, and other places have failed. The
great obstacle is the impossibility of producing it as
cheaply as in China. It is now cultivated only in
five provinces of the great empire, generally on hills
which will not produce corn; and there is not the least
difficulty in increasing the production so as to meet
the greatest possible demand. England, in 1700, imported about one hundred thousand pounds ; in 1800
twenty millions, and in 1835 no less than forty-
seven millions, and yet the prices in China have
undergone hardly any variation. Black and green
teas are only varieties of the same plant, indeed are
plucked from the same shrub ; the best and dearest
are the buds of the spring ; the most inferior are the
leaves of the fourth gathering, which takes place in
autumn. Black tea is cheaper than green, and less stimulating. Of the abovementioned sixty-five million
pounds, there are about fifty millions black, and fifteen millions green. The Chinese, the other Asiatic
nations, and the Russians, drink hardly any green
tea; the English, one part green to four black;
the Americans, two parts green to one black.   As
early as the year 1660, a duty was laid upon tea;
i. e. upon the amount of the liquid infusion; a proof
that, at that time, each family did not prepare it at
home, but bought it ready made, like beer. The
amount and the manner of collecting the tax underwent many subsequent changes, and at length rose
far above the prime cost. Many reasons are adduced for laying the same duty on all tea, without
reference to quality (as in France); and this method
has certainly the recommendation of simplicity; but,

on the other hand, it is contended that the duty on the superior sorts would be much too low, on the inferior, much too high.

LETTER XV.

Different ways of regarding Poverty—Experiments of antient Legislators to equalize Wealth—Moses, Lycurgus, Solon, Servius
Tullus—Influence of Christianity—Historical Sketch of English
Poor-laws—Law of Settlement—Increase of Poor's-rate—Scotland—Increased consumption of England—Diet of Poor-houses
—Remedies proposed—Mr. Sadler—Report of the Poor-law Commission—Allowance System—Moral effects—Functionaries—
Overseers—Law of Bastardy—Plans for Reform—Poor-law Commissioners—Objections to the Poor-law Bill—Prevalent errors
about England—Right of the Poor to relief.

London, April 27th, 1835.

IF you expected nothing but amusing chat from my letters, you will have found yourself much mistaken. I am here irresistibly, and as a part of my vocation, led into the consideration of serious, perhaps even melancholy subjects ; and, this time, I have deter-mined to write you a long letter on the condition of the poor, and the much-debated poor-laws. If you are terrified at this threat, I must tell you that it were much easier to write a thick book on the sub-ject, than to compress the essential facts into a few pages. And however I may wish to spare room, I find it absolutely necessary to your understanding anything of the matter, to begin *ab ovo.*

There have always been two very different, or rather opposite, systems with regard to poverty. According to the one, it has been looked upon as a predestined condition of mankind; as a divine ordi-nance, and therefore wholly blameless; as an un-

alterable *datum*. It is only from this point of view
that any one can look with calm indifference at the
Sudras and Parias of India, and say that God and
nature have assigned them their fit station.

The second and opposite system assumes that
God has formed all men equal; that He has appointed an equal share of happiness to all. That
wherever this equality has disappeared (from whatever cause), where poverty and distress have broken
in, they can and ought to be entirely uprooted, and
the golden age of equality restored. Upon this system rest, in their various shades and degrees, all
plans for community of goods, agrarian laws, the
schemes of the Anabaptists, of the Jesuits in Para-
guay, the St. Simonians, and others.

There is a third system which (as opposed to the
first) regards poverty as a great evil, but denies
(as opposed to the second) the possibility of its extirpation. Its advocates affirm that its existence
is necessary, that it remedies itself best when it is
left entirely to itself, and that all means to avert
it are useless, since they cannot change the laws
of nature; and mischievous, since they raise false
hopes, relax energies, and beget discontents.

Such are the extreme systems, each of which appears to me to contain errors. The first rests on a
bad theology, which ill conceals pride and selfishness: it stamps circumstances as sacred and unchangeable, which the diviner part of human nature
regards as the fit subject of its beneficent influence
and activity.

The second goes too far in the contrary direction,
and, from a want of humility and resignation, aspires
to mould anew, with human hands, the work of the

divine Creator, and to reduce the variety of his works to one pattern. Everything is to be governed by external and forcible means, or (as with the Jesuits) the most artificial calculations. Every diversity is to be regarded as an injustice; and a dead uniformity to be introduced, and maintained, by the hardest and most impracticable tyranny (as among the St. Simonians).

The second and third systems are right, in so far as they hold poverty to be an evil; but the second errs from superabundance of remedies; the third, from indifference and neglect. Medicine cannot banish death from the world, but has it, therefore, been renounced as useless?

If, to leave theory, we look at the practice of the greatest legislators, we find that, from the earliest times, extremes of poverty and riches were regarded as an evil and a danger which various means were devised to counteract. The division of the land in Palestine, the sabbath, and the year of jubilee, instituted by Moses, were mainly directed against this; although, from causes which I have investigated in my lectures on ancient history, they could not answer the purpose for which they were designed.

Lycurgus made a still more direct attempt to establish equality among his citizens; and a multitude of institutions, customs, and laws were framed to support this fundamental principle. But they were frustrated not only by the existence of the unfortunate Helots, but by the insufficiency of mechanical means (such as the division of land) to subdue the activity of the counteracting causes. Hence Solon and Servius Tullus adopted what I may call dynamic

means,—moving regulators, which were designed
perpetually to check the growth of excessive riches or
poverty. That is to say, they gave the rich greater
rights, but, at the same time, they laid upon them
heavier and more costly duties; they abridged the
rights, but they also lightened the burdens of the
poor. By such measures, existing relations were
not suddenly changed (as by the jubilee or the division of land), which can never produce more than a
momentary equality; but gentler and steadier means
were applied to maintain, in some degree, the
balance of fortune. The less abrupt contrasts of
the Athenian division of classes disappeared still
more rapidly than the Roman; and the Licinian
rogations were just as little efficacious in preventing the extremes of wealth and poverty in a conquering state, as that altered employment of the
public lands which the Gracchi proposed in vain.
Then followed revolutionary schemes of a general
partition of property, and, at last, military proscrip-
tions and confiscations. With these ended all the
legislative experiments of antiquity, and universal
intellectual bankruptcy went hand-in-hand with
universal decay and misery.

With christianity arose a totally new set of feelings and principles on this subject, in common with
so many others. From the Agapæ to the mendicant
monks, we may trace views of property, of the individual enjoyment, or the participation of it, which
deviate entirely from all that had hitherto existed.
Even the rigidly exclusive Roman system of private
property was compelled to give way to a doctrine
which (in idea at least) established the temperate
use and the fraternal interchange of riches. This
was a great advance. Charitable endowments, volun-

tary almsgiving, and a church no less wealthy than bountiful, mitigated the sufferings of poverty in the middle ages, more effectually than is commonly believed.

This state of things has, from a thousand causes, entirely changed; and great reforms (such as the abolition of slavery and villenage) have been accompanied with great evils in relation to the poor, and the provision for them. Countless questions pressed upon the consideration of legislators or rulers, and demanded instant answer. Who are the poor? What succour is the most efficacious? Must the poor be left to voluntary alms, or have they, as against the rich, a right to support which governments are bound to enforce?

On all these points, no nation has made so many efforts and experiments as England, and therefore I proceed from this long, but I hope not useless introduction, to the English poor-laws.

The first feeling with which one considers them is, that of astonishment at the contrast of the greatest affluence and the greatest poverty; of the vast gains, and the urgent want. Is this accidental, or is it the result of successive mistakes? or is it the inevitable consequence of so high a state of civilization, and such enormous national power? Have not all nations reason to congratulate themselves that though their station is humbler, they have not fifty millions of thalers to pay as poor's-rate? that though they are without many comforts and enjoyments, they have fewer wants and miseries? that though they have some partial or local maladies, they are not threatened with a universal and consuming plague? Lord John Russell* exclaims, " Our poor

* On Government, p. 213.

form an army four times as numerous as that with
which we resisted the empire of France !"

I might, perhaps, conclude with repeating these remarks, so often and so confidently made; but you must
be content to follow me through that longer path
which I have entered upon for my own instruction.

The laws concerning the poor, which existed in
England in the middle ages, related chiefly to
wandering beggars, and were harsh, not to say cruel,
towards them, from the persuasion that enough was
done for the poor in the way of voluntary almsgiving. A compulsory tax for their support was not
thought of. According to a law of the year 1388,
no husbandman or labourer could leave his place of
abode and travel about the country, without the permission of a justice of the peace, nor unless he could
obtain no work there. Laws were passed in 1495
and 1504, to the same effect; and one of the year
1531, empowers justices of the peace to grant leave
to "impotent persons" to beg within a certain district. "Able-bodied beggars," on the other hand,
were to be whipped and sent back to the place where
they were born, or where they had passed the last
three years, and there made to labour. Later enactments of Henry VIII. and Edward VI. show that
after the suppression of monasteries, and the alienation of so much church property, begging, whether
by the impotent or the able, could not be kept under;
hence the parishes were exhorted to provide wholly
for the former, and to punish the latter.

More important, however, than all previous enactments, and more varied and permanent in their
effects, are those of Queen Elizabeth, A.D. 1601.
The most material are as follows:—The church-

warden, and from two to four of the householders, appointed by the justices of the peace, shall provide for the employment of the children for whom their parents cannot find work or food. Parents and kinsfolk are bound, under pain of imprisonment or other punishment, to provide for the helpless members of their families, for the old, the sick, the lame, the blind, &c. The overseers are to find work for all able-bodied persons who are without employment. If these things cannot be accomplished in single parishes, several are to be united for this purpose. Those who will not work shall be imprisoned. A tax for the poor shall be levied, but not exceeding a very moderate sum; the overseers to be responsible for the disbursement of the funds. All begging, except by the inhabitants of the parish, is still rigorously forbidden; but those who are unable to work may be allowed by the overseer to ask alms in their own neighbourhood.

These enactments of Queen Elizabeth are regarded by many as the source of all the evils and sufferings,—the Pandora's box; while others, even very recently, have warmly defended them: the Marquis of Salisbury, for instance, said in parliament, in the year 1830, that the law of Elizabeth was admirable and beneficent, and that the evils complained of had arisen solely from its maladministration. Lord Teynham, too, remarked that Elizabeth's regulations were wise and benevolent; they, like all the laws of her reign, were framed with a view to increase the happiness of her people*.

Undoubtedly, wise provisions are not to be confounded with blundering or abuse in the application

* Hansard, l. 376, 689.

of them. What did the law contemplate? First, to support the miserable and helpless whom their families were unable to support; and to provide the able-bodied, not with money, but with work. Secondly, to lighten the burden, by the extension of the circle from which succours were to be drawn. Thirdly, to punish the lazy. Fourthly, for these purposes, to levy and to apply a tax not exceeding a certain amount.

These provisions seem so natural and so simple, that it appears as if no objection (apart from mal-administration) could be made to them. So far, however, as they relate to a disease, the entire removal of which is impossible, they must have some weak points inherent in them, and these we must not conceal. One is, the direction to find work for all those who can do it. But in a simple state of society, the difficulties attending this might be less than in a complex one, and the punishment of the indolent is the best means of making them labour for their own support. Further, the very important question here first occurred, whether, when voluntary alms are insufficient, the state acts wisely and justly in levying a tax for the support of the poor? We shall be more able to answer this question when we have seen what the English have done, and what left undone.

In the first place, immediately after the restoration of the Stuarts, the simple principles above stated were departed from; and the freedom and facility of obtaining work and subsistence were greatly abridged by the laws relating to "settlement." In virtue of these, the place of birth must be regarded as the place of settlement, till another

is gained. This is done, first, by the residence of
the parents, or by marriage : secondly, by a residence
of forty days, after notice having been given to the
magistrates of intention to settle : thirdly, such
notice is held to be given, 1. by hiring a house
of the yearly rent of 10*l*.; 2. by paying the public taxes; 3. by undertaking any public office
in the parish. Unmarried and childless persons
needed to give no such notice, and apprentices
gained a settlement as such. Every person who did
not gain settlement by one of these means might be
sent away by the magistrates. But in order to
diminish the number of cases in which persons
coming from other places were sent away, the
parishes often invented pretexts for receiving them
as parishioners. They could then only be passed
home to the first parish, in case they became actually
chargeable to the second *."

London, April 28th.

I see that if I were to go into accurate details
concerning the state of the poor and the poor-laws
of former times, I should weary you. I shall therefore only advert to one or two earlier institutions,
and then describe to you more at length those more
recent events which have given occasion to the poor-
law which was passed last year.

To be brief : spite of all precautions and expedients, the evil went on increasing; and, for want
of going to the bottom of it, people came to the
conclusion that the increase of poverty was actually
and irremediably in the same ratio as the increase

* Blackstone, 1. 363.

in the amount of the poor's-rate.   This was as follows :—

1750	about	£500,000
1800	„	£3,860,000
1812	„	£6,580,000
1817	„	£7,890,000

Scotland, though so much poorer, required, even in
a year of scarcity, only £119,000; of which £70,000
was raised by free gift, and only £40,000 by rates.
It was justly deemed advantageous to Scotland that
the management of her poor was committed, not to
officers annually changed, but, permanently, to the
landlords, clergy, &c.   But this one favourable circumstance by no means explained the enormous difference between that country and England*.   Dr.
Chalmers, in a work on political economy, says, that
all alterations in the laws of taxation or provision
for the poor are vain and futile ; that there is but one
main and fundamental remedy,—a sound christian
education of the people.   True ; and yet not true.
Certainly, this vital matter has often been entirely
overlooked, or rated far beneath its importance ; but
there are a multitude of circumstances independent of
it, which have a material influence on the prosperity
and adversity of a nation ; such as the price of commo-
dities, &c.   The poorest man in a civilized country is
not so destitute as an inhabitant of a desert; and it
is demonstrable that the incomes, the comfort, and
the luxuries of the people throughout Europe have
increased within the last century.   In England the
produce of the national industry has risen six-fold
since the year 1770, while the population has only

* Lowe, p. 345.

doubled in the same time. The consumption of wheaten bread, of beef, &c., has increased, while the mortality has greatly diminished ; fifteen millions sterling are deposited in the savings banks*.

These facts, among many, would seem to prove the impossibility of the pauperism talked of, and yet it existed, and grew to an overpowering height. In the year 1800 †, there were, in Salisbury, 312 poor in the house, and 2436 receiving out-door relief. The amount of the rate was £4,481 ; the number of householders 1353, of whom 475 were unable to pay to the poor's-rate ; so that each of the remaining 878 householders paid £6 13s. 4d. yearly in poor's-rate. By the side of this fact I must place another from the same period. The inhabitants of the poor-house at Bristol had, for breakfast, oatmeal-porridge, or rice-milk ; for dinner, a pound of beef, or mutton, or a rice-pudding, &c. In Shrewsbury, for breakfast, meat-broth, or milk-porridge ; for dinner, five times in the week, meat, with vegetables ; once bread and cheese, once potatoes, or dumplings, or a pound of wheaten bread, with milk ; and for supper, alternately, meat, peas-soup, milk-porridge, or potatoes ‡.

These two statements, placed in contrast, are sufficiently instructive. An expenditure like that in Shrewsbury would reduce the whole continent of Europe to beggary in two years ; and if every man is a pauper who fares worse than the inhabitants of these poor-houses, certainly we ought immediately to provide such receptacles for nearly the whole

---

* M'Culloch's Dictionary, *Ale*, p. 15.   † Göde's Travels, ii. p. 365.
‡ Göde, v. 9.

body of the German peasantry,—and perhaps for some of the German writers on pauperism.

These single traits of light demonstrated the necessity of an extensive investigation, and the poor-laws came frequently under discussion in Parliament. In one of these debates, Mr. Sadler* maintained that the existing poverty did not arise from over-population, for that, though there was less work in winter, particularly in the country, in summer there was a want of hands. The chief sources of the wretched condition of the lower classes were, according to him, the following :—

1st. The want of small landed proprietors.

2nd. The increase of large estates.

3rd. The loss sustained by the small tenants from enclosures and partitions of common lands; in which the wealthy proprietors get almost all, while the poorer can hardly ever formally substantiate their rights.

4th. The increase of day-labourers employed in the cultivation of the large estates, and the crowding of several families into small houses.

5th. The establishment of the greater number of manufactures in cities.

6th. The introduction of machinery.

A motion of Lord Winchilsea in November, 1830†, on the means of employing the poor, pointed more distinctly to the real and radical evil. Yet opinions remained so confused, that many sought the cause of all the suffering in the calling in of the small paper currency; while others looked for help in a kind of poor insurance-office for the whole empire. Since that time, the facts have been so fully and radically

* Hansard, viii. p. 506.   † Ibid., i. p. 371.

examined and elucidated by some writers, but more particularly by the Parliamentary Commission in their admirable Report, that the truth has been completely brought to light. I will endeavour to extract from that Report, and from other sources, the most important facts, more especially those which may serve to correct some prevalent errors.

The subject may be viewed in relation,—1st, to the support of the "able-bodied;" 2nd, to the support of the "impotent."

Let us begin with the former, and, in England, the more important and more dangerous, part.

The "able-bodied" were maintained, either at their own homes by "out-door relief," or in the workhouses, where they were provided with lodging and other necessaries. The relief granted in money has assumed various shapes. The first of these consisted simply in alms given to those able to work, without requiring any service or labour in return. This found the more ready acceptance, because it caused no further trouble (such as the providing work), and was usually connected with the condition that the alms-receiver was not soon to present himself again. In fact, however, it was a premium given to indolence and even to vice, and soon became more costly than had been imagined.

A second class of aids in money was comprehended under the name "allowances," although the word is applied to very different cases. Sometimes, occasional help for definite purposes, such as the buying of shoes, was understood by it; sometimes, a general addition to the ordinary wages of the labourers; sometimes, a succour granted according to the number of children, or to the price of wheat.

The two latter modes, in particular, were so important, that, in many places, the several gradations of
relief were officially calculated; and the rates raised,
and disbursements made, in accordance. In many
parishes the birth of a child, or the rise in the price
of corn, immediately conferred a right to demand a
larger allowance, without any inquiry into the income
of the parents.

The third mode was called the system of "rounds-
men," or of tickets. According to this, the parish
(by the overseer) bought the labour of one or more
paupers, and gave those who hired them a certain
sum towards the wages : this was not determined by
the goodness or the market price of the labour, but
generally by the wants of the labourer, the number
of his children, and the price of corn. The labourers
were often put up to auction, and knocked down to
the bidder who required the smallest advance.

Fourthly, the parishes themselves employed and
paid the unemployed, but able-bodied poor, though
the law of Elizabeth refused all assistance to the
able-bodied, and aimed only at finding them work :
this was in fact seldom done. In the year 1832, of
7,036,968l. paid to the poor, only 354,000l. was paid
for labour actually performed (whether within or
without the houses). This is to be accounted for,
partly because it is too much trouble to devise and
furnish suitable work ; partly, because no persons can
derive any *immediate* advantage from it, as they did
from getting labourers at low wages. The gain to
the whole parish was indeed very small, and dis-
obedience and revolt were often produced by congre-
gating the labourers, or rather the idlers. Everywhere the free labourer had harder work, and, pro-

portionally, less pay; so that many wished—and the
wish was easily fulfilled—to be transferred into the
ranks of paupers. But more of that presently.

While so extravagant a provision was made for
those who were able to work, the assistance granted
to the aged, the sick, and the helpless, (necessarily
so inconsiderable in amount,) was comparatively
inadequate. And yet these are just the persons
who stand most in need of help; and for whom it
is much easier to provide relief than for the first
class.

The maintenance and employment of both classes
in poor-houses (" in-door relief") was also liable to
many objections. The apparent humanity of allowing the paupers a very bountiful diet was perhaps
among the most pernicious abuses. Mr. Lee, who
had been for seventeen years master of a workhouse
containing above a thousand persons, said,—" It is a
common remark among our poor that they live better
in the workhouse than before;" and this seems really
to be the case, if we consider the spaciousness and
cleanliness of the rooms, the goodness of the beds,
and the variety and good preparation of the food.
A so-called pauper, says the writer of an article in
the ' Quarterly Review *,' in a poor-house in Kent,
has " meat-days" from three to five times a week,
his bread is better than that which our soldiers receive, and he has as much of vegetables as he will
eat. While but too many are thus enticed into the
workhouse (where hardly any work is done), and
their residence there seems agreeable enough, the
whole weight is thrown into the scale of the animal
part of human nature, and the noble feelings of inde-

* No. cvii.

pendence, self-support, attachment to home, to family, to neighbours, are lost. The greater number, says the same writer, do nothing, love nothing, hope nothing, fear nothing; they sit listlessly in the same place, like blocks of wood rather than men. England, with all her wealth, has uselessly expended immense sums in this stall-feeding of her so-called poor; has sustained the bodies and destroyed the souls of her people, and has created more misery than she has removed. The ancient Greeks reverenced even the ashes of their fathers; the English teach their peasantry to bury father, mother, and kindred in a workhouse, unmoved; and to look upon roasted meat as a compensation for all losses. The free labourer lives much worse than he who by lies and trickery obtains relief from the poor's-rate. Nay, those who pay to the rates are often far worse off than those who receive them*.

Two hundred and four persons in the poor-house at Margate, cost fourteen thousand thalers yearly. The poor, or, I must repeat, the pretended poor, who generally live in entire idleness, receive (as at Swanscombe and Stone, for instance)—

" Four hot meals per week :

Half a pound of butter per week:

One pound of bread per day :

Vegetables of various sorts, as much as they can eat:

One pint of beer per day :

Pudding on Sundays."

Although the effects of such a system must be sufficiently manifest from the mere statement of it, I shall add some facts from the Report of the Commissioners.

---

* The reader will observe that all these quotations are re-translated from the German.—*Translator*.

The abuses which have hitherto existed have been but too popular. In the first place, the labourers receive lower wages, but they have no need to look about for work, care nothing for the approbation or disapprobation of their master, need not seek for any further help, and, if they have nothing to gain, have nothing to lose. Secondly, the employers have favoured the system, because, though they could get no diminution of rent on account of high wages, they do on account of high poor's-rates; and the landlord, again, finds means to shift his own loss upon the whole parish, or to gain when the poor are occupants of his houses. This gain is, however, only transient and apparent.

One example from among the thousands afforded by the southern counties of England will make the matter more clear. A farmer reduces the wages of his labourers from 12s. to 10s. The labourer goes to the overseer, shows, by a reference to the abovementioned estimates and tables, that he wants 12s. for the support of his family, and receives 2s. The other farmers follow the example of the first; the first then lowers wages again to 8s., and so it goes on, till wages are run down to the very lowest sum on which a single man can barely exist. What follows? or, rather, what does this imply? First, that wages are no longer regulated by free competition for the supply of the fair wants of a moderate family, but are artificially depressed. Secondly, that this difference is most absurdly made up in the form of poor's relief. Thirdly, that this relief is raised with the birth of every child, and is generally apportioned to the numbers of a family. Fourthly, (a crying injustice,) that all the parishioners, the clergymen, &c., must contribute to make good what those who employ the labourers squeeze out of their wages.

Meanwhile the evil of necessity increased so rapidly under such a system that the inevitable Nemesis overtook the selfish and the ill-judging. Rents fell, the value of property thus burthened, decreased; the farmers paid enormously in the shape of poor's-rate, and sometimes actually emigrated from one county to another less heavily taxed.

The system of "allowances," or the making up artificially depressed wages out of the poor's-rate, at length not only impoverished the payers, but made the receivers lazy, careless, and vicious. They tried to avoid all work, and to live at the public cost; while masters often rather took a lazy workman who was partly paid by the parish, than an industrious one who lived by his wages. Reckless marriages, and indifference to the training of their children, were the inevitable consequences. The effect of "allowances," says Mr. Stuart, is to loosen, if not to sever, all bonds of affection between parents and children. If a young man, sometimes a boy of fourteen, receives an allowance on his own account, he may indeed continue to live with his parents, but he does not contribute his earnings to the common stock; be buys his bread and bacon and eats it by himself. The most revolting quarrels arise from mutual accusations of theft, and as the child knows he will be supported by the parish, he loses all dependance on his parents. The parents are not less thoroughly degraded and demoralized; they neglect their children, and do their utmost to prevent them from getting work, for fear the overseer should hear of it, and diminish their allowance.

The monstrous waste of money (says the Report)

vanishes as unimportant in comparison with the
frightful effects of this system on the happiness and
the morals of the lower classes. It is as difficult to
give the mere reader a distinct impression of the
powerful and pernicious influence of it, as, by any
description, to convey an adequate idea of the terrors
of the plague or of shipwreck. One must associate
with the poor, visit poor-houses, question the inhabitants, be present at the paying of the allowances,
in order to have an idea of the moral debasement to
which this system has given rise. One must hear
the pauper threaten that he will desert wife and
child if he does not get more money; that he will
put his old bedridden mother into the workhouse,
or lay her before the overseer's door till he is paid
for taking care of her; mothers come without shame
to demand the wages of their daughters' inconti-
nence; wives declare with the utmost coolness who
are the several fathers of their children—and then
say whether the expenditure be the greatest evil
produced by the Poor Laws.

Let us now observe the persons and authorities
connected with the administration of these laws, viz.,
the overseer, the vestry or parish-meeting, and the
magistrates; for the form is closely connected with
the substance of the institution. The overseer is
bound to decide how much money is required, from
whom and how it is to be levied, and how it is to be
applied. In the country this office is generally filled
by farmers; in the towns, by shopkeepers and manufacturers. They are elected for one year; sometimes for only three or four months. If they refuse
to serve they are subject to a fine. They receive no
pay or compensation for loss of time.

These overseers are, of course, often hindered

by their business from paying due attention to
the poor; while even the most zealous are not in
office long enough to acquire the requisite knowledge and experience. Still oftener, indirect motives
are in operation; partiality, dislike, share in jobs
and undertakings, desire of popularity, fear of unpopularity. When, for instance, the overseer sold
articles of food, he often found those only deserving
of relief who bought of him, and so on. The only
check on partiality, extravagance, or dishonesty,
was the duty of laying all his accounts before the
rate-payers and the magistrates. But this, from
various causes, lost its efficacy. The frequent
change of the overseer made the amount of blame
due to any individual appear too inconsiderable for
notice; or, as I have said, the rate-payers thought
they gained more by low wages, than they lost
by high rates; there was no rule or model for the
form of the accounts, and nothing distinct could
be gathered from a cursory inspection of them.
Above all, they feared to irritate the paupers by
rigid economy, and to render themselves objects of
their formidable vengeance.

The Commissioners close this section on overseers with words to the following effect :—" What
can be expected of officers who enter upon their
office unwillingly, have no requisite knowledge, no
time for the business, and who are exposed to
innumerable temptations? They distribute or refuse the public money to their workmen, creditors,
debtors, relations, friends, and neighbours; they
are exposed to every kind of pillage and menace;
they find themselves popular and beloved for
prodigality; hated and abused, nay, their property

and their persons exposed to danger, for care and frugality."

The parish meetings are either "open vestries," or representative. The former consist of all the actual inhabitants who pay poor's rates. Non-resident proprietors have no seat in these meetings, the chief object of which has been to diminish wages at the expense of others. The representative meetings (from five to twenty householders, chosen by the whole parish) have generally been found to work better than the open ones; but even here, partiality and antipathy, or fear of the consequences of a more rigorous administration, have manifested themselves. The plan of subjecting the overseers and parishes to the control of a superior authority—the justices of the peace—was very just; but it was impossible for the latter to go into all the endless details; and the paupers too easily found protection and favour with goodnatured magistrates, however false and unjust were their complaints of the parish officers. Every statement or correspondence became so tedious and diffuse, that people preferred adhering to the decision, though this generally entailed an increase of expenditure.

From the year 1794, when the principle, that a part of wages were to be paid out of the poor's-rate, and that a sort of premium was to be paid for every child born, became generally diffused, and was adopted and enforced by the magistrates, from that time, the evil spread with redoubled force. After a thoroughly false direction had thus been given to the whole system, the inquiry into errors of detail was of little avail.

A peculiar train of evils proceeded from the laws

XV.]LAW OF BASTARDY.143

of settlement already mentioned, which secured to
hired servants, apprentices, labourers, &c., a settlement as above described. Various expedients were
resorted to to prevent such burthens falling on the
parish. People hired only those already belonging
to it, or, if strangers, for less than a year, or did not
allow them to sleep in the parish, or sent them out
of it on the thirty-ninth day. Thus each village
became a sort of poor-enclosure; assumed a posture
of suspicion and hostility towards all others, and
settlements were gained or refused by every possible means, deceit and perjury inclusive.

London, April 29, 1835.

In but too close connexion with the poor laws
stands the theory, or rather the practice, of illegitimate children. Queen Elizabeth's laws decreed that
both parents should provide for the child; or, in
case they deserted and left it to the parish, should
be liable to imprisonment. A law of James I.,
in a severer tone of morality, made all such breaches
of chastity penal. The mother was condemned to
be imprisoned for a year; and, on a second offence,
until she could find good securities for her future
conduct. But as the mother often absconded,
and the child was left on the parish, a law was
passed in the reign of Charles II. empowering the
magistrate, before the birth of an illegitimate child,
to seize so much of the property of the parents as
would suffice for its support. Lastly, by a law of
George III., it was enacted, that if a woman declared herself pregnant, and named the father of the
child, the magistrate, at the request of the overseer,

might immediately imprison the man till he had given security for its maintenance. The declaration of any woman was sufficient ground for such a proceeding ; the magistrate was not bound, nor even authorized, to make the least inquiry as to truth or falsehood, guilt or innocence, nor even to listen to the defence of the accused.

The consequence of this senseless and unjust law of course was, that loose women soon learned to regard natural children as an easy source of gain ; and, according to one witness, out of ten such, nine were sworn to wrong fathers. The accused had only the wretched alternative of marrying or paying. The parish allowed much more for illegitimate than for legitimate children, so that two or three such were a good portion, by means of which many women got husbands who did not scorn to live on the wages of their wives' shame. " I am persuaded," says one witness, " that three-fourths of these women would not be seduced, had they not the certain prospect of allowance or marriage in consequence." Mothers have even been known to facilitate the seduction of their daughters, in order to get them off their own hands upon those of the parish, or of a husband.

The notion that any good can be done by foundling-hospitals has long been given up. In the magnificent and expensive establishment of that kind here, at its very commencement, (between the 2nd of June, 1736, and the 31st of December, 1737,) not less than 5510 were received *.

I pass from this brief survey of the existing evils to the measures for their removal, which have been proposed, accepted, or rejected.

* Quarterly Review, No. cv.—*See* Translator's note, p. 137.

Firstly. Some, as I have mentioned, thought that they had discovered a remedy in the return to a small paper currency. This extravagant scheme was, however, with great justice, rejected *.

Secondly. Others proposed that the care of the poor should be entirely taken from the parishes, and be under the sole management of the Government, as a state charge. Thus all the difficulties respecting settlement, want of work, over-population, &c., would be put an end to; time and money saved; unity introduced, instead of the innumerable different modes of management; burthens equalized and lightened, &c. To this it was replied, that between the distinct parish system, and a general government system, a middle course might be taken: that innumerable details could not be managed by a central authority; the operation of parishes and counties was useful, indeed necessary; and that the Government should beware of assuming the least appearance of being able to establish a sort of universal insurance office against misfortune and poverty, improvidence, laziness, and vice. Moreover, the workhouse would then remain almost the sole, and yet the inadequate, form of equal relief; and the supply of money would be neither certain, nor to be taken out of the ordinary funds of the empire, since Scotland and Ireland have no concern with the poor-laws.

Thirdly. Many thought it the most simple and effectual mode to grant the poor small allotments of uncultivated or common land. In this manner, they urged, the poor's-rate would be, if not entirely abolished, yet greatly diminished; suitable labour pro-

* Hansard, xvii., 497.

vided; a taste for work engendered; production increased, &c. The obstacles to this scheme were alleged to be, that farmers or peasants of this kind would be regarded by the parish as an inconvenient new body, within itself; that such allotments of land could not be made in the existing state of the laws without great difficulties, &c.* If, indeed, all these obstacles could be removed, great good might be expected to result from such a scheme.

Fourthly. The system of a labour-rate was warmly recommended. According to this, every payer to the poor's-rate should have, instead of that rate, a proportionate number of persons allotted to him to employ and to pay; or, in case he did not employ them, he should pay the amount of their wages to the poor's-fund. This system has worked well in certain cases, but is liable to great objections. Every sort of compulsion to employ persons at a certain rate of wages diminishes or disturbs the difference between free labourers and paupers; confounds wages with relief; and gives work to a man, not because he is a good labourer, but because he is chargeable to the parish. Every man is subjected to a disadvantage, indeed to a tax, as long as he has any property, or has too much pride to put himself on the pauper list. Besides the division of paupers, according to the poor's-rate, presses most unfairly and unequally; while, for instance, it is light to the manufacturer, the farmer has insufficient employment, the clergyman or physician none, for the men assigned to him.

Fifthly. But the heart of the evil was much more clearly laid open by the following principles, than by any of these or other particular schemes:—

* Hansard, i. 1319; ii. 606; iv. 262.

That the condition and the fare of the poor man receiving relief ought to be, not better, but, on the contrary, more rigid and scanty than that of the independent labourer.

That the system of raising wages by means of the poor's-rate is utterly bad.

That the number of children, and the price of corn, affords no just standard whatever for the relief of able-bodied persons.

That the system of management of poor-houses, as well as the laws of settlement and bastardy, stand in need of essential reforms.

As these and other propositions formed the basis of the new Poor-Law Bill, laid before the House on the 14th of August, 1834, I will proceed to give you the most important contents of it, and then close my long report with a few general remarks.

1st. Three commissioners are to be appointed to direct and control the whole system of pauper management throughout England. They are empowered to nominate nine assistant commissioners for the several districts ; to issue directions for all measures and changes connected with the poor; to remedy abuses, inspect accounts, to order the erection of poor-houses, &c. In a word, they form an effective and powerful central authority, but are of course subject to Parliament and to the ministry.

2nd. Wherever the union of parishes appears advantageous, several may be united for the management of the affairs of the poor, and, with the aid of chosen guardians, render the levy of the rate more uniform and equable.

3rd. The three chief commissioners to decide on the appointment, dismissal, and pay of the officers

of the poor, and on expenditure and affairs generally.

4th. Persons able to work who come upon the
parish, to be taken into the workhouse, and compelled to work hard ; out-door relief, generally, to
be gradually abolished.

5th. Persons unable to work, to be maintained by
their relations; natural children, by the man who
marries their mother.

6th. Hired servants and apprentices to gain no
settlement.   This can only be gained by payment of
poor's-rates.

7th. The laws concerning the parents of illegitimate children to be repealed.   The child to follow
the mother's settlement, and she to be chargeable
with its whole support, and to have no legal plea
against, or demand on, the father.   If the child
become chargeable to the parish, the parish to have
the power of compelling the father to pay for its
support; but the mere declaration of the mother as
to the paternity must be supported by the testimony
of at least one witness.   This money paid by the
father to go exclusively to indemnify the parish for
the support of the child, not to the mother.

These few principles do not indeed give the contents of the one hundred and four printed pages of
the law, but they show the main points and general
tendency.

London, April 30th, 1835.

In the debates on this bill, a few obstinate voices
were raised against that, as against all other alterations.   These persons were of opinion that the existing laws were sufficient; the more so, that they were

certain to be better administered in future. The great majority, on the contrary, were convinced of the necessity of new laws; and directed their objections only against certain points, which led to various modifications of the first scheme. Objections were, and still are, made; which, however, did not change the decision of the majority in Parliament, and of which I give a few by way of specimen.

Objection 1st. — The central board will be all-powerful, or utterly powerless; either superfluous, or mischievous; and the authority of the established magistracy is too much abridged and degraded by that of the assistant commissioners, and by other provisions of the bill.

Answer.—Without a vigorous central control, it were impossible to have any general inspection, or to put an end to the boundless disorder and caprice which has hitherto existed; nor is it very consistent in those who see such immense advantages in the centralization of all judicial business, to be the vehement opponents of centralization as regards the affairs of the poor. There can be no danger of the omnipotence of public functionaries who are subject to the control of ministers, parliament, and public opinion; nor of their powerlessness; since their powers are established and accurately defined by law. The authority of the magistrates is not, as hitherto, decisive in the last resort; for the precise reason that the incoherence and anarchy resulting from it were the very things to be removed. It was only under such a system that it would have been possible for the south and the north of England to take a totally different course, and for the consequent misery in the former so far to exceed that in the latter. While

the poor's-rate (calculated upon the income and pro-
perty-tax of 1812) rose in the south to 6s. 9d. in the
pound, in the north it fell to 1s. 7d., and, on an average, the difference was as four to one.   All this was
not the effect of existing misery, but the misery was
created in the south by the adoption of all the false
principles which I have explained above.   By prudent, though, indeed, very rare measures, the immoderate poor's-rate was reduced again.   In Ashford,
it amounted in 1818 to 3,450l., and in 1834, to only
1160l.* ; and in Manchester and Sheffield it was in
ten years reduced one-half.   It will be the business
of the new laws and the new authorities to convert
these scattered examples into a universal practice.

Objection 2nd.   An equalization of the rate, and
a union of parishes is impossible.

Answer.—It is by no means the aim of the new
system to introduce an absolute, and, indeed, impracticable, equality, without regard to local circumstances, but to abolish the innumerable and
senseless diversities which prevailed under precisely
similar circumstances, and oppressed the one whilst
they unduly favoured the other.   Thus in ten neigh-
bouring villages, there were nine different modes of
assessment, and in seven districts of the same city,
five.   The difficulty of uniting several parishes for
a beneficial end generally arose from these diversities: thus, a well-ordered village refused to unite
itself with an adjoining one, which was overrun with
paupers and dissolute persons.   In future, most of
these objections will be removed, and many useful
objects, such as the building of poor-houses, be
facilitated to each.

* Quarterly Review, No. cvi., p. 517.

Objection 3rd.—The new law lays far too great a stress on these workhouses.   They are too expensive, and lead, in another way, to the old evils.

Answer.—If the labour in them is harder, and the diet mo re scanty, than an able-bodied man can obtain out of them, the pressure upon them will diminish ; and also, after the removal of all restrictions on the free circulation of labour, it will be much easier for a man to maintain himself.

Objection 4th.—The abolition of allowances is cruel and impracticable.   Wages have been depressed by the maladministration of the laws, and will rise again very slowly, and the father of a numerous family reckoned on legal relief which ought not to be suddenly withdrawn.

Answer.—The law empowers the authorities to proceed gradually, and free intercourse will soon equalize wages in the north and south of England.

Objection 5th.—Some provisions of the new law are contrary to the laws of God and nature, which impose the support of children on both parents. The law of God commands the man to marry the woman he has seduced, of which nothing is said in the bill.   The mother of a natural child justly looks to its father for support.   If this is denied, either she grows hardened in vice, or she destroys the child she despairs of being able to support.   The new law is repugnant to all the natural feelings of the people, and gives the men a licence for profligacy.

Answer.—The ordinances of the Mosaic law are not to be regarded as the absolute laws of God. The compulsion on a man to marry any woman who declares herself with child by him is not the

way to produce many good and Christian marriages.
That all natural and moral feeling impose on both
parents the duty of maintaining their offspring, no
one has ever thought of contesting; the only question is, how far *legal* compulsion is expedient or
practicable? Where that feeling exists, all compulsion is needless; where it is wanting, experience
shows that unchastity, recklessness, perjury, and a
host of evils are produced by an attempt to force it.
When breaches of chastity are not the way to pecuniary aid, or to marriage, seduction will be better
and more constantly resisted. Lastly, if the parish
chooses, and the father is ascertained, he may be
made to pay, as before; only, as is just, for the sole
advantage of the child. But, in general, the new law
will probably operate as a wholesome check on vice.

So much for the several objections and their con-
futation. On the whole, matters stood so that they
could not be worse, and that any alteration must be
an improvement. I hear, too, that the first annual
report will exhibit very satisfactory results.

And here I should close my long report, but if
you have followed me patiently thus far, you will
allow me a few general remarks.

First.—There is an idea widely diffused on the
continent, that England, spite of her apparent
wealth, nay in consequence of that wealth, is falling
into inevitable poverty and decay. This is a great
error. There exist no natural causes for such
poverty, and as soon as the mistakes in the poor-law
system are corrected, it is far more probable that
the natural condition of the country will prove to
be far better than even Englishmen anticipated.
But where, from absurd institutions, the pauper

lives better than the free labourer, the thief better
than the pauper, and the transported felon better
than the one under imprisonment*, how is it possible that all the bad results I have enumerated
should not ensue ? and what less opulent country
would not have gone to utter ruin in a much shorter
time, under such a system as that pursued in England ? Unquestionably England's progress and
elevation is, in some respects, attributable to her
laws, and her customs, which have almost the force
of laws ; but it is impossible to repeat often enough,
or emphatically enough, that these laws and customs
have, perhaps, as often impeded, cramped, nay, destroyed ; that therefore all sweeping admiration or
sweeping condemnation are shallow, and all imitation or rejection founded upon those sentiments are
erroneous and mischievous.

Secondly.--Just as unfounded is the common
assumption that manufactures have created and en-
hanced the poverty, and that agriculture would have
led to less suffering ; from which a vast many hasty
inferences have been drawn, about the value or the
worthlessness of manufactures, about protective or
prohibitive legislation, and so forth. In the year
1826, on the contrary, the poor's-rate was highest in
the agricultural county of Sussex, and lowest in
Lancashire, the centre of manufactures.

Another common assumption, that pauperism always increased with the increasing population of a

* Bulwer's England, i., 222. This is the reference given by Herr
von Raumer, who was doubtless ignorant that the original source
of the information he quotes is to be found in the ' Selections of
Reports on the Administration of the Poor Laws,' p. 261, Report of
Mr. Chadwick; by whom the evidence establishing these facts was
collected.—*Translator.*

place is equally destitute of confirmation. In the hundred largest cities in England, the population of which amounts to 3,196,000, the poor's-rate amounted to 7s. 6d. per head. A hundred smaller towns, with a population of 19,841, paid 15s. per head. The hundred smallest villages, with a population of 1708, averaged 1l. 11s. 11¼d. per head. In the first hundred, 1 in 13, in the second, 1 in 8, in the third, 1 in 4, was a pauper. The increase of pauperism was, between 1803 and 1813, in the first, 1½, in the second, 2½, in the third, 8½, per cent. In Liverpool and Manchester the greatest manufacturing towns, the poor's-rate amounted to only 4s. 2d. and 5s. 8d. per head*.

But that people may not, from these facts, rush with equal precipitancy to the very opposite conclusions, I must say this:—The greater distress in the country seems to me to proceed, partly from the far more general adoption of the bad system of allowances there than in the towns; partly, from the far more injurious consequences of the restrictions imposed by the law of settlement on small places than on populous ones. Under a rational system, the greater apparent distress of the peasantry would be gradually removed, or the contrast would at least be diminished. The fact, that landed property is much more heavily charged with poor's rate than fluctuating income, has had some, though not much, influence on the numbers of the poor. In June, 1823, 1,760,000l. of the poor's rate was laid on houses; 4,602,000l. on land; and only 247,000l., (or about a sixth) on manufactures †. This difference appears still greater, when the question is,

* Extracts concerning administration of poor laws, p. 345.
† Hansard, xxii. 444.

whether the landowner or the manufacturer be most highly taxed? whether they want prohibiting duties or corn laws, &c.? Doubtless, however, the burthen on the land will be considerably lessened.

It is objected that any legal provision for the poor is destructive of all Christian piety and beneficence. That this is not true is proved by the example of England, where those sentiments have never ceased to operate; while in Ireland, where there is no poor's rate, so little is done by the wealthy to alleviate the sufferings of the poor.

We come now to the general and inevitable question—whether the poor have a *right* to relief? If the main end of all society is the protection of the helpless, and the increase of the total sum of civilization, happiness and virtue, it seems to me that it is impossible to deny to the poor this right; nor to the rich the corresponding duty.

A more intricate and difficult question is that of the measure and limits of the claim; and how far it is expedient to enforce it by the legal sanction. Nothing can be predicated generally, or *in abstracto;* in every case it must depend on a thousand considerations. It is certainly heartless and stupid to look with indifference at distress, under the pretext that it is inevitable, and means may be devised (without falling into the extravagances of some systems of poor's taxes) to extort something from those rich, who will give nothing voluntarily; and it is equally certain that the funds so obtained might be usefully applied without increasing idleness or vice.

I must close these remarks with the—*radical*—assertion that most of our laws and institutions have a tendency to favour the rich and the power-

ful, and to bear hard on the poor; and hence
follow arguments for changes, alleviations, voluntary alms and for the imposition of poor laws. As
a proof of this I will only mention a few facts.
All immovable direct taxes cease with time to operate as taxes; all indirect press proportionally more
on the poor than the rich. Machines and horses,
those arms of the rich, are not taxed equally with
the arms of the poor man; while a large proportion
of the earnings of the latter go to the capitalist.
Mr. Bulwer* affirms that every labourer pays a third
of his earnings in taxes : if this be true, what opulent man does not enjoy an immense advantage over
him? Besides, the corn laws raise the income of
the landholder at the cost of the poor; and the fund-
holder has made corresponding gains by the rise
in public securities.

In order, therefore, that well-meaning benevolent
men (like the St. Simonians) may not run into essentially absurd theories, and the poor into wild and
destructive practices, it is the duty of our lawgivers
to call to mind the examples of Moses, Solon, Lycurgus, and Servius Tullus, and to endeavour to find
out remedies or mitigations for this fundamental evil.
To refuse to do this altogether, or to give it up in
indolent despair, would be no less wrong than to
attempt to regulate every detail by countless laws,
and thus to throw everything into confusion by over-
governing. A wise direction from the supreme authority, a lively feeling of humanity in the opulent,
and a Christian resignation to certain diversities of
outward condition in the poor—all must combine to
ensure a real progress towards security and happiness, and to avert a dissolution of social order.

* England, vol. i. 187.

England has made important steps in the career of improvement; may other states consent to learn from her example before the evil reaches an equal height with them, which perhaps they may not find equal resources to overcome.

LETTER XVI.

Party prejudices of England—Peers for Life—Aristocracies of France and England—Lawyer Peers—Eligibility of Peers to sit in the House of Commons—*Ex officio* Seats in the House of Commons—Difficulties attending the formation of a Ministry—Balance of Parties—Negro Slavery—Objections to Emancipation—Notions on private Property—New Ministry—Causes of Changes in England—Tory Blunders—" Measures not Men"—Freedom of the Press—English Newspapers—Speeches of Sir R. Peel and Lord John Russell—Lord Melbourne and O'Connell—Corrupt practices at Elections.

London, Saturday, April 18*th,* 1835.

RECENT events in England have given occasion to the agitation of questions and the starting of possibilities which were not so much as thought of in the last century, mainly because the Revolution of 1688 was held to be " a final measure." But this security, this faith in the immutability of human things, together with the general admiration of English institutions, were precisely the causes that many defects passed unnoticed—many measures were left incomplete—many which had a principle of life were allowed to petrify; till at length the censure grew louder than the praise, and the demand for change more powerful than the principle of conservation. Doubtless much of what is attacked is still valuable and vital, and the problem often consists only in the means of freeing this vitality from what oppresses and chokes it; yet there are also such crying evils, such mischievous chasms in legislation, such rooted prejudices, that to a German, and especially a Prussian, it is often impossible, at first, to understand the facts or the arguments he hears. I find here a world of violent contradictions, which require to be solved and harmonized by more lofty and comprehensive principles. But so long as most Englishmen regard their own point of view as the sole, unalterably, and inviolably right, and that of their opponent as absolutely wrong, each party loses sight of that higher ground which overlooks both, and which it ought to be the aim of all civilization and all government to reach.

I am brought back by these reflections to my last letter but one, and to the question of the expediency of peers for life. This has been discussed in the French Chamber of Peers, with a depth, solidity, and real liberality rare in Paris. The state of things in France, however, materially differs from that in England. The hereditary aristocracy there enjoys nothing like the consideration and influence of the English. It is poor, and not strengthened by the laws of inheritance as this is—not to advert to other causes. Hence it sunk under the weight of the opinion of the day; and the people, in their anti-aristocratic fervour, did not perceive that their new institutions greatly increased the once dreaded power of the king.

The introduction of peers for life into the Upper House is vehemently opposed by many, for no other reason than that it is new. But it may be maintained that there is long and abundant precedent for such an institution. The English and Irish

bishops, the Scotch and Irish peers, are nothing
more nor less than peers for life; the former, nominated by the king; the latter, by the whole body
of the nobles of Ireland, for life, and by those of
Scotland, for only one parliament. The abstract
principle, that one chamber should be hereditary,
and the other elective, has not therefore been
strictly adhered to: a middle course has for years
been the practice. These nominated or elected
members of the House of Peers are by no means
untinctured with aristocratical opinions; on the
contrary, they are often their most vehement champions; while many of the heads of the oldest and
richest families incline strongly to the opinions
generally called liberal. It is remarkable that
new-made lords are more commonly violent aristocrats than men who are more tranquil on the
question of their descent, as well as more familiar
with the possession of wealth. No class, for instance, contains such stiff-necked defenders of all
existing things (existing abuses included, *bien en-
tendu*) as the lawyer-peers. One cause of this is
that from the habit they have acquired of regarding
law exclusively in its administrative details, they
find it impossible to attain to the comprehension of
the variety of, and the necessity for, national legislation : examples of this may be seen in the debates
on schools, churches, and universities. The French
Jacobins fell into the contrary faults.

The Reform Bill has certainly stripped the aristocracy of many of its means of influence; these,
however, are still very great, particularly in the
counties, as the nearly equal strength of the parties
shews. The eagerness to be admitted into their

circles is still extreme in the higher *bourgeoisie,* and
marriages between nobles and commoners tend to
render the line which divides them less striking.
Unquestionably open war between the two Houses
cannot long endure without evil consequences to
each; but it is quite a mistake to imagine that England is on the verge of equalization, *à la Française.*
There is far too much *à plomb* in this country for
people so lightly to turn things topsy-turvy.

That lords should not be able to sit in the Houses
of Peers and Commons at once is obviously reasonable. But whether they might not be admitted into
the latter, if they were elected and chose to resign
their seats for the time in the former, is a question
deserving further consideration. The effect of this
absolute and unqualified separation, is, to throw
many distinguished men out of their place. Who
deserved the peerage more than Burke? yet he
would have been as little suited to the House of
Lords as Chatham or Brougham. Both these distinguished men were taken off their natural ground,
and their extraordinary powers, to a great degree,
crippled. The question mooted above only goes to
this—are there no means of conferring the reward,
without cramping the activity?

The inquiry becomes still more important when
we regard the constitution of the ministry. Lord
Althorp's elevation furnished the reason, or the
pretext, for dissolving the Melbourne administration,
in a manner as precipitate as it was *maladroit.* If
the constitution permitted a peer to remain at his
post in the House of Commons, on a temporary
renunciation of his hereditary seat, every statesman
might be employed in the place for which he was

best fitted.   Sir Robert Peel's self-devotion—or his mistake, if you will—in the struggle for the Tories, surely gave him a stronger claim to a peerage than most men can urge; but would not this be putting him into a false position for the rest of his life?

Another inconvenience is, the necessity for those of the ministers who are not peers to be members of the House of Commons.   This limits the king's choice; indeed, it makes it depend upon the will of the electors.   You may say that the man who cannot secure a seat at a general election must be insignificant or unpopular,—in short, unfit for office; but temporary unpopularity is no proof whatever of unworthiness; and a minister ought not to have to consult the opinions and the wishes of any particular constituency.   The simplest remedy for this inconvenience seems to be, that ministers appointed by the king should, in virtue of their office, have seats in the House of Commons.   But this would probably appear to many Englishmen an awful violation of the representative system; just as, from fear of the power of the crown, almost all magistrates and official men are ineligible; though the royal prerogative is the last thing from which danger is now to be apprehended.

All these things add to the difficulties attendant on the formation of a ministry,—which are extreme.   The two great parties are now so violently opposed, and, at the same time, so nearly balanced, that the division rests with the Radicals, or rather, with those victims of long injustice, the Irish. Without their co-operation, Lord Melbourne will be as little able to command a majority in the House of Commons as Sir Robert Peel; and thus the main question is—how far the former and O'Connell can or will act together? If Lord Melbourne and his friends cannot form a ministry, probably Sir Robert Peel, with a somewhat different following, will return to the weary way he left. But how he can succeed, after his open hostility to all changes in the Irish church, is just as unintelligible, as how the Duke of Wellington could imagine that all political reforms were to be disposed of by such means as his unqualified opposition.

To a man who is placed without this English party circle, what is here thought impossible appears so easy. If Whigs and Tories would agree on the only wise and just policy with regard to the Catholics, there were an end to all talk of injustice, spoliation, agitation, rebellion, and what not. If they will not, no ministry can last, whoever be at its head.

Strange!—the so-called private property of the West Indian slaveholders has been annihilated; twenty millions have been applied by the nation to indemnify them, and to secure freedom to some hundreds of thousands; yet, to apply any part of the property of the church or the state to the giving a sound and religious education to five or six millions of Irish, is called impious and revolutionary!

Now that I have touched on the subject of slavery, I must say a few more words on it. That it is a necessary or salutary institution, as the great men of antiquity thought, nobody now maintains. The modern objections to its abolition turned entirely on two points. First, that the slaves were well treated and happy;—that the humanity and kindness of their masters rendered their condition not a hard one, &c. These speeches are the echo of those of our shallow defenders of villenage. The slave upon whom duties are imposed while no corresponding rights are conferred, is subject to force alone; and it is the indisputable office of legislation and of civil society to constitute for him a legal status which may indicate the rules and the limits of that force. It is true that law will not do every thing; but the abolition of slavery will by no means remove occasions for the practice of the virtues and the charities which the slave-owners are said to possess in so eminent a degree, and which will be sure never to want exercise.

These flowery descriptions of the happiness of the slaves are not however always confirmed by nearer investigation, which too often discloses, on the one hand, the barbarism and demoralization resulting from ill treatment, on the other, the cruelty begotten by power. The black population, since the importation of slaves into the British Colonies has been prohibited, is said to have fallen off as much as twenty-two per cent. in ten years; while the white and coloured population, notwithstanding the unfavourable climate, increases *. These facts are sufficiently significant.

It is most lamentable that, in spite of all prohibitions, the slave-trade to the colonies of the Continental powers continues. Between the years 1815 and 1830, six hundred and eighty thousand slaves were imported into the Havannah and the Brazils; and between 1824 and 1827, ten thousand eight hundred and fourteen slaves were captured by British cruisers and set at liberty.

The second main objection to all interference of the legislature in this affair is based on the asser-

* Hansard, iii. 1410.

tion of the planters, that the slaves are their private property, with which no one has any right to interfere.

This notion is a perfect focus of confusion, injustice, and absurdity. In civil society, it is by no means true that every man may ' do what he will with his own ;' on the contrary, the very idea of law includes *restraint* as well as *protection*. Abusive employments of property are forbidden; divisions of it are sanctioned, or prevented; incomes are taxed, and so on.

But if this argument of absolute private right is stupid and uncivilized as applied to things, how much more barbarous when applied to men! and what a *salto mortale* do these defenders of slavery make from Christian benevolence, to the depths of such inhumanity as this!

In the year 1823, the British Parliament required of the colonial legislatures to draw up and submit proposals for the cure of these evils; but the mother country was afraid of interfering too much with the colonial legislatures, and thus the latter did nothing effective. The Whig ministry, therefore, in 1833, took this important matter in hand, with the purpose of cautiously abolishing slavery and of indemnifying the planters. Hitherto no slave could purchase his freedom; and the severest punishment for the utmost cruelty of a master was, that he was compelled to sell the slave—and pocket the money.

The two principal points of the plans adopted by Parliament are,—

1st. The master receives a compensation calculated upon certain average prices of slaves.

XVI.]   EMANCIPATION OF THE SLAVES.   165

2nd. The slaves are at once free; but are bound to serve their masters for a certain time, at certain wages—which are determined by the sum the master demands as compensation *.

The Duke of Wellington opposed the emancipation of the slaves, on the ground that they were no better prepared for freedom in 1833 than in 1830—a position which is equally true of 1933, if their condition remains unaltered, and no attempt is made to educate them. The Duke further asserted that the abolition of slavery would cause only ruin to all parties. Even Peel opposed it; yet in the last King's speech they were compelled to insist upon the happy consequences of this measure of their opponents †.

Great have been the controversies about the relative merits of ancient and modern forms of government, and the real progress of mankind in the higher regions of policy and legislation. But it can hardly be denied, that freedom, independence, humanity, and the education of the masses have advanced; and particularly, that the abolition of slavery is an immense stride. I can only agree with one objection of the opponents; *i. e.* that the sum granted as compensation is too high. In the same way the loss sustained by the abolition of hereditary jurisdictions, and of other feudal privileges among us, was over-rated. But better be too generous than grudging and unjust.

So the new ministry is launched, and with few alterations, and without any coalition with the Tories. This re-appointment is a fresh proof how great a

* Hansard, xvii. 1194.
† Hansard, xviii. 518.   Edinburgh Review, lii. 297.

mistake was their dismissal, which has had the worst results; personal offence, universal irritation, dissolution of parliament, loss of time, &c. Whether or not the Whigs be enemies of their country, their opponents have clearly lost the campaign, and they remain (for the present) masters of the field. This is a serious loss to the Tories, for whatever the future may bring forth, their means of warfare are permanently diminished, and will be yet further impaired whenever the laws on Ireland and the corporations pass.

The events and wants of the age have, doubtless, mainly hastened on the changes which have taken place in England; but next to these, the most active cause has been the bad tactics and strategy of the Tories: just as the French Revolution was precipitated by the opposition of the French nobles to Turgot's plans of improvement. Of this I will only mention one or two proofs.

The Tory system stood unshaken and triumphant during the French war, and even up to the time of Lord Liverpool's death. Canning, a Tory, Pitt's ablest disciple and follower, and an opponent of parliamentary reform, was disdained and rejected by Wellington, professedly, because no true Englishman could ally himself with a minister who advocated Catholic emancipation. Canning was thus driven into the arms of the Whigs, while the very men who denounced emancipation as ruinous were those who carried it. The Whigs very properly supported a measure they had always approved, and which, at the same time, strengthened their chances for power, by removing an obstacle so long existing between them and the king. The high Tories, on the other hand, were offended with Wellington and Peel for deserting long-cherished principles on the ground of necessity; and predicted, very truly, that Catholic emancipation would not be a final measure, as Wellington and his allies believed, or at least affirmed.

This ecclesiastical question was closely connected with political ones,—especially with that concerning East Retford. Instead of transferring the franchise from this borough, convicted of gross corruption, to a large manufacturing town, (as Mr. Huskisson proposed,) it was given to a county, where it went to increase the aristocratical interest. This denial of even the smallest reform drove people to keener inquiries and higher demands. Another blunder of the Tories,—which occasioned the rupture with Mr. Huskisson and his friends.

The last and most fatal was the Duke of Wellington's declaration against all and every reform. This mistake was the ruin of his ministry, and opened a free course to the Whigs. All attempts to arrest the Reform Bill were fruitless. If we regard this as an evil, the Tories have to bear, at least, half the blame; if as a good, they can claim none of the merit.

Precisely in the same manner, the rejection of the Tithe Bill last year,—that boasted triumph of the Peers,—has been no less injurious to their own interests than to those of the Irish,—Catholics and Protestants. So much, by way of proof that the Tories, in spite of the greater knowledge of business for which they have generally credit, frequently act with all the imprudence and *maladdresse* of passion; often injure themselves, and sometimes prejudice a good

cause. Never would such men as Pitt and Canning
have so ordered a campaign; never so pertinaciously
have defended an indefensible post.

We may conclude that the new ministry have
come to some understanding with the king and the
Irish. From the latter they have probably little
opposition to dread, as they must see that Ireland
has nothing to hope but from the Whigs.

It is assumed that the choice of the ministers rests
with the king. It is, however, in a great measure,
dependant on the electors. This has, no doubt, its
good side; it shows confidence, gives occasion for a
sort of popular assent, justifies a man from the charge
of giving up principle for place, and so on. But
on the other hand, it places the decision of a general
question in the hands of a particular constituency;
and (not to mention objections I have before stated)
gives peers who are appointed to office an undue
advantage over commoners. So long as both parties
had boroughs at command, there was no difficulty,
but now it may become a serious one. It were
certainly advisable to inquire into the expediency of
this institution, as well as into that strange chronological rule, that no man can be elected to serve in
Parliament who accepts a place created since 1705.

The favourite cry of " measures, not men," is unmeaning. At the fountain of authority they must
be one,—inspired by one spirit. Where they diverge,
some serious objection lies, either against the measures, or the men.

A just mean must result from the perfect unison
of measures and of men, and must rest on broad
and comprehensive foundations. Both must have
positive (not merely negative) objects and purposes.

These conditions are wanting, when (for instance) Stanley and his friends support all political, and oppose all ecclesiastical, reforms. They do not form the living, vigorous, and all-ruling Aristotelic *Energeia*, but a fluctuating party, which, though it may come in here and there to decide in favour of a sane opinion, is totally incompetent and inept for the consecutive and harmonious direction of *the whole* machine of government.

I cannot believe in the justice of the opinion which a clever man expressed to me the other day, " that this was all mere talk, and that the sole source and end of all movements and changes was, desire for place." This desire may co-operate with other causes, but, in England, the questions at issue are vast, real, and important; whereas, in France, the *objects* of the strife are often scarcely intelligible.

Unfortunately, so much time is lost here in debate, that, of many important and needful laws, not above one or two can be got through the Commons. What will happen in the Lords, nobody knows.

After what I have said concerning censorships of the press, and what others, without my knowledge or consent, have printed of mine on that subject, I have a right to say, on the one hand, that I am a friend to freedom of the press, and, on the other, that I am not ignorant of the difficulties which attend all the means hitherto used to check its licentiousness. I see, then, that *here* matters cannot be otherwise than they are; but I am as little delighted with the results as with those at Berlin.

Let us, this time, put aside the *form* and the legal supervision, and look only at the *matter:* we shall find that, in the newspapers of this country (of which I see a great number at the clubs), either in jest or in earnest, with reflection or with passion, eloquently or vulgarly, acutely or stupidly, every thing possible and conceivable, for and against ministers, is said. Every truth, every incident, presents various points for thorough investigation; and the many-sided is (as the higher) justly opposed to the one-sided. England thus certainly enjoys the great advantage of more varied and profound inquiry, than if a censor erased before, or a magistrate punished after, printing. It by no means, however, follows that the sum of all these discussions involves no error or no passion. Every newspaper has its own spectacles, and represents the colour under which objects appear to it as the only true one; while readers attach themselves with violent partiality to one of this or that tinge. It is astonishing how dexterous these writers are in seizing every fact or argument, principal or secondary, under this one colour, and presenting it so to the eyes of others. They trouble themselves much less than with us about rival political colourists. This practice engenders the most intense, the most unconquerable prejudices and oppositions; such as have existed among the English (spite of all their wisdom) for centuries.

If the judgments pronounced on ministers rested on careful examination and profound thought, these diversities would be, if not just, yet pardonable; but one too often sees exaggeration and sinister intention; and one is, to use the gentlest term, displeased: till, after long familiarity, one comes to regard these party clamours as mere empty and dis-

cordant sound. But how can we expect that, in so
plenteous a harvest, there should not be some
blighted ears and some worthless grain? That
mode of culture is still the best which produces the
largest crops.

The addresses of Sir Robert Peel and Lord John
Russell to their constituents rise far above this
gossip of the day, and have a historical importance.
They exhibit a remarkable difference, even in form.
The one, eminently clever, employing all the arts of
language, form, and power of expression; the other,
written with more feeling than rhetoric, and trust-
ing to a simple chronological enumeration of facts.
The one suggesting the fairest hopes, showing
the brightest, noblest aims in the remote distance;
the other distinctly pointing out the immediate and
the necessary, with its essential conditions. Lord
John has one great advantage over Sir Robert:
namely, that he quietly pursues the same path he
has trodden for years; and that the future is, with
him, only the immediate continuation of the past.
Peel, on the other hand, had, in fact, to give up his
earlier course, and to promise to pursue a new one,
more enlightened and more suited to the times;
which promise some hear with incredulity, and others
with disapprobation. Lord John Russell spoke out
decidedly on the two subjects which must now be disposed of before all others,—the Corporations and the
Irish Church; Sir Robert Peel said, in fact, nothing
about either, and only mentioned his project of reforms in the English church. This was putting
forward a lesser evil in order to slur over a greater;
and it has not succeeded.

Lord Melbourne denies having come to any compromise with O'Connell; and no doubt his assurance is *literally* true. Both, however, know what they mutually wish, and what they have to expect from each other; and upon this alone rests the possibility of the duration of the present ministry. The applause with which the Tories received this assurance of Lord Melbourne's was given the moment before he declared, to their astonishment, that he should bring in Lord John Russell's clause as a *government measure*. It was evident, therefore, that the king had consented to it; and that the support of the Irish members depends on it, follows of course.

Why all the several posts are filled as they are, and no otherwise, can be satisfactorily answered only by the initiated;—but Lord Palmerston's appointment, by preference, to the post of Secretary for Foreign Affairs, proves that his popularity (which was not great before, even in England) has increased, precisely because he is disliked by the three great Northern powers. On this ground he has, perhaps, a better chance at this election than at the former; most assuredly all insinuations from abroad will be perfectly thrown away upon English electors.

There is one fact which shocks me; namely, that the papers mention, with great praise and exultation, that patriotic societies have subscribed large sums to pay the expenses of the new elections. Ordinary and inevitable expenses, for travelling, loss of time, &c., electors and elected might surely defray themselves; and that expenses of any other kind should be publicly acknowledged as at once

necessary and ruinous,—that no disgust at this
should be expressed,—is the greatest scandal, and
the way to resolve all popular representation into
a traffic and a system of corruption, analogous
to the Polish regal election, and equally fatal.
The hereditary boroughs, bestowed by a few individuals at their pleasure, were a great evil; but
not a greater than this monstrous abuse, which
seems to have increased with the change of the elective system. Perhaps a time will come when people
will discover a bright side in this defect of the English constitution, as they did in that. Then it will
be, a fair tribute or tax which unfair riches pays to
oppressed poverty; a laudable, voluntary means of
equalizing unequally divided burthens; a sabbath
or jubilee year for the children of toil; joyful satur-
nalia for those who have otherwise no share in the
pleasures and luxuries of " high life."

These corrupt practices inevitably lead electors
daily more and more vehemently to enforce upon
their representatives the duty of voting for annual
parliaments; and will make the whole business of
election, and the form of government, depend upon
the accident whether, in the struggle between buyers
and sellers, those who pay or those who receive shall
get the upper hand. At present all parties are
agreed in finding plausible excuses, or in passing
over the evil in silence, because each hopes to have
the *elixir vitæ* of the heavier purse on his side.

LETTER XVII.

Climate of England —Houses—Fires—Museum—St. Paul's Cathedral—St. Peter's—English Drama—English Law.

London, Sunday, April 19th, 1835.

I HAVE often, and with reason, described and boasted
how much I see and learn here; but that you may
not fall into the foul sin of envy, and undervalue the
comforts of your country and your home, I must send
you a few hints of the shady side of the picture.

The root of most of the miseries is the London
climate,—such, at least, as it has exhibited itself to
me from my arrival up to the present day. It is
true I see the sun, but not in his golden radiance ;
for though here is wealth enough to gild everything
else, he alone appears red as a copper kreuzer, or
pale as a silver groschen. The atmosphere of Italy
is so transparent, that it heightens all colour, but
this bounds the view, or quite conceals the distance.
The thick fog which generally prevails is thoroughly
impregnated with water, and this, blended with the
air, is chilling and penetrating to a degree of which
we, in Berlin, have no idea. I must now admit
that clear dry frost is, without comparison, less injurious than this damp, wetting, ice-house air. The
doors and windows are not quite so bad as in Rome,
but much less carefully constructed, and less close
than ours. We do not want them, say the English ;
and when I try to contradict them, my voice trembles

with cold.   Although the grates consume a monstrous quantity of coals, the temperature of the
rooms is never equal.   If by dint of a great deal of
heaping on, stirring, raking out ashes, &c., I have
at length succeeded in making a good fire, I am
scorched on one side, while, if I turn my head on the
other, I see my own breath.   If I let the fire go out,
the room is cold instantly, from the constant draught
through the enormous chimney.

When I go to the Museum there is an end to all
these sufferings—for there is no fire at all; or, if
there is one, I have never been able to find it.   In
spite of woollen stockings, my feet are ice-cold, and
I am obliged from time to time to warm my hands
in my pockets.   The consequence is tooth-ache,
with all its agreeable caprices and varieties.   To-
day the tooth is quiet; and now the climate has
seized upon one leg, so that I can hardly walk.

London, April 20th, 1835.

I went yesterday to St. Paul's Cathedral, which I
had only seen from without.   The effect it produced
on me was, I confess, very meagre and poor.   It
forces comparisons with St. Peter's, and every one
of these comparisons is to its disadvantage.   In the
first place, every imitation falls short of its original.
That this is the case as to size, is less important than
the total want of variety, of internal decoration, of
harmony or grandeur of colour, or of pictures; which
is ill compensated by the cold white monuments to
Britain's naval heroes, scattered through the cold
white waste.   As often as I entered St. Peter's church,
a feeling of harmony, of a sublime satisfaction and

enjoyment, took possession of me. The architecture, without any distinct influence on the mind, vaguely excited pleasurable emotions, and called up thoughts and feelings which other places had never produced, and which St. Paul's church is certainly not calculated to give birth to. It is a *puritanized* St. Peter's; and however great may be the excellencies of puritanism in other respects, to Art it is, if not fatal, at least barren and cold. These impressions are heightened by the very poetical situation of St. Peter's, the utterly prosaic, of St. Paul's.

Yesterday I became acquainted with Mr. R——, a lover of German literature; our opinions coincided on a number of literary questions. Unfortunately he confirmed the report of the decline of the English stage, and the monotonous reign of the modern Italian opera.

Mr. H—— assured me that the structure and administration of English law were so intricate, so unsystematic and irregular, that no foreigner could possibly understand them: bad hearing for me—but worse for Englishmen. Yet I think I have learned many of the more important points from Blackstone, though not the quirks and finesses.

LETTER XVIII.

Exchange—Bank—Lloyd's Coffee - house—Naples and London—
    Commercial Spirit—West India Docks—Absence of Soldiers—
    Standing Armies.

London, April 22nd, 1835.

YESTERDAY, as I was on my way to visit B——, I
met Mr. N——, in an omnibus, and he had the
goodness to show me the Bank, the Exchange,
and Lloyd's Coffee-house,—the centre of the world
of money and of trade. What one sees, and
what, though unseen, necessarily presses upon one's
thoughts and imagination, make an impression as
peculiar as it is vast. When Sir Roger Gresham
founded the Exchange, his most sanguine wishes or
his boldest conjectures could never have anticipated
the mighty amount of business which has since been
transacted within these walls. Boundless treasures
flit invisibly from side to side; gain and loss, prosperity and adversity, joy and grief, pass in rapid and
often unexpected succession. All the arrangements
bespeak the greatest simplicity, fitness, and completeness. The numbers and letters of the bank-
stock, or public funds, are inscribed above the head
of each clerk in the Bank. At Lloyd's, close to the
dial which tells the hour, is one still more interesting here, which tells the direction of the wind, and
is connected with the weathercock on the roof. Intelligence of the arrivals and departures of ships, of
the existence and fate of vessels in all parts of the

world; reports from consuls and commissioners resident in every foreign town; newspapers and gazettes from every country, are here to be found, arranged in such perfect and convenient order, that the entire actual state of the commercial world may be seen in a few minutes, and any of the countless threads which converge to this centre may be followed out with more or less minuteness. The whole earth,—or the whole commercial machinery of the earth,—appeared to me to be placed in the hands of the directors of Lloyd's Coffee-house.

Mr. N——, whose principal business consists in underwriting, *i.e.*, insuring ships, remarked to me how much there was for them to learn, to know, to reflect, and to decide upon; for example, the ship's build, her lading, the time of year, the place of her destination, &c. How often they are obliged to draw elaborate conclusions from vague and scattered accounts of danger or of safety, and how much might be won or lost according to their decision. It is, he concluded, an incessant intellectual activity and excitement. Where can anything like this be found except in London? and how small does everything else appear in comparison with the magnitude and extent of these operations !

I was in the best disposition in the world to find out and observe all this for myself, but the last remark flung me suddenly into opposition; and I said to myself,—And so, then, these pursuits which, whatever be their vivacity or magnitude, go at last only to split the world into two parts, the debtor and the creditor;—these views, which resolve everything into questions of distance and of money,—do really

embrace the highest possible intellectual activity
and excitement! And all former nations and races
of men were intellectually poor and contemptible,
because they did not devote their whole souls to the
business of catching the ships of every sea in the
nets of Lloyd's Coffee-house, and of pocketing premiums on insurance! And the human mind, then,
has attained its widest reach when it embraces the
papers from Hamburg and New York on the one
hand, those from the Cape of Good Hope or Cal-
cutta on the other, and the next moment can learn
whether or not thievery goes on flourishingly in the
rogues' colony of Sydney!

With all the rapidity of an underwriter, I put on
my wishing-cap, and transported myself to Naples.
When the Neapolitan stretches himself on the
shores of his sea of chrysophras, and indolently
sucking the crimson pulp of his golden oranges,
sees Vesuvius in its glowing and awful magnificence before him, and over his head the eternal
blue, would he exchange this "excitement," this enjoyment, for all that Lloyd's Coffee-house, all that
dingy London, could offer him? And then, turning
my arms against myself, I asked, with melancholy
and vexation, why I could not be satisfied with my
little hazel-bower, but must run after English "ex-
citements," like a fool?

Commerce has been the grand discoverer and
conqueror of the world: it has produced a community of knowledge and of interests, which is invaluable, and which will strengthen the bonds between
man and man: but its apparent boundless extent,
all the calculations of latitude and longitude, all the

hopes built upon the points of the compass, vanish
before one glance into the starry firmament, before
one pulse of generous love, nay, before one sigh
from the breast, which, like Memnon's pillar, re-
sponds to the touch of some ray from heaven.

April 22nd, 1835.

I rose this morning in better strength than if I
had raked away more of the night at ———g; and,
indeed, I wanted it, to go through a London day.
I was in a mercantile English humour, and suscep-
tible enough to everything new and remarkable.   I
have delivered a great number of fashionable letters
to fashionable people here, who, being occupied with
more important things, naturally take no cognizance
of me, and will readily forgive me for doubting
whether I have any great loss.   Mr. C. B. (an
eminent merchant), with whom I accidentally made
acquaintance on the road between Prague and Dresden, on the contrary, devoted to me a whole day of
his time, here so precious, and has appointed another
for a similar undertaking.   We drove first to the
West India Docks, an immense basin, artificially
dug or hollowed out by machinery, long, broad, and
deep enough to contain a great number of the largest
merchantmen, and flanked on both sides by immeasurable warehouses for sugar, coffee, rum, dye-
woods, mahogany, &c.   There were some trunks of
the latter of such enormous size, that, in our country,
pilgrimages would be made to an oak of the same
dimensions.   From hence we crossed the Thames to
see the Tunnel, a wonderful work of human audacity
and skill, compared to which, the cave or passage

cut through the soft mountains at Pausilippo appears a mere trifle.

We next went to the celebrated brewery of Barclay and Perkins. As to the Tunnel, the plan gives a short but sufficient account; the brewery has been described by all travellers, so no repetition. I saw a hundred and fifty gigantic horses for carrying out the beer, in the stables. The carters here do not yet seem converted to the faith in the superiority of the thin-legged blood-horses for draught. This brewery contains and supports more men than many small towns; and far surpasses them in capital. It was here quite clear to me that the English, with their unrestrained competition, have the start of the continent for a long time to come, from their immense capital, and the saving effected by the minute division of labour in the great machines and manufactories; and that they make large incomes with small profits, whilst many a manufacturer in other countries will starve with high interest on his small capital.

While rowing up the Thames, from the Tunnel to London Bridge, our boatman told us that, on Easter Sunday, a steamer had taken 2375 people from London to Greenwich, where the sum of 50*l.* was taken from 12,000 persons, who paid a penny a head for seeing a new railway.

From the brewery we went to the Custom-house, to see the great room, where the principal duties are paid. The proceedings are as simple as they are expeditious. The merchandise is unloaded in the docks, valued, booked, and warehoused. As soon as anything is to be withdrawn from the warehouse for inland consumption, the merchant pays the regular duty at the Custom-house, and receives the goods on showing a receipt or order. Almost all sales follow immediately upon examination, and always with the intervention of a broker. The usual difficulty of taxing goods according to their value, is diminished by the great experience of the sworn officers, and by the forfeiture of the goods, with a fine of ten per cent., in case of too low an estimate being given. For example : about six sorts of sugar of different qualities were laid out as samples; the hogsheads or bags were brought in rapid succession, and the valuer pierced a hole in each with a semi-circular iron, and drew out a sample : this he compared with the sample on the table, and called out the number on the hogshead or bag according to which the duty was fixed. All this passed with the greatest quiet, uniformity, and rapidity.

Not a soldier or sentinel is to be seen ; generally speaking, soldiers are hated, and their interference still more so. A just respect for liberty, a just feeling of the necessity of maintaining order by law, and by the civil power alone, is certainly at the bottom of this. Doubly just is the aversion to a paid standing army, which often consists of very ignoble soldiers. On the other hand, a national force is absolutely necessary to the nations of the continent; and our system destroys all antipathy between citizen and soldier, inasmuch as every man unites both characters in his own person.

It would be easy to show that this union and reconciliation of the civil and the military spirit, thus giving tone and firmness to the one, and humanity and mildness to the other, is a higher form, and produces a better result, than can be obtained by severing them, or leaving them to take different directions.

LETTER XIX.

Radical opinions and Tory saws—Concession—English Church—Incomes of Bishops—Voluntary System—Education Expenses—Steam Printing-press—Intellectual power—Westminster Abbey —English Manners—Education of Women—Covent Garden—Macbeth — Richmond — English Architecture — Fashion and Flattery.

London, April 23rd, 1835.

I FIND it much more easy to appreciate and understand the exaggerations and mistakes of the Radicals, than the principles which I hear from many high Tories. Thus, for example, when the former cry up the United States, overlooking the dark parts of the picture, such as slavery; or the peculiar geographical advantages, such as boundless space for fresh colonization, and draw inferences which, as applied to England, are false. Here I have something before me; I see land, and can pursue my inquiries into the details; such as, what institutions are worthy of imitation? what require to be modified and altered? whether those of Europe be stronger or feebler through age? whether an elective president be preferable to an hereditary monarch? which is the best system of taxation, provision for the poor, &c. &c.?

But what can I say when well-meaning, and, in other respects, sensible men daily preach to me that in a state (and more especially in England,) nothing whatever must be conceded, because every concession excites fresh demands, and general ruin will be the inevitable consequence.

When such saws as this appear to my adversary pregnant with truth and wisdom,—when they seem to him the point from which the world can be firmly held together, while I, on the contrary, think them absolutely null—" without form and void,"—how can we come to any understanding? I must doubt, if I do not contest, every word he says. In the first place, what does he mean by " concede?" Do I " concede " that only which is entirely dependent on my own will? But what in the world does depend on one will, without reference to the wills of others? Or if I concede that only which is agreeable to me, why, then, all one can say is, that the unconceded comes to pass quite as often as the conceded. Is it with my consent that time rolls on and that every thing changes with time? Did the Pope consent to the Reformation? or did his non-consenting retard it? Did the Venetians consent to the new direction taken by the commerce of the world? or did the English " concede" independence to America? If concession depends upon individual will, that surely has its limits. Within these limits I may have some influence; without them, my efforts are but wasted.

The first question therefore is, how far our powers extend; and this is the true starting point of all political inquiries. The Impossible can never be a rational object of endeavour. When this first question is decided, the next that offers itself is, what is right or just? If I owe a

man a hundred pounds and have not a farthing,
I cannot, in practice, " concede" to him what I owe ;
but my inability in no way affects his right. If I
say, " If I grant him ten pounds, he will only ask for
more and more, till at last I shall be obliged to pay
him the whole hundred—therefore, I had better
grant nothing," I am a fool, or a knave, or both.

In like manner, in public affairs, a concession is
generally the consequence of a demand ; and neither
is the result of any individual will. The *formal
right* of expressing the will (such as that possessed
by the lords, or the king, of throwing out bills)
has no effect in deciding the *thing*, and gives no
answer to the question of wisdom or folly, justice or
injustice. It is often maintained in letter, when it
is dead in spirit. Such maxims as, that a government ought to grant no demand, or to grant
every demand, are equally null. Because it is
possible that the concession of a just demand may
be followed by an absurd and unjust one, I am in
no degree absolved from the first ;—on the contrary,
the concession of the just, is precisely what will give
me strength to withhold the unjust. When, on the
other hand, one just principle gives birth to a whole
series of new conclusions, we ought not to be
alarmed, but should learn to understand how and
why such was the natural, the inevitable, and the
proper result. This ensued upon the abolition of
the slave-trade, of villenage, of commercial restrictions, of exclusive class or corporate privileges, and
so on. New forms of disease, as well as new vital
energies, are doubtless connected with every new
stage of development, but the latter cannot be re-

pressed, nor can the former be cured, with old nostrums.

Never was a universal ruin brought about by the concession of what was just and suited to the age (which, indeed, inquiry proves to be identical); what was destroyed by such means had lived out its life. Never, on the contrary, have senseless and untimely changes borne the fruits hoped for by lovers of revolution. Therefore let every man who has a share in public affairs exert his understanding to the utmost, and lay aside his prejudices, that he may see *where* it is fit to concede and where to withhold; and not fancy himself a statesman because he can repeat a few phrases out of Haller or Bentham.

General changes, moreover, are not effected by mere personal springs of action. If Luther's opposition to the sale of indulgences proceeded (as some Catholics falsely assert) only from envy and avarice, the Reformation would not the less remain a mighty turn in human affairs—an event belonging to universal history. Supposing that O'Connell's efforts in behalf of his countrymen spring from ambition or from avarice, — the discovery or the proclamation of this fact will neither tranquillize Ireland, nor settle the question of the justice or injustice of their demands. If immoral springs of action are really at work, the way to render them impotent is to withhold nothing that ought to be granted.

The first part of the Report of the Commission on the English Church has appeared, and confirms, in the main, what people knew before. For instance, the vast disparity between the bishops' sees.

The number of parishes they contain varies from 94 to 1234, and the population from 127,000 to 1,688,000. The incomes, which are in no degree regulated by the business, are no less unequal. The least favoured of bishops has only about 924*l.* a-year, the richest 19,000*l.* The see of Canterbury yields the latter sum; York, 12,000*l.*; Winchester, 11,000*l*; London, 13,000*l.*; Durham, 19,000*l.* The gross amount of all the sees of England is 157,000*l.*, thus twenty-seven individuals receive 1,090,000 thalers. This indeed explains the zeal with which certain aristocrats assert the inviolability of ancient institutions, and the duty of regarding church property as private property. A Presbyterian division of these funds would rob many younger sons of their fairest prospects. The commissioners observe that bishops are subject to many expenses; that those incomes only should be reduced which exceed 31,500 thalers, and that none should be raised which now amount to 38,500. This seems to them the maximum of possible or prudent reform. How would our bishops and superintendents rejoice if it were possible to put them on such a *reduced* establishment as this!

I do not deny that ecclesiastics may have, and may usefully expend, incomes like those formerly possessed by our prince-bishops; that ecclesiastics very often expend them better than laymen; that an equalization of all benefices is unjust and inexpedient: but it does not at all follow that reforms are needless in the English church, or that trifling reforms will do. Those who deny that certain individuals have too much, will hardly deny that a vast many have too little; and, indeed, taking these into the account, the Church of England seems to me rather too poor than too rich.

Several people to whom I have said that the present system seemed to be impractical if carried to its full extent, immediately replied, " Oh, *then*, you are an advocate for ' the voluntary system ?' " This " *then*" is, however, utterly unsupported by any of the opinions I have expressed. On the contrary, I repeat, that a really worldly, that is, a careless, dissipation of church property is an abomination in my eyes; that the alienation of it from really spiritual uses can be excused only by absolute necessity; and that I look upon those recommendations to leave the church of Christ to the chances of voluntary contributions,—like a card club or a reading-room,—which some seem to consider proofs of the highest wisdom and intelligence, as proofs of nothing but either misguided fanaticism or covert hostility. What would become of all our schools and colleges, if they were left entirely to the voluntary contributions of the scholars? And yet many people who think School necessary, regard Church as superfluous.

April 24th.

A well-informed man observed to me, that this report on the incomes of the bishops included, in fact, only their fixed incomes; and that if the immense patronage, the undetermined dues, which are seldom estimated high enough, and especially the large sums paid on the granting of new leases were calculated, the estimate might nearly be doubled, or

certainly greatly raised. Moreover, that a great part
of the aristocratical power of the bishops rests not
on their personal office, but on their patronage.

Doubtless, patronage is frequently abused; but
election is equally liable to objections; and if there
is no church property, no endowment, the clergy
fall into a very pernicious dependence on the opinions and the wishes of their flocks.

*   *   *   *

I mentioned to you the impression which the public subscriptions for defraying the cost of elections
made upon me, and the inferences which suggested
themselves to my mind. It is, therefore, my duty to
communicate to you what I have heard on the other
side of this matter. You must carefully distinguish
bribery (said a man who knows England more accurately than I do) from necessary and legally recog-
nised expenses. Since the number of polling places
has been increased, and the time allowed for voting
abridged, these expenses are, indeed, considerably
diminished; but by no means abolished. There
is the cost of the booths, hustings, desks, travelling
and board of voters, law expenses, and so on. If
these were thrown on the voters, the partition and
collection of them would be attended with great
difficulties, and many would abandon all share in
the business of elections; thus leaving the whole in
a few, and by no means the purest hands. It is
better, therefore, that the candidates should be left
to pay something for the honour and advantage of
a seat in the legislature. That poor men are thus
deterred from offering themselves the English
think an advantage; they wish that none but opu-

lent men should represent them. The facility for individual bribery has been greatly lessened by the Reform Bill, because the number of voters is greatly increased, and it is easier to buy few than many.

I could but defer to the justice of some of these remarks—and, indeed, even the defenders of rotten boroughs have a good deal to say for themselves: yet thus much I must maintain in spite of them. Certainly morality and disinterestedness cannot be forced by laws; but these forms, and this doctrine of expenses legally and necessarily thrown upon the candidate, lead almost inevitably to *indirect* bribery ; and it is hard to prove exactly where the limits have been transgressed. How can 280,000 thalers (40,000*l*.) be spent in the lawful expenses of an election ? How can it be necessary for one individual to subscribe 1000*l*. for planks for polling booths, and such like? As to the second point, it is certainly good that legislators should be men of property ; but this might be secured by much better means than extravagant election expenses, the direct effect of which is to diminish the very wealth regarded as a recommendation.

Thirdly, the exclusive predominancy of money is as one-sided as that of birth ; and if it is true that it is more difficult to bribe many electors than few, it is also true that small gains are more important to the mass, than larger ones to persons of a higher class ; and perhaps, therefore, the sum required may be the same, only more subdivided. But that the great question of the duration of parliaments should turn so much upon money, is a very serious, not to say alarming, thing. From all this it seems, that a mere general, abstract view of the English law and customs of election will not suffice; and that, in practice, many things work very differently from what one would anticipate. Nevertheless, I cannot but maintain that both theory and practice exhibit something essentially false and artificial; and that here exists morbid matter of which both parties are conscious, and which both turn to account; but for which both ought to combine in devising a timely remedy.

April 24*th, Evening.*

When I have closed or sent off my daily register of events, I always recollect a number of things which I ought to have mentioned. Then it is too late,—what I have omitted finds no appropriate place. But it really is impossible to devote more time in a day to writing than I do. This being Easter week, I have, indeed, literary holidays at the Museum; but I have visits to pay and various things to see, for which I have no leisure at other times. Lastly, you must not forget that, from the enormous distances, everything takes double as much time as in Berlin, even if you ride. Of this I had experience yesterday.

I went with Messrs. M—— and O—— to Lambeth, to see the steam printing-presses by which the 'Penny Magazine,' among many other things, is printed. It was a very interesting sight, both as a whole and in detail. Twenty presses, moved by steam, worked with such unwearied rapidity, that a thousand sheets were printed in an

hour; *i.e.*, in ten hours, by the twenty presses,
200,000 copies; the number which the ' Penny
Magazine' sells.

Revolving cylinders are covered with printers'
ink, which they spread over a horizontal surface,
with greater evenness than could be accomplished
by the most careful hand-labour. The machine
takes the sheet, passes it over the types (after these
have received the necessary quantity of ink from
the blackened horizontal plate), prints it on one
side, then turns the sheet in the most intelligent
manner, prints the other side, and deposits it before
the hands of a workman who has nothing to do but
to take it away. And all this goes on more rapidly
than one can tell it! In the time required to write
these few lines, the machine prints some hundreds
of sheets.

If we compare the snail's process of transcrib-
ing with this communication and communicabi-
lity of thought, idealism and realism,—those reconciled antagonists,—seem to have acquired
such force as no human being could have imagined, even after the invention of printing. How
do the rapidity and operation of speech, which can
extend but to so small a circle, sink in the comparison! how feeble seems the influence of eloquence which can act upon hearers alone! A steam
printing-press like this would strike terror into an
army of censors; they would flee before it as the
savages of America fled before the new and terrific
horses of their invaders. You will tell me, that
the Indians no longer run away from the horses;
but you must remember that they ceased to fear

them, because they learned to ride and to master them. Horseman against horseman, then; that is to say, an enlightened steam-press sending forth wholesome knowledge, is the only equal, nay, superior, force by which to make war upon steam-error and licentiousness. Two hundred thousand sheets read by some millions of people may become the source of such infinite blessings, or such infinite calamities to mankind, that a society of high-minded and enlightened men, combining to diffuse really " useful knowledge," would exercise a far more powerful tutelary influence in the state, than the whole body of those negations, censors and censorial boards.

After I had seen and admired the operations of the machine as a whole, I learned many curious details: for instance, how the single types are formed, how they are placed together and transformed into stereotype plates; how plaster-casts are taken from the blocks of wood-cuts, lead and antimony again cast into these matrices, and thus plates produced, which are used as substitutes for the blocks.

I said just now, or I meant to say, mind alone can advance or impede mind. A positive force must be met by positive means; otherwise little or nothing is effected, and the ground gradually slips from under the feet. All the censors in the world could not stop the movement of the steam-press, but would be hurried along, or torn in pieces by its resistless force. If there *were* a force which could effectually obstruct this infinitely accelerated power of diffusing thought, or

VOL. I.

could direct its operations at will, this would involve the possibility, indeed the actual existence, of a tyranny such as is unknown to history. In comparison with this, the red ink of censors were but milk and water.

So, then,—these excerptors will say,—you are a defender of the licentiousness of the press; you think that it is right and wise in a government to allow the poison of pernicious doctrines to be disseminated among masses, and to infect the whole people. On the contrary, gentlemen, I have the greatest disgust not only at what you strike out, but very often at what you leave in: but I am of opinion that these ineffectual restraints serve but to whet the desire for the forbidden fruit. The waggon, heavily laden with poison, rolls down the hill with resistless rapidity, while the fly of a censor, perched on the wheel, fancies that his weight will be sufficient to avert all danger. Vain presumption, or well-meaning delusion! A Penny Magazine of really valuable and useful matter were a far more effectual dragchain!

From the present and the future we turned to the past;—to Westminster Abbey and Henry the Seventh's Chapel. If what I have just written gets me into disgrace with some, what will others think of the confession I am now going to make? Westminster Abbey, as I saw it in Paris,—the painted Westminster Abbey of the Diorama,—made a grander, more sublime, and more harmonious impression on me, excited and touched me, far more than the reality. There I saw the solemn edifice at one glance; the whole extent

was before me, and an awful stillness seemed
to invite the mighty dead from their tombs, although those tombs were not visible.   Here, on
the contrary, is a perfect labyrinth of wooden
partitions, doors, screens, railings, and corners.
Nowhere a grand general effect; nowhere a feeling of congruity, and of regard to the main object,—the architectonic character of the building.
It seemed as if all these nooks and swallows'
nests were contrived merely to increase the number of showmen and key-bearers who lurk in
them.   I made all possible efforts (disregarding
the building or intentionally looking away from
it) to elevate my thoughts and feelings by the
recollection of the immortal dead who rest within
its walls; but most of the prominent monuments
are so utterly tasteless, so devoid of all artistical
beauty, that one inevitably falls into a discordant
key from a feeling either of the ridiculous or the
vexatious; I could hardly keep my mind in the
right frame even when looking on the altered
face of Mary Stuart, and the stern features of
Elizabeth.   Both were no doubt intended as
portraits.

If Shakspeare and Handel (the two greatest
among the artists immortalized here) were such
pretending, affected coxcombs as Roubilliac has
made of them, the French of the last century, and
the Italians of this, must be right.   If their
works were to be judged by these statues, small
indeed would be the truth or the beauty of either.
It is no answer to this to say that they are like-
nesses—if, indeed, that be the case.

The style of Henry VII.'s Chapel has been justly called rich; but is not the interior somewhat overloaded? Do not the traceries, and the short interrupted lines on the outside produce an effect rather of littleness than of variety? But I am fallen into such a strain that if I do not break off I shall be stoned. Chantrey's monuments in the abbey have certainly a very different character from the others; his statues are human beings: yet in my opinion they are still far behind the German school, both in poetical conception and in technical finish.

Yesterday I went to call on Miss G——, whom I met at Lord M———'s. She has a handsome person and a cultivated mind, an air of great good nature, and is rich into the bargain; in short, she combines every quality fitted to inspire a fatal passion,—if I were my own son. Her mother too made a very agreeable impression on me; her father was not present. The daughter was better informed about German literature than many German young ladies. Indeed I hear on all sides that young English-women are generally educated with great care, and learn more in proportion than their brothers. This would at once explain why Englishmen are so pre-eminent in some things; in others, for instance, the fine arts, so far behind. But I have spoken of this before. You must pardon occasional repetitions; these very repetitions show that circumstances have called my attention to the fact anew, and confirmed my former opinions.

When I went away, mother and daughter cordially shook hands with me, as is done with us on great occasions only, and scarcely ever by young women. I know that the custom is universal here, and means no more than " Guten tag," in Germany; in spite of that, it gave me great pleasure. I felt as if our acquaintance had thus made great progress, and as if a ray of human sympathy had fallen upon me in my solitude.

I was afraid yesterday, as I went rather late to see ' Macbeth,' at Covent Garden, that I should not get a place. What a mistake!

The house is just like Drury Lane, only rather less ornamented, and rather dirtier. And the performance?

Mr. Vandenhoff had certainly caught some of the psychological features of Macbeth; the subtle, sophistical inward debate, the doubting, wavering purpose; but nowhere did I catch a gleam of that originally heroic nature which alone could have rendered him an object worthy of such high and elaborate temptation.

Lady Macbeth, Mrs. Sloman, a fiendish shrew, who must have been the torment of her husband's life long before the predictions of the witches. Even in the sleeping scene she betrayed only fear of discovery and of punishment; and the exaggerated action, the rubbing of the hands, and seeming to dip them in water, and the rhetorical " to bed!" were very little to my taste.

To sum up my impression of the whole—an excess of effort, of bustle, and of accentuation; with every now and then, by way of clap-trap, a violent and yet toneless screaming. Exactly those passages in which these stage passions were the most

bóisterous and distressing were the most applauded.   There is not a single well-frequented
German theatre (such as those of Vienna, Berlin,
or Dresden) in which so bad a performance as
this would have been exhibited.   The three
witches were represented by three men; and to
give greater variety and interest to Shakspeare,
a long unmusical singsong was introduced, which
only retarded the action of the piece.   Well as I
know Macbeth, I often could not understand the
clipped and compressed English articulation; if
the fault is partly mine, it is also partly that of
the language.   Why did I understand every
word last year in Venice?   Why did Erminia
Gherardi intrance me as she did, while Mrs.
Sloman produces no effect upon me?   I have no
passion for playing the dissatisfied.   After Lady
Macbeth's last scene I went home, and lost the
rest of Macbeth and a grand melodráma—or lost
nothing.   Carlmilhan, from what I read in the
newspapers, is one of the tasteless monstrosities
of the modern unschooled school.   My indulgence in dramatic art cost 1 thaler, 8 gr.   It
was not worth so much as the mackerel I had at
dinner.

One other observation about Macbeth.   In
the banquet scene two tables were placed along
each side of the stage, and thrones erected for
the king and queen, in the centre at the back.
Neither of them took any share in the feast; there
were neither places for them at these side-tables
nor any table of their own.   Lady Macbeth remained seated alone upon her throne, and de-

claimed from thence till she led out her husband.
He, on the contrary, took a chair, brought it to
the front of the stage, and seated himself upon
it, till he became engaged in the dialogue with
his wife.   When he rises, Banquo glides in from
the side-scene, and sits down in this same chair.
The second time, he calls out from the opposite
side-scene and places himself in front of Macbeth.
The whole action and combination of this scene
is far better ordered in Berlin ; though even there
the appearance of the bloody ghost savours a
little of the peepshow.   If Macbeth sees a dag-
ger and clutches it, without the necessity of sus-
pending one by a wire from the ceiling before
his eyes and the public's,—might not he and they
see an invisible ideal Banquo and tremble at his
presence ?   Or if this be too much to ask, could
not a shadowy figure be produced by some opti-
cal means, as Enslen once did ?   The effect of
this, if properly managed, would be far more
ghostlike and supernatural.

Sunday, April 26th, 1835.

Yesterday, after I had very industriously
written letters, I bought a map of the environs
of London, studied it, and then drove to Richmond with Mr. and Mrs. T.   We went first down
Oxford Street, then to the left through Hyde
Park, through Kensington and Hammersmith,
and past Barnes and Mortlake to our place of
destination. The country is, as you may imagine,
highly cultivated, and exhibits a universal neat-
ness and elegance. The numerous villas and

gardens are very inviting, and often have an Italian air, from the luxuriant ivy and creepers, the balconies, verandahs, and the like. Though in Italy many things are more striking and poetical from the favouring climate, the forms of the hills and mountains, the character of the ground, and the luxuriant vegetation, yet the melancholy observation obtrudes itself, that the proprietor is poor, and that the poetical charm but too often resides in ruins, ancient or modern. It is thus in the neighbourhood of Rome, along the Brenta, and around Venice. Here, on the contrary, every door and window, the most trifling arrangements, show that the greatest care is bestowed on them, and can be bestowed, because wealth is universally diffused.

The Hammersmith Suspension Bridge is a fine and useful work. In whatever depends on mechanical fitness and precision, the English are masters; where taste is required, they seem frequently to confound the merely extraordinary with the poetical, and to prefer the fantastic to the artistic. A very severe judgment may be passed on many of the London buildings; they only produce effect by mass, and by being surrounded with other masses : for example, what an extrordinary *coiffure* is that stuck upon the Mansion House! And where is one to seek the school of architecture in which the man studied who is now constructing those strangest of buildings at Charing Cross? Vicenza, within her narrow walls, contains a greater number of beautiful and stately palaces than are to be found in all gigantic London.

From the terrace at Richmond the eye wanders or reposes with delight over the expanse of country as far as Windsor; and the winding course of the Thames, and the changing lights and shadows of England, increase its variety and beauty. Unfortunately the weather was extremely cold, which contrasted strangely with the splendour of the bursting spring. The plants seemed as if they would wait no longer, but would defy the unusually long and obstinate winter. Everybody says that such weather at this time of year is quite extraordinary.

—— told me that admission to a party at the Duke of D———'s was a thing so eagerly sought after, and so important, that I was most fortunate in having obtained it; and that, if I could prove I had been there, I should pass for a man of fashion all over England—if, only, my fashionable, does not share the fate of my literary, celebrity! A short time ago a gentleman, who presented me to a company, mentioned my name, and most politely added that it was unnecessary to say more, for that this was sufficient distinction, recommendation, and honour. But before I had time complacently to pocket this *testimonium morum et diligentiæ*, I heard my host (for my ears are sharper than my eyes) whispering, not to Englishmen, but to some Germans, that I was the author of the 'Hohenstaufen,' and so forth. So I was preserved from having my head turned, and had the joke into the bargain.

LETTER XX.

Museum—Philharmonic Concert—Police-office—Summary Proceeding—Morning Concert—Concert-room—English, French,
and German women—Royal Military Asylum—Chelsea Hospital—Hyde Park.

London, Monday, April 27th, 1835.

To-day, after a week's holiday, I resume my
labours at the Museum, with which I am very
well satisfied. I shall continue thus to divide
my time between the past and the present, as it
beseems a Professor historiarum.

If I could but divide *myself,* and read manu-
scripts in the Museum, the Chapter House, and
the State-Paper Office; books and newspapers in
the clubs; make visits, look at galleries and collections, wander about the parks, and write letters
at home, at one and the same moment! In spite
of the utmost economy of time, I do not know
how all these things are to be accomplished.

Last night I went to the Philharmonic Concert,
and heard,—

1st. Beethoven's ' Symphony in B.' It went
very well,—better than before.

2nd. ' Dies Bildniss ist bezaubernd schön,' sung
by Rubini. His voice is twice as powerful as that
of Mantius, and his facility in executing trills,
roulades, and quavers far greater. But as he
thought proper to introduce all these tricks, and
entirely to disregard the simple musical elocution,

he produced far less effect upon me than I expected. Here this imperfect style, which, spite
of its apparent variety, brings down everything
to the same level, is extremely admired.

3rd. Concerto Hummel in ' A Flat,' played
by Neate. Extraordinary clapping, because the
performer is an Englishman. In Berlin people
would say, the touch wanted power, the expression
was indistinct ; in short, that there was much still
to learn. It seemed to me as if I could play so
after a week's practice ;—and my vanity is not
great on the side of music.

4th. Terzetto from Otello,—' Ti parla amore,'
sung by Grisi, Lablache, and Rubini, and much
admired; though the composition, as adapted to
those words, is perfectly absurd—particularly the
running passages.

5th. Overture to the ' Jungfrau von Orleans,'
by Moscheles ; with the three principal elements,
the Pastoral, the Martial, the Religious. Conception and execution meritorious, but perhaps
not sufficiently intelligible to those not previously
acquainted with the drift.

6th. Symphony—Haydn.

After such a musical supper, and that at the
close of such a day, you will not wonder if I had
enough, and left the rest unheard. Otherwise I
should not be sitting here, but must have lain in
bed. It is also my firm persuasion, that nobody
can listen with full attention and enjoyment to
music (especially undramatic music) for more than
two hours, or two hours and a half.

Wednesday, April 29*th,* 1835.

To-day Mr. S——, police magistrate for the —— district, took me to his office or court. Most of the affairs that concern the police are decided by one magistrate, the more important by two, and those which require the decision of a jury are referred to the law courts. Questions of police and of law are not so rigorously divided as with us—indeed many are referred to the same persons. The magistrate sat at a table; before him, at another, were two clerks or protocollanti. Behind the bar, or separation of the room, was the complainant; on the left, in a place assigned, the accused. The business was conducted with great quietness and acuteness; questions asked, defence heard, and judgment pronounced. First were brought in the persons who had been apprehended and confined in the course of the night.

A. B. was so drunk that he could not stand. Does he admit this?—Yes.—He must pay 5*s.*—Dismissed.

This gentleman broke a pane of glass in my omnibus.—When did you see this pane whole last?—I can't exactly say.—Has he any witnesses?—No, but the gentleman was drunk.—Fined 5*s.*—Dismissed.

C. D. was drunk, and is very often drunk.—Fined 5*s.*—The next time to be sent to the House of Correction.

Remarkable:—that the shabbiest-looking fellows could all pay down their 5*s.* at a moment's notice; and that men very well to do,—" respect-

able men" as the English call them,—were found
drunk about the streets.

That woman brought me a begging letter with
testimonials, which, for such and such reasons,
are false.—That man writes petitions complaining
of his extreme misery, his wife is ill, his children
without food, &c., &c.—Where does he live?
—I don't know the exact house.—Shall I send
for his wife and children, and hear?—No.—Guilty
of deception, and obtaining money under false
pretences.—Both sent to the House of Correction
for three months.—And they went off without
any attempt at reply or remark, and the business
was done; and all the decisions seemed to me,
and, as far as I could observe, to the offenders
themselves, perfectly just.

After I had heard these summary and efficient
proceedings with great interest, and had postponed kings and queens to knaves and drunk-
ards, my historical conscience took alarm, and I
went to work at the Museum from two to four.

Saturday, May 2nd, 1835.

Although I was greatly delighted with the
spoil I gathered yesterday at the Museum
from the letters of Randolf and Bedford during
their embassies, and would gladly have stayed
longer, I was obliged to break off after three
hours' work, because Mrs. T—— had had the goodness to promise to take me to Moscheles' *morning*
concert, which began at two in the afternoon.

Though I am no friend of concerts in general,
yet as Mr. Moscheles' is one of the choicest and

the best attended, I determined to hear it, as a sample of what the London public likes, and what it can obtain, in the musical way.

The Concert-room in the King's Theatre has a steep orchestra, reaching to the ceiling at one end, and tiers of boxes at the other. On the right is a bare wall; on the left, three narrow windows for lighting the whole room. The space in the centre is filled with benches, but only every other row has a back—a sort of training for the outside of the stage coaches. The room has neither size nor beauty to recommend it. The walls are shabbily and tastelessly painted with arabesques, more like those on a china tea-cup than those of Raphael's Loggie. So rich a people as the English might really afford to have these scratched out. A white wall would be better than such pitiful scrawls. The concert began at two and ended at half-past five, for there were no less than seventeen pieces. I shall give you a list of them, accompanied by a few scholia, or marginal glosses.

1. Overture to the ' Jungfrau von Orleans.' I prefer the peaceful and religious part to the warlike; or at least I should strike out some resolutions and discords from the latter, in order to give greater simplicity to the whole, and perhaps greater historical consistency with that period of musical art. For musical war and peace have a different character in different ages, and yet each belongs to the other—relates to, and illustrates the other. The martial part of this overture employs all the arts of music in use at the present

day, and is thus out of keeping with the pastoral music, which is manifestly of a former age.

2. Scena from the 'Freischütz,' Miss Robson. I have bad luck with this scene in foreign lands. In Paris, I heard it sung very accurately, but without the least expression, by Damoreau Cinti; and there are at least a hundred Demoiselles in Berlin who could accomplish the task as well as Miss Robson.

3. Duet from Rossini's 'Donna del Lago,' sung by Grisi and Rubini. Grisi's voice is powerful, and cultivated according to the true rules of art; but her musical elocution, nay, even her tone, has, occasionally, something vulgar, which you never hear in German singers. Less voice, with more elevation and sentiment, would produce more effect. Rubini trembles when he holds a note ; whether he takes this defect for a beauty, or whether his voice is growing old, and he cannot help it, I don't know. Much less lungs, voice, art and expression are required for all that trickery of whispering and shouting, piping and quavering, than good-natured admirers think.

4. ' *Concerto pathétique*' for the piano-forte, by Moscheles. I will only put two questions as to this. First, would not every piano-forte concerto be the better for being delivered from such powerful accompaniments as drums and trumpets? Is not the contrast too violent, and the effect of the principal instrument enfeebled ?

Secondly. The piano-forte is, in many respects, inferior to all stringed and wind instruments ; but it has one great advantage—that the player can execute several parts at once, according to the rules of harmony. Why is this peculiar advantage, of which the old German school invariably availed itself, now utterly neglected, both by composers and performers?

5. Air, 'Ah quando in regio talamo,' by Donizetti, sung by Madame Caradori Allan. A hodge-podge of unconnected phrases, tacked together with solfeggios, sung with accuracy and facility, and greatly applauded.

6. Aria, 'Largo al factotum,' sung by Lablache as admirably as before. But it is better suited to the stage than to a gentleman in black, with white kid gloves, in an orchestra.

7. Quintet, the dirge of 'Rosabelle" composed by Horsley, Mus. Bac. A simple ballad, requiring a simple, lyrical, touching melody, cut up into recitative, solo, trio, and quintet; and, to my taste, utterly spoiled by the employment of all sorts of complicated scientific expedients.

8. Terzetto, 'Ambi morrete,' from Donizetti's 'Anna Bolena,' sung by Grisi, Lablache, and Rubini. One must have resigned all idea of dramatic music, and have lost all memory and trace that such a thing ever existed, before one can give one's admiration to the senseless roulades, the dancing rhythm, the starts, screams, and die-away whispers, with which a royal tyrant, his wife, and her lover amuse themselves and others in the hour of death. The stupidity of opera composers has now become so audacious, and their audacity so stupid, that art will probably once more raise itself from these disgusting tricks to a pure and

noble style.   At the present moment this cholera
rages, as it seems, all over Europe.

9. Concertante for piano-forte, violin, and vio-
loncello, Beethoven, played by Moscheles, Mori,
and Lindley.   Beethoven's daring flights occasionally border on lawlessness; but he is a man
who has a right to ask of Art what he pleases; or
rather Art must ask him in what new dress and
adornments she shall present herself.   With
dithyrambic frenzy does this high-priest of Art
cast the jewels of his vast treasury into the air;
and even the broken fragments which fall to the
ground would suffice to compose many a costly
ornament.   But when impudent bajazzos fling
dirt and stones at our heads, are we to fall on our
knees and humbly thank them for their favours?

10. Duet ' Cedi al destin,' from Meyer's
' Medea.'   Miss Masson and Rubini.   Dramatic
intentions, means and ends, thank God, not so
entirely vanished as in more recent productions.
For the fourth time I heard Rubini conclude with
exactly the same cadence; thus :—violent effort in
the lower notes, then a soft squeaking up to the
very highest—sugar on sugar—and, last, a very
forcible accent which set the hands of the audience
in motion, with as much certainty as the foot of the
bellows-blower moves the bellows of the organ.

11. New ballad, ' Go, forget me,' by Mortimer,
sung by Parry.   The composition simple and appropriate, enounced with feeling and expression.
More of vocal music, that is, the human voice
speaking to the heart, than in a thousand instrumental pieces for the voice.

12. 'Heart, the seat of soft delight,' from 'Acis and Galatea;'—say, rather, from another world of music; well given by Miss Clara Novello.

13. Scene, 'The Battle of Hohenlinden,' by Smith. I was glad when peace was restored.

14. Concertante for four violins, by Maurer. A difficult task, considering the small compass of the instrument; but if such must be set and undertaken, well enough accomplished.

15. Aria, ' Dal asilo della pace,' Costa. A 'solfeggio,' perfectly sung by Grisi. Formerly people sang solfeggios as a preparation and training for singing; now, it seems, the solfeggio is the beginning and the end of art.

16. 'Fantasie improvisée,' by Moscheles, in which, among others, an air from the ' Muette de Portici,' and one out of ' Euryanthe,' were introduced and treated—all with great skill and science; round, clear, brilliant, attractive. The question whether different themes should be blended in a fantasia is intimately connected with another: whether, in an overture to an opera, various motivi from the work itself should be introduced? The greatest masters have adopted opposite principles, and I have not now time to discuss the merits of the two methods.

17. Instrumental piece of Mozart—omitted: indeed, the quantity was already too great; though it is most certain that the quality would have been materially improved by Mozart. Donizetti is not a dish from which any man of sense or discrimination will endure to be helped twice; and Rossini's operas have been so often repeated,

that any thing else would have the charm of
novelty in the comparison. But the public, perhaps, will have it so; and, still more, the one-
sided and meagre education of the singers may
make it inevitable.

What infinite odds between such a concert and
Sebastian Bach's mass in A flat, well executed!

The greater part of the audience were ladies,
as is generally the case at morning concerts.
The men are too busy to go. All, even the
youngest, wore bonnets; their dress was simple,
but rich and elegant; without eclat,—nothing
extravagant or glaring.

I must say, in general, that I cannot detect any
trace of personal vanity in English women. This
sin, or passion, or what you will, seems to give
more trouble to the French and Germans. It
appears to me that the women and girls here bestow less time on their persons; esteem it less of
a duty or an important business to dress and
trick them out, and then to delight and exult in
them till they cry " *Vivat sequens!*"

Monday, May 4th.

YESTERDAY I worked at home till eleven o'clock,
and then (as a relief from my sedentary employments during the week,) I was six hours on
foot. First, I saw the Royal Military Asylum
at Chelsea, that is, the great establishment
founded by the Duke of York for the sons of
soldiers. It formerly contained a thousand boys,
but, in consequence of the peace, there are now
not above three or four hundred. Every place

was remarkably clean, orderly, spacious and airy.
The boys make every article of clothing that they
wear, and are trained to different trades, and then
bound out apprentice.   They looked uncommonly
healthy and full of fun; I only wish I may see
the children in factories wear the same appearance.   There was a place for gymnastic exercises,
and the old woman who showed Mr. B. and me
about, invited us to go some Friday and see the
boys' feats.

From hence we went to the hospital for invalids
hard by; a large building, with beautiful gardens
and convenient arrangements.   It would certainly
cost less to pension these invalids at home; but it
is more humane to have such an asylum for those
who would rather stay among their old comrades,
and, as far as in them lies, keep alive the tradi-
tion of the glories of the British army.

We returned to the beautiful St. James's Park,
went through the Green Park to Hyde Park, then
into Kensington Gardens, and back to Hyde
Park, favoured by the weather, and cheered by
the freshness of spring.   A man like Laine might
beautify Hyde Park very much.   To-day the
grand thing to see was the endless line of
equipages, the beautiful horses, the riders, good,
bad, and indifferent, and walkers of every kind
and degree, who thronged the park from four to
six o'clock.   All the women of the lower classes
very simply drest, chiefly in black or dark colours;
but few remarkable for beauty.

LETTER XXI.

French Communicativeness—English Reserve—Prussian ' Staatszeitung '—' Wochenblatt'—Exhortations to Peel—' Thorough'
—Insignificance of the Theatre—Political Press in Berlin and
London — Whigs and Tories — Primogeniture — Husband-
catching—Religious Bigotry—New interpretation of the Apocalypse—Hansard's Debates—English Society—German Joviality.

London, Tuesday, May 5th, 1835.

YOUR remark, or reproach, that my letters contain
very few personal details, has some justice.   But,
in the first place, I have such a hearty disgust at
the practices of several modern travellers, that I
could not even think, much less write, such ungrateful gossip.   I am afraid every company I go
into should suppose me capable of entertaining
such designs and principles.   In the second,
within the last few weeks, scandal sent to Berlin
in private letters (I do not choose to give any
names) has travelled back to London, and produced very unpleasant consequences.   In the
third, the English do not give themselves out
like the French, who let you into their whole
history and sentiments at the first sitting, so that
you have nothing to do but to pack it up and
send it home.   The English neither feel the
same want to make these immediate and circum-
stantial disclosures, nor have they the same facility in making them.   I learn from everybody,
and everybody touches on various topics ; but if I
wanted to connect what I have learned with the

persons of my informants, and give you an account of every conversation, every dinner, &c., this mosaic would have no unity or coherence, and would afford no general view of any subject. I must collect the scattered details and opinions; examine what is contradictory; sift the truth, wherever it is possible, from party evidence; and not connect this with persons, but gradually gain a distinct view of the great questions which are here under discussion.

This reminds me of ————'s article in the ' Staatszeitung.' Excellent intentions, and generous feelings,—only too English; that is to say, all directed towards one person and one side; the opposite views either not mentioned at all, or in such a manner as if they were not worth mentioning. Nevertheless, ————'s representations and opinions are a hundred thousand times better and more enlarged than the absurd lecture which the Berlin Wochenblatt, with its condescending pedagogical air, reads to such a man as Peel; telling him that, with the support of the King and the Lords, he ought to have blown the whole reformed House of Commons to the winds, and have restored things to the condition they were in at I know not what good old times. Such a scheme supposes an incredible ignorance of the state of England, and a stupid *borné* fanaticism into the bargain. Peel has more sense in his little finger than such politicians as these in their heads; his patriotism, his humanity, his disinterestedness, his moderation, would all conspire to preserve him from so desperate a course: just as Wellington laudably relinquished his opposition

to the Catholic claims, rather than incur the risk
of civil war. The defect is not in the place where
the Berlin tinker thinks he has spied it. The
alarming thing is, that certain British prejudices
push opposite opinions to a point where they can
no longer mutually serve to correct and to de-
velop each other (like the regular and alternate
action of the lungs), but where their excited and
irregular motion becomes wearing and destructive. Were I inclined to look on the black side
and play the prophet of ill, I should say that as
the *royalistes purs* and the constitutional royal-
ists ruined each other, and thus became subject to
the Girondins and the *Terroristes*, so Whigs and
Tories are here playing the game of the Radicals.
It grieves me to think (and this grief is more
generous than the indoctrinations of the Wochenblatt) that Peel, under different circumstances,
and with modified—I will say, with Germanized
—views, might have commanded a majority of
two hundred, and have put an end to all these
pernicious vacillations; that the best that can
now happen will be, to reach the point by a cir-
cuitous road, which those who had the power had
not the capacity or the knowledge to reach by the
straight. Such heads as Peel's (a very different
one from that of the theorist Posa *) cannot be
inactive whatever be his situation. Lord Stanley
is in a still more false position when he opposes
all changes in the church, and supports them in
the corporations. Very naturally, replied some one ;
he would have to give up livings worth 22,000*l*.

* This alludes to the character of Posa, in Schiller's Don
Carlos.—*Translator*.

The sage of the Wochenblatt concludes somewhat in this wise:—Our proposal is certainly contrary to the usages of Parliament, but the whole
origin and course of the Reform was contrary to
them ; and it is necessary to make head against
revolution by those portions of the constitution
which are yet unreformed. What logic ! what a
hocus-pocus of words and ideas, made with
greater rapidity than the conjurer, Philadelphia,
could have done !

In the seventeenth century, however, wisdom
was reduced into still smaller compass; squeezed
into a nut-shell. The one word " Thorough "
was used as the ruling substantive, the pass-word,
the expression of the aim of the initiated. Straf-
ford and Laud, the high priests of civil and ecclesiastical absolutism, conclude their letters with
this word, as if it were a charm, a *salve* against
all dangers.

And what were the consequences of their so-
called anti-revolutionary " Thorough " ? That
they brought on the revolution they pretended
to avert, and lost their own heads. God grant
that those who fancy themselves statesmen may
not attempt to carry matters in the same way !

*　　　*　　　*　　　*

Here, where the theatre is so insignificant, its
importance in Berlin might perhaps appear to
me puerile and ridiculous, did I not reflect that
the enthusiasm of the Greeks for the drama, and
for art generally, was far nobler than the military
enthusiasm of the Romans; and that there has
been no lack of the latter in Germany when the

times required it; nor ever will be. I shall therefore return with great complacency from this capital of the world to stall No. 102; and shall not even be deterred by the ———, which has such a contempt for my criticisms on art.

At any rate I understand more about that than about England, spite of all my pains to get at a broad and clear view of it. When I see what nonsense many travellers write about Germany, I lose courage to say anything about England ; though I may venture to say that I came here better prepared by previous study than many come to Germany.

*   *   *   *   *

Political hand-weaving has long been abolished here, and not only the presses, but the pens and brains employed on the newspapers are moved by steam-engines, which send out the greatest possible quantity of goods " to order," in the smallest possible time.

At Berlin, a newspaper article, *à la* ———, is an outpouring of the heart for the writer, an *évènement* for the readers ; here one such wave courses over another, and all break and disappear upon the shore. But then here is indeed a political ocean, whose depth and contents must be tried by other means than by a mere observation of the surface, curled or tossed by the winds. As the times are over when the writer on religious questions could assume that Catholics or Protestants were exclusively right or wrong, so ought the political observer of Europe to endeavour to raise himself above the region of those subordinate differences which, arrayed in opposition, mutually annul and destroy each other, and leave a mere vacuity of thought, a paralysis of action. But certainly nothing is so convenient and so easy as one-sided predilections, and a complacent nursing of these predilections, combined with a sublime determination to ignore all other modes or points of view. If, unluckily, these measures of security do not suffice to pre-serve from all attacks, a loyal or a liberal mantle (as the case may be) is thrown over the armour, and this is more impenetrable to reason or con-viction than India-rubber cloaks are to rain. Let nobody laugh at the ostrich for hiding her head in a hedge, when span-new nobles who travel to Paris make it their wisdom and their '*gloire*' not to see or speak to any but Carlists. Just as silly as if some democratical *privat-docent* would not visit or listen to anybody but the editor of the 'Tribune.'

Where so many see the sole reality and truth of a subject, I can hardly ever see *a whole*. Viewed in this manner, it seems to me a mere semblance, and one semblance opposed to another leaves, as I said, nothing behind. Tories without Whigs, conservatism without any principle of movement, republicanism without monarchical bond of union, landed interest without monied interest, and so forth, are quite unintelligible to me. Their very existence and significancy de-pend on their antithesis ; they belong to each other like body and soul, day and night, right and left, income and expenditure, right and duty,

ruler and subject, rich and poor; in short, like all
ideas which can only attain their full existence in
their contraries, and can never by any possibility
have an independent being.

Thus, for instance, the author of the eulogy on
Peel forgets that the sower's labour is as useful
as the reaper's; and that the living movement of
the political body must proceed from the centripetal force of Conservatism, and the centrifugal of Whiggism. It were not difficult, indeed,
to represent such measures as the repeal of the
Test Act, the deliverance of Ireland from pro-
tracted tyranny, and the like, as the true sun-
light of political wisdom; and if people must
reduce every thing to halves, *this* is certainly the
one in which lies the pulse and vitality of future
Europe;—not in the close corporations, the ex-
clusion of dissenters, the maintenance of slavery
or commercial monopoly; not in the exclusive
schools; not in aristocratical church patronage,
or laws of primogeniture.

I have studied the middle ages more atten-
tively than most men; I have defended some of
its institutions, which many, both wise and foolish,
joined in abusing, and have endeavoured to place
them in their true light: I have, therefore, a
right to be regarded as, at least, impartial, when,
resting on a knowledge of the past, I try to
investigate the character and the wants of the
present.

The contest really is, whether England shall
Germanize herself;—shall enter, at least in part,
on the German career of civilization. This is the

real point for which Whigs contend and which
Tories resist;—though neither know enough of
Germany to be aware of the fact. In regard to
all the measures just alluded to, Germany stands
exactly at the point towards which Whigs are
steering, and at which Tories can discern no
land. Without helm or motion the ship is lost;
with bad pilotage she may, indeed, be run on the
French rocks, instead of reaching the German
port: but to avoid this danger by doing nothing
is a very ostrich-like precaution. The same
danger impended over us; we did not shut our
eyes to it, but have averted it by vigorous
and efficient changes, and by dint of these have
attained a powerful and positive security against
the invasion of foreign opinions or foreign swords.
And so (I end as I begun) the writer of the
Berlin Wochenblatt is no statesman, because he
does not understand that to refuse reform is to
precipitate revolution; to remain motionless is
an indication of disease or of approaching death.

Yesterday somebody, I know not who, sent me
a pamphlet on primogeniture. This is just one of
the points I alluded to, in which some different
direction requires to be given to social institutions. The question is, whether the aristocratical
policy, which attaches such enormous advantages
to the accident of primogeniture, is to be adhered
to; or the democratical regard to individual justice,
which enjoins an equal division of property, is to
be preferred? In Germany and France, the latter
(with the exception of the reigning families) has
conquered; in England, the former still prevails.

The author of this pamphlet is of opinion that the laws are defective in allowing a father to leave his whole property (with few restrictions) to his eldest son; nay, more, if the father dies intestate, the eldest son takes the whole of the real estate. It is not only possible, but actually in practice, that one of ten children may have 10,000*l.* a-year, and the other nine be destitute. This remnant of feudalism is productive of so many evils, that it must be removed; since the causes of it, which were to be found in the nature of feudal service, no longer exist. The increased wealth of the elder sons has no effect in stimulating them to greater mental exertions; on the contrary, its natural tendency is to make them indolent and indifferent. Society would gain by a more equal division, and the powers and talents of all its members be more equally and efficiently called forth and encouraged.

It is unquestionable that large accumulations of wealth are productive of many advantages which are incompatible with divided property; such as the erection of castles and mansions, the forming of collections of pictures, &c.; but these are often only useless demonstrations of pride, and distressing contrasts to the miserable dwellings by which they are surrounded. In many families, too, the law of primogeniture has afforded motives and temptations to mortgaging property to a ruinous extent.

National galleries contribute much more to the enjoyment of the public, and to the cultivation of taste, than the splendid but inaccessible collections of the English nobility.

The law of primogeniture is an artificial elevation on the one hand, which necessarily involves a
corresponding artificial depression on the other.
The worst of its consequences are those which
regard the relation of the sexes, and marriage.
I must give you some idea of the extraordinary
picture the author of this book draws of the state
of English society in this respect. The competition for high prizes in marriage; the intrigues
and manœuvres of mothers to catch elder sons
and to keep younger ones at a distance from
their daughters; or, if a girl have the folly or the
magnanimity to prefer the latter, the tyranny or
the falsehood resorted to to separate them;—in
short, as elder sons alone are considered eligible
husbands, the supply of wives in the market, in
economical phrase, exceeds the demand. Hence
arises the noble science of husband-catching.
The more generous and amiable half of the
human race is transformed into bait with which
to catch heirs. Frivolous accomplishments are
substituted for solid instruction; care of the person, for culture of the mind; and instead of singing being pursued as an agreeable relaxation, or
dancing as a graceful exercise, they are made the
great ends of existence. The whole soul of the
mother is absorbed in schemes for procuring for
her daughter a good ' establishment;' no time
must be lost, and the girl must apply herself dili-
gently to the business of captivating a husband.
But as the market is notoriously over-stocked,
invisible lines must be laid out in various directions. The youthful and inexperienced object of

these arts bites, the bait is drawn up, and he is caught. Too often follows the discovery of the manœuvres by which he has been caught, and of the objects by which they were prompted—his wealth and station;—to which the empty, heartless being to whom he is united considers him a mere appendage. The consequences may be imagined.

Perhaps this picture is too highly coloured. However, the author maintains that this law of primogeniture nourishes a spirit of rapacity, and of animosity in families, where the interests of all the others are sacrificed to one. Such are the statements of the English author, for which he, not I, is responsible.

Thursday, May 7th, 1835.

Mr. —— described the way in which the Catholic priests in Ireland try to induce parents, in mixed marriages, to bring up their children in that persuasion; a thing which, as Prussia shows, is determined less by law, than by custom and the habits of the clergy.

The cry of " No popery" is stimulated by means of every kind. Thus, for instance, a political writer demonstrates, by figures which seem incontrovertible, that the number of Catholics in North America has, of late years, increased in a vastly greater proportion than that of the Protestants. These millions it is said are seduced by the diabolical arts of proselytizing, and have fallen away from Christianity. A similar danger now impends over England, and must be averted by the overthrow of its author, Lord John Russell, and his party! &c. &c. This is the cry.

I rather doubted the boundless power of pro-
selytism ascribed to the Catholic priests of America, and looked beneath this array of figures for
something like reason and coherence.   And what
came to light?   That this increased proportion
of Catholics was not the work of the priests at
all; but resulted, first, from the shoals of Irish im-
migrants, who are nearly all Catholics ; secondly,
from the fact, intentionally suppressed or carelessly overlooked, that Louisiana and Florida,
with some millions of Catholic inhabitants, have
been annexed to the United States since the
former calculation was made.

And these are the arguments with which party
men seek to oppose the Christian doctrine of
toleration and charity, and to defend their prejudices,—or, more frequently, their incomes !

     *   *   *   *   *

I told you that Mr. ———, my companion at
dinner, defended my views concerning Elizabeth
and Mary, and that I was delighted with his
acute historical criticism.   Yesterday I was quite
alarmed, when, at the end of our dinner, he told
me, in confidence, that he was going to publish a
new explanation of the Apocalypse of St. John.
The seven trumpets, he said, were the fall of
Paganism, of the Roman empire, the Albigenses,
Luther's Reformation, the English Reformation,
the expulsion of the Protestants from France, and
the revolution of July.   With as much certainty
as he knew that I was sitting opposite to him, he
knew that, on the second day of some festival, (I
think Easter,) in the year 1843, Christ would re-

appear in Jerusalem. Nobody, he added, or very few, would believe in this interpretation, but this is the very *proof* of its truth; for Christ says that he should come unexpected, " as a thief in the night." Spite of all his earnestness and conviction, he did not take amiss a little raillery.

Although Mr. ———'s inferences and explanations were immeasurably more daring on this subject than those of Mr. ——— on the oft-mentioned controversy about the two queens, yet his conviction had to me something imposing in it. Not that I attached any importance to his interpretations, analogies, calculations, historical comparisons, and so on; but in the *thought—Christ will appear in* 1843! or be it when it may—lies such power, such omnipotence, and infinitude of new conditions of human existence, that all the parties, passions, and agitations of our days vanish before it like the most miserable trivialities. Were He to appear,—were He to be, and to be acknowledged as the Christ,—what another world must arise! Where, then, would be the petty arts, the articles of faith, the party feuds and persecutions, the French *côté droit* and *côté gauche*, the English Whigs and Tories, Conservatives and Radicals, the Berlin watchmen of Zion and Demagogues? All this would be scattered like froth before the wind, and all who would not turn to him would be destroyed; or,—better,—all would be rescued by the almighty power of regeneration. Dreams—or perhaps not;—for what thought or fancy here compresses into a moment, lies hidden in the future history of man, to be gradually evolved by the hand of time. The seed-corn is in the ground, and the race of man cannot all be lost, or all go astray, so long as His word and His promise endures,—to abide with us to the end of time. So far as we live together in love, this promise is daily fulfilled. Let this, then, be the corner-stone on which the new legislation for church and state shall be built; not on the delusive calculations of the statisticians, or the false inferences of Ultras of any party.

Friday, May 8th, 1835.

As I accidentally remarked to Mr. ———, that I had been assiduously reading Hansard's Parliamentary Debates, by way of gaining information, he exclaimed, " Hansard's is a hateful, abominable book." " How so?" " If you said a word ten years ago it is picked out, taken from its connexion, misinterpreted," &c.

Bad,—thought I; but not so very bad either. What if we could quote ———'s vote for the abolition of the censorship, and ———'s recommendation of the sale of the royal demesnes, out of some Prussian Hansard?

If I compare English society with that of other countries, many remarks present themselves. If the number of guests exceed three, there is seldom any general conversation; that is to say, I do not see or hear that any individual, whether from talent or from conceit, takes upon himself to lead the conversation, makes himself the prominent person, keeps possession of a particular subject, or battles it out with some other intellectual fencer; people very seldom address themselves farther than to their next neighbour, and the conversation is carried on in so low a voice, that those who sit at a distance can hardly hear it. Subjects of great general interest are, as it seems to me, very seldom subjects of social talk. What an eventful time ! A change of ministry! the approaching opening of a new parliament! &c. &c. Not a trace of all this in society: the saying, out of the abundance of the heart the mouth speaketh, seems not to apply to the English. In days like these, even if their mouths were corked tight and sealed down, the French would have gone off like Champagne bottles; their thoughts and feelings would have forced a way. In parliamentary discussions the French are very inferior to the English; in social, superior; and I should have learnt more if the English were, in this respect, more like their neighbours. What passes in parliament we get from the papers ; but a foreigner is glad to pick up in company the commentaries and additions of individuals. To have to extract everything by questioning, *tête-à-tête*, is always somewhat disagreeable and " boring."

What is more, eating and drinking seem to produce no effect upon the English. I do not applaud inordinate and boisterous talking after dinner; but that people should be just as cold, quiet, and composed, at the end as at the beginning; that the wine should produce no apparent effect whatever, is too dry and formal for my liking. Perhaps the old-fashioned tippling was so disgusting, that people now shun the slightest approach to joviality; or perhaps sherry and port oppress rather than elevate, and have little power in transforming gloomy fogs into sky-blue fantasies. In short, I am for the German plan—frank, lively conversation, even though it be a little too long and too loud; light wine and a light heart; and at parting, joyous spirits, and only just mathematics enough to perceive that five is an even number.

LETTER XXII.

English and French Society—Scene in an Omnibus—House of Commons—English Oratory—Poor Laws for Ireland—O'Connell—Public and Private Law—Repeal—Lord John Russell—Devonshire Election—Sir R. Peel's City Speech—Fifty-fourth Birth-day—'King and Constitution'—King of Prussia, the First Reformer of Europe—Fogs—English Orthography of German.

London, Sunday, May 10th, 1835.

MY observations on many English societies are, with reference to the point from which I contemplate them, and to the feelings with which they inspire me, unquestionably true at the moment. But are they not, for that very reason, one-sided? and have I not neglected to seek for the causes of the appearances that strike me? That no Englishman may come and set me right, I will,

therefore, rather compose an answer to myself,
and put it into his mouth.

" The French conversation which Herr von
Raumer seems so much to admire and covet, is
generally a light and insignificant bandying of
words; ' a chit-chat,' which it is very easy to carry
on in general formulas and phrases; the more so,
as the speakers flatter each other's vanity, and
studiously avoid all sustained argument and all
violent opposition.   But a man who regarded
this as the highest and most instructive, or
even the most agreeable, sort of conversation
were greatly mistaken; the German earnestness
and prolixity, nay, sometimes blunt and grace-
less manner, would be more to our English
taste.   The important events of the time are not
so entirely passed over in silence as Herr v. Raumer imagines; but, as they are the subject of daily
discussion in speech and writing, out of society,
a few words are sufficiently intelligible to the
English; though they almost escape a foreigner,
with his inadequate acquaintance with the language.   The English, who are permitted, nay,
obliged, to speak their sentiments on these
points in a thousand places, do not make society
an arena for discussion, merely for the pleasure
or instruction of ignorant foreigners; and an
' English gentleman' would as soon think of
boring people with what he had already
thought, heard, and read, as a well-bred German
employé would entertain them with the details of
his official business.   An Englishman, if Herr
v. Raumer will address himself to him, *tête-à-*

tête, will reply to all his questions with pleasure and courtesy; but will give them no encouragement in a place where they would be tedious to other hearers. Lastly, if Herr v. Raumer exults in his countrymen's enjoyment of wine, we will not seek to spoil his pleasure; but we must observe, that the chief cause of this is, that the poor Germans drink but little wine, and that therefore it produces upon them an effect to which we have long been insensible, and which we are not disposed to purchase by abstinence, or by drinking Berlin *Weissbier.* We fancy the loss might be greater than the gain."

After this speech, I might surely play the judge, weigh each side with great dignity, and pronounce sentence; but it seems to me better to show my impartiality, and leave the judicial function to others.

*　　*　　*　　*　　*

Soon after I had seated myself in the omnibus, a well-dressed man got in, and was instantly followed by an equally well-dressed woman, who seized him by the hair with her left hand, while, with the right, she gave him a box on the ear which made the omnibus ring. As she was proceeding in her ill treatment of him, the neighbours, like good Christians, interposed. To my shame, I confess I was more inclined to call out "Go on," that I might see the end of this "untoward event," and then hear the history of it. The man sat quite still, like a *pauvre honteux;* from which I inferred, spite of the sinister appearance of the slap, that he was the offending party. The lady promised him, by very significant gestures, that the performance should be resumed at home, and played to the end.

Wednesday, May 13*th.*

Yesterday I was present at the opening of Parliament. The House of Commons is a long square room, lighted by lofty semi-circular windows by day, and by chandeliers at night; the walls wainscotted, and painted of an ugly ochre-colour; benches on either side for the members, and galleries for the public. All the members were in their ordinary dress, most of them with their hats on; the Speaker alone, as a sample (or rather as a caricature) of former times, was adorned with a long white wig of great amplitude, and was perched on a high seat. Below him, a table with clerks, papers, &c. Probably the noise to-day was greater than usual, from the number of new members taking their seats; it was, however, not always accidental, but increased beyond measure with the growing ennui. The members seldom listened; probably because what was said did not seem to them of any importance. The only persons whom I understood at all were Messrs. Hume, Cobbett, and Spring Rice, and those I could not follow. I was only conscious that the others were speaking from their gestures. Two Englishmen near me were in the same predicament; so that, this time, it was not the fault of my ignorance of the language or the pronunciation. None of the speakers seemed to attempt to produce effect by external demeanour, attitude, gesture, or such arts of oratory. Demosthenes, Cicero, and Quintilian would have been sent back to their schools of rhetoric. The imposing effect of the English House of Commons by no means lies in externals; it lies in the thought of the results to England, nay, to the whole globe, from words thus unartistically and negligently uttered.

I must now pass to other subjects; for though these starts and breaks prevent any profound or connected discussion, you must be content to take what the day forces upon me, and make what you can of the Mosaic.

In the first place, I wish to add a postscript to my letter on the Poor Laws, with reference to a speech of O'Connell's just printed. He abjures his opposition to the Poor Laws on grounds of a most singular nature, which are closely connected with the peculiar circumstances of Ireland, and with the future government of Great Britain. When he calls the Poor Laws " a solecism and an anomaly," and declares it to be highly dangerous and destructive to all civil order, that one man should have a claim to support out of the private property of another man, he is much less of an " Agitator" than he might be, indeed than he *ought to be*. This doctrine (which I have so often attacked), of an absolute, unconditional, exclusive private right, is far more destructive of social order; and, if followed out to its consequences, leads equally to helplessness and heart-

lessness. No State can either avow this doctrine
in theory, or follow it in practice; as the daily
demands made on life and property by all governments more than sufficiently prove. Its
duty is only to set legal limits to the claims of
selfishness, injustice, and violence; and, among
other things, to put an end to robbery and to
beggary by means of a legal provision for the
poor. That the very words should frighten
people here is natural enough, after the abuses I
have detailed to you; but they ought to distinguish these from the essence of the thing, and
not to cover hardness and selfishness under a veil
of political economy. O'Connell's conversion,
therefore, is no solecism, but a renunciation of
errors.

The course of his conversion, however, is a
proof of my favourite opinion of the reciprocal
influence of public and private law, and the necessity of looking at the consequences of every individual enactment on both sides. So long as the
elections in Ireland depended on the ten-shilling
voters, the landowners subdivided their land in
order to secure to themselves a preponderating
influence. Since the constitutional law has been
altered in this respect, and the qualification is
raised from ten shillings to ten pounds, the small
farmers and cottagers are, in virtue of an unqualified civil right, relentlessly driven from their
homes, in order that the landlord may conso-
lidate his farms, and thus secure ten-pound
voters. Thus this public reform leads to incalculable private misery, and O'Connell is right in

saying that the national legislature must, in some
way or other, interpose.   It were unquestionably
just, humane, and Christian to enact poor-laws,
purified from errors and abuses, which should
compel wealthy land-owners to support those
whom they have plunged into such unequalled
wretchedness, by availing themselves of a law so
favourable to their own interests.

Lastly, O'Connell's declaration is politically
important.   He entirely relinquishes the idea of
the Repeal of the Union;—indeed, he avows that
he has only regarded it as a means of extorting
justice from a reluctant government.   It is now
clear to him that Ireland will never obtain this
from the Tories, and that the effect of his opposition to the Whigs would be to bring them back
to office.   The present ministry, for the blessing
of Ireland, will therefore stand better with the
Irish members than ever it did before.

Another matter I wish to call your notice to, is
Lord John Russell's defeat in Devonshire.   The
county has given him a " *démenti*," which, in
France, would be seriously injurious; here he is
elected for another place, and, in general popularity, he gains by being a sort of martyr to the
rancour of an intolerant party.   The thing is
clear enough.   Wherever the largest landed
properties are in the hands of Tories, a Tory
member must be returned.   The tenants are
threatened with being turned out of their farms,
and their wives are privately advised to keep
their husbands from ruining their families; they
had much better go to such a shop where they may

choose clothes for their children; they need not trouble themselves about paying,—and so forth.

My third topic is, the addresses to Sir Robert Peel, and his speech in the city. The latter is certainly, in a measure, sincere; but you seem to attach a far too great political importance to it, in Berlin. Peel knew, better than you, that he had no chance of founding his power upon this incident. The address of the lawyers, say many, proves nothing but the inveteracy of their prejudices, and the extent of their selfishness; they dread reforms that may diminish their gains. The city address comes chiefly from persons connected with the old East India monopoly, West India slavery, and so on. All see in Peel the champion of their prejudices; but all together have not votes enough to return one of the six hundred and fifty-eight members to parliament. They are, therefore, in this respect, quite insignificant, and can do no more than express their opinion and give it influence,—or not,—as it may be.

But does Peel, then, really share their opinions? This it was hoped he would declare at the dinner. But has he declared it? Certainly, say some of the papers; his speech is only the old Tory *refrain*. I cannot assent to this. Peel calls his speech simple, artless, unrhetorical; to me it appears extremely dexterous, artful*, and rheto-

---

* I ought to remark that the word *artful* is not used here in the corrupted sense it usually bears in English. It means, the skilful application of art to a given end, and neither implies cen-

rical. It was a most difficult task to satisfy his hosts, himself, and the future electors, and to hint at a future administration according to his own views. This task he has fulfilled with great skill. But when we extract the real contents, the *argumentum*, from this work of art, what does it amount to? Nothing more than that the entire old system of the high Tories is impossible and irrational. Reform, with its necessary consequences, must be adopted, and a return to old principles is not to be thought of. Their own influence on the elections is quite insignificant; the royal prerogative cannot afford them any protection; the king cannot appoint any ministry at his own pleasure; the House of Lords cannot maintain any struggle with the House of Commons. The great business, on the contrary, now is, to win back a majority in the Commons by moderation and talent, and by conciliation and union with the moderate.

It is only on the subject of the church that Peel seems to cherish all the old opinions; but this is only *seems;* for he acknowledges the right of parliament to legislate for the church; he would govern the church according to the standard prescribed by law, but would maintain the Protestant as the predominant, granting to the Dissenters equal civil rights. All this is in perfect conformity with the principles and the practice of the King of Prussia, and can hardly

sure of the end, nor of the means, as it does in English. A few lines further on, in like manner, the speech is called a *kunstwerk,* —a work of art.—*Translator.*

be made to stand for a profession of intolerance. In short, since Peel has gotten rid of his tail, he moves in a very different manner; and whatever compliments the Tories of the old school may pay him, he has, in truth, shaken them off. The wisdom of the Berlin Wochenblatt, in particular, has been as entirely and singularly confuted by him as if he had had its presumptuous schooling in his eye. This unknown Berlin authority will hardly have a colleague and *socius malorum,* even in the D—— of C———.

London, May 14*th,* 1835.

To-day I miss your friendly morning greetings, and feel more lonely than usual; yet I hope you will think of me as affectionately as I think of you. A fifty-fourth birthday gives occasion to long and serious reflection; above all, the *carpe diem* is pressed upon one,—and more in this place than anywhere. The mass of work before me, instead of decreasing, grows with every day, so that I hardly know where to begin, or how to get on. The past asserts its right, and, not less, the present: I can give up neither, nor society, and any one of the three would suffice to fill the day.

At a party at ———'s the toast ' King and Constitution' was vehemently attacked, and in part by Germans. It was abominably radical; the second part was superfluous, and was understood of course, &c. I took the part of the proposer; as even the objections showed that the objectors perfectly understood the sense, and did not regard the two halves as synonymous, though they are inseparable. In like manner, man and wife are one; drinking the health of both is no offence to either, but an equal compliment to each. Such pointed contrasts and nice distinctions bring on the very thing they seek to avert. England's political health rests on the totality of her great institutions, and the man who drinks cordially to the actual constitution can hardly aim at its overthrow.

At last it came to my turn to give a toast. I gave "The King of Prussia, the greatest and best Reformer in Europe." The latter half of my toast of course excited the scruples of the opposition; but I knew what I said, and what I meant; and my meaning was a good one; and further details concerning England will prove that the King of Prussia has a greater claim to be placed " à la tête de la civilization," than many (especially on the other side the Channel) who pay themselves this compliment with great self-complacency.

Friday, May 15th.

I cannot say much in favour of my birth-day yesterday. In the first place the weather was horrible, as it has been for several days. Thick fog, rain; everything cold, wet, grey, miserable. On my complaining of this in company, a gentleman maintained that there had not been a fog in London for the last two months; that nobody thought of calling it foggy, so long as he could see the houses on the other side of the street by day, or the lamps burning by night. Another added, that last winter, out of a party of two-and-twenty invited to dine in the Regent's Park, only four arrived; all the others were afraid of losing their way.

Saturday, May 16th.

Yesterday at P———'s the conversation was much more lively than the day before, among the ' Gelehrten.' These gentlemen are generally not the best or the most amusing company. Their mill will grind no corn but what is of their own growth. The varied and many-coloured world interests them little; and they have seldom the facility and address requisite to vary their own intellectual position, or to talk on any subject but their own. Of course, minds of the highest order are in a very different category from those exclusively addicted to a particular science.

Among other things we talked about the poor Irish, the English system of letting farms, and Lady Macbeth.

My English seems, like an ague, to have good and bad days alternately. Yesterday, I heard and spoke with much more ease, perhaps because I fell into the right step. But even on the fever-days I should not spell the titles of English books quite so badly as they are spelt in the Report of the Education Committee, printed by order of government: I give you a few specimens—not to mention names which are entirely wrong.

Schmidts kleine Biblische Geschulter, und Grosse Biblische Gerschichten. Ferrenner Volksshulrunde. Rauscherbusch Gotielungs Büchlein (I cannot guess what this means); Krouse Versuch planmüssiger und natürlicher Deskübungen. Türk die sinnlichen Walrnehmungen. Anleitung zu Deux und Sprechübungen. Harnisch Roumlehre. Pestalozzi Tapeln. Kaweron Leitfoden, &c. &c.

If the Prussian government were to print such things, what an outcry there would be (and justly) about negligence—if not ignorance!

LETTER XXIII.

Reform in Parliament—Historical Sketch of [English Parliament —Spiritual Peers—Creation of Peers—Changes in the House of Commons, from Edward I. to George III.— Projects of Reform — Mr. Pitt— Duke of Wellington's resistance — Its consequences — Lord John Russell's Bill—Remarks on the Debates — Rejection by the Lords—Resignation and Return of Whig Ministers—Final passing of the Bill.

London, May 1 *to* 16, 1835.

ALL I have hitherto communicated to you concerning reforms of the church, the poor-laws, the corporations, &c., is essentially connected with the subject of reform in parliament, out of which, indeed, those measures mainly sprang. For this reason, and because the recollection of old and scattered newspaper articles is not sufficient, I must venture to say something on the history, character, and consequences of this most weighty and difficult measure.

Though a history of the English parliament can find no place here, it is necessary to revert to a few of the incidents which have recently been the subject of praise or blame, and have called forth the conflicting demands for conservation or for change.

Since the end of the 13th century, parliament has consisted of the King and the three estates of the realm, viz., the spiritual and temporal

VOL. I.

Lords, and the House of Commons. The two former, however, have long constituted so completely one body,—the Upper House,—that a division of the votes has never taken place, and a decision of the majority is binding, though all the spiritual Lords vote against it.

There was a time in which the number of the latter was greater than that of the temporal lords. Their number and influence, however, greatly declined at the Reformation, thirty-six being abolished, while the kings were continually adding to the nobles. Under Henry VII., only twenty-nine Lords sat in the House; under Henry VIII., and Elizabeth, fifty-one; under James I., ninety-six; in the year 1640, one hundred and nineteen; in 1661, one hundred and thirty-nine; in 1826, three hundred. There are now three hundred and fifty English peers, twenty-eight Irish, sixteen Scotch, and thirty-two bishops, including the Irish;—in all, four hundred and twenty-six. These numbers sufficiently show how extremely weak, compared with its condition in the middle ages, is the spiritual part of the House of Lords; and yet many are of opinion, that it ought, as at the rebellion, to be entirely thrown out, and the whole power left in the hands of the temporal lords.

I can by no means adopt this opinion. When, in our days, every grocer and pastry-cook lays claim to political rights, either immediately or by representation, and must have a voice and a hand in everything, why should the highest interest of

society, that of religion, have no voice? Certainly,
every man is or ought to be, in some sort, an organ
of this interest; but he is so in the same sense
only as of that of law, of agriculture, trade, &c.
The clergyman has his peculiar knowledge and
calling; and this calling by no means lies so out
of the world and the state, that no point or direction of salutary influence and useful co-operation
could be marked out for him. If this is denied
in theory, and yet permitted in practice, an illegal
interference is almost inevitable; and generally
becomes more powerful and more dangerous
than when it is moderated and controlled by its
connexion with other parts and powers of the
state. The objection, that ' Christ's kingdom is
not of this world,' has its just and useful accepta-
tion, and even the powerful clergy of the middle
ages knew that there were some things, such,
for instance, as the command of armies, which
were not suited to their character. But it does
not in the least follow from this, as many infer,
that a poor and dependent clergy, existing merely
upon voluntary contributions is the best; that the
temporal legislature needs no spiritual aid; that
State and Church have no connexion whatever,
and so forth. Abuse of wealth, party intrigues,
exclusive power and privilege, ought to be prevented; but it were very inconsistent in an age
which vaunts its liberality and universality, to
exclude altogether from public life the most important element of civilization; and it were
equally at variance with all historical experience.
    It is not the twenty bishops in the House of

Lords, it is not this inconsiderable minority, which has occasioned the defects of the English Church. It is, that the temporal lords have seen their own advantage in maintaining everything as it is : as, in the 17th century, others found theirs in overthrowing everything. On the other hand, the bishops are frequently men of aristocratical connexions, and generally vote with the government. That.they have deviated from this course several times lately, more on party than on religious grounds, has not tended to make them popular, and has altered their position with relation to the government.

If, however, the spiritual portion is to be entirely excluded from parliament, instead of giving it a broader foundation and more liberal views, either some form of convocation or synod must be devised, or that must be abandoned to accident, which ought to be guided and governed by law. The same thing does not suit all, and I am far from wanting to fit all institutions to one precise model ; but the war with the clergy carried on with mere common places and abstractions is a shallow proceeding, and may be turned by analogy against the temporal peers, professedly for the interest of the House of Commons, till this latter becomes the prey of a Cromwell, or a Napoleon, and apparent omnipotence is suddenly changed into miserable nothingness.

I have already mentioned in another place propositions of particular reforms in the House of Commons, and will no longer refrain from looking at the subject in a more general way.

The House of Lords was certainly wrong, in endeavouring, in George I.'s time, to limit the right of the king to create peers. The bill was thrown out by the Commons, who perceived that an exclusive narrow-minded oligarchy, predestined to speedy decrepitude, would have thus arisen; and that any renovation, or any introduction of popular opinions, would have been rendered infinitely more difficult. Once only, in the time of Queen Anne, peers were created, in order to secure to the ministry a majority in the Upper House; since that time this perilous expedient has been avoided; and affairs stand so, spite of all threatening appearances, that collisions and disputes of the two Houses are settled without any fundamental alterations in the constitution of the peers. But things will not continue on this footing, unless both parties preserve reason and moderation. Whether the Lower House required reform is the question we have now to discuss ; a question which has received such contradictory answers.

The House of Commons was generally regarded by the one party as a body which had been unchanged from time immemorial, and, therefore, as one in which no change was ever to be made. I might urge that the principle, " a certain state of things ought to be preserved, *because* it is old," may (like most abstractions) be converted into the equally true or equally false proposition, " a certain state of things ought to be altered, *because* it has been so long without alteration." But setting aside this, history shows a very gradual and various development of the elements and powers of the House of Commons. At first, for instance, the latter were so trifling, the expense of sitting so great, and the office of voting supplies so ungrateful and disagreeable, that many endeavoured to avoid being summoned by the king. So long as the summons depended on the king, this involved a principle of change and mobility; and it was not till the restoration of Charles II. that a general conviction arose, (without any express law to this effect,) that the balance and the significancy of the several powers of the state would again be lost, if the king could call members to the commons as well as create peers.

In the time of Edward I., about one hundred and fifty members sat in the Lower House; in that of Henry VIII., about two hundred and twenty-four *.

Henry VIII. restored	2	votes, and created	33
Edward VI. „	20	„	28
Mary „	4	„	17
Elizabeth „	12	„	48
James I. „	16	„	11
Charles I. „	18	„	6

Since Charles II., no king has, as I have said, granted new charters; but the addition made by the Scotch and Irish unions in 1706 and 1801, was a great and important reform of the English House of Commons. Since that

* Hallam, iii. 50. Archenholz, Annals v. 15—43. Stockdale, xxx.

time it has consisted of the following members :—

[These details are so familiar to English readers, that it has been thought advisable to omit them. The author goes on to describe the form of election which existed before the passing of the Reform Bill, the different sorts of qualification for voting, and the qualifications for sitting in Parliament. These details, also, I have taken the liberty to omit, and to pass on to the observations.]—TRANSL.

These short notices will render more intelligible many of the attacks on the one hand, and the defences on the other, which I shall soon lay before you. I must find room here for two or three prefatory remarks :—

First,—Up to the latter half of the seventeenth century, the House of Commons was subject to still greater changes than the House of Peers; and the settled and immutable character which it afterwards assumed, rested neither upon express laws, nor upon philosophical reasons, nor upon practical necessity; or it would be easy to invent arguments to show why the aristocratical, conservative House of Lords *must* be more unchangeable and inaccessible than the democratic House whose vocation it was to represent the progress of opinion among the mass. Although George III. did not create Lords, *en fournées,* for certain definite purposes, yet, in the course of his reign, two hundred and thirty-five new peers were added to the House, while seventy-four became extinct; thus leaving an augment of one hundred and sixty-one members! Such a proceeding as this would have appeared, to the hereditary nobles of Venice or of Berne, or even to Queen Elizabeth

(who was so sparing of elevations of rank), a reform of the Upper House more radical than all
that has been effected, or even proposed, in our
times, for the reform of the Lower. These large
additions, however, tend to correct the defects
of an hereditary nobility; introduce into it the
greatest talent of the Commons from time to
time, (especially the holders of the highest legal
offices,) and thus give to the peerage a great
and appropriate weight. But in whatever way we
view this matter, we can collect from it no historical nor philosophical indication why the Upper
House should be moveable and changeable, and
the Lower, immoveable and unchangeable.

Secondly,—The same applies to forms of election and qualifications of electors. It is just as
absurd to run into an idolatry of an abstract uniformity on these points, or of a useless variety,
which is generally the consequence merely of accident and caprice. Increase or decrease of population, of wealth, of education, &c., which, in
all the affairs of life exert their influence, cannot
be wholly inoperative on the number and the
circumstances of the electors or the elected. Or,

Thirdly,—Those vast changes which enter into
all the relations of private life, cannot remain
without influence on public affairs; and it is
one of the greatest and most fatal errors, either
completely to dissever public and private law,
as many high Tories desire, or completely to mix
and confound them, as the Jacobins attempted
to do.

The idea of reforming the House of Commons

is by no means the modern offspring of selfishness and rancour; it is old, and had its source in the desire to restore that principle of life and motion which, up to the middle of the seventeenth century, lay in the hands of the king; but, from that time, fell asleep, or died. From this it is clear, that no measure relating to *forms* could possibly be a " final measure;" since that idea exactly plunges things back into the lifeless immobility out of which the very object was to draw them. The assertion, that the adoption of this principle must inevitably throw every thing into ruinous confusion,—that nothing would be secure or stable for an hour,—is just as rational as that the House of Peers is threatened with a swift destruction, because no new-made lord can be a " final" lord; since the king retains the *droit du mouvement* here, though he lost it in the Commons. If the Upper House had remained, from the year 1640, like the Lower, shut against all renovation, the aristocracy would indeed, long ere this, have sunk to nothing.

But how I speculate, instead of narrating!

Since Pitt's repeated motions for a reform in Parliament, the idea has never been dropped. If that great statesman renounced his own projects during the most frightful years of the French revolution, this was no proof of inconsistency; it only proved that he, like Solomon, saw that there is a time for everything. But the reasons which were valid in the year 1793 did not exist in 1830. When, therefore, the Duke of Wellington declared, on the 1st November, 1830,

" that he was opposed to all and every reform, because the existing forms were sufficient for every purpose, and possessed the perfect confidence of the country*," he said what was agreeable neither to prudence nor to truth. This was the firebrand, or, if you will, the safety-bringing light, for England for many years; it produced the very spirit it meant to quell, and was more pregnant with consequences than the speaker imagined. In October, 1831†, he said, in justification of his former declaration, " that he had spoken as the king's minister, whose duty it is to maintain the institutions of the country." This seems to contain the *petitio principii*, that everything he thought right to maintain, was worth maintaining. But the office of the statesman is a quite peculiar one; he has to watch over and facilitate the birth of present opinions and events, and to prepare an honourable grave for the past. The Duke's protest put an end to legislating on the subject: the contest now became merely one of time. A conditional declaration would have placed the course and shape of the reform in the Duke's hands; an unconditional one threw them into the hands of his adversaries.

The East Retford business, which the Tories celebrated as a victory, appeared to every clear-sighted observer a defeat, inasmuch as it increased the number of their enemies; but this and similar things were mere matters of detail.

Wellington's general declaration of war natu-

* Hansard, i. 52.   † Hansard, vii. 1187.

XXIII.] LORD JOHN RUSSELL. **251**

rally and necessarily led to a general rising. It has often been said in his defence, that he spoke in haste : I cannot be of this opinion, when I look at the course of things, the circumstances, and the words. I have rather explained the matter to myself thus :—In 1829, the Duke carried the question of Catholic emancipation, by the help of the Whigs and the Radicals. In 1830, he kept his place by granting a repeal of taxes, after having refused it. In the third year, the Whigs demanded reform; but the Tories would agree to no further concessions, and the Duke was forced to adopt their views or lose their support. Whatever were the motives that decided him, he was mistaken in thinking that a display of resolute resistance would change public opinion. His ministry fell; and on the 1st of March, 1831, Lord John Russell brought forward a comprehensive plan of reform. I abstract for you the most essential contents of his speech.

[I have thought the reader would rather not go through this abstract of the debates on reform, however clearly and concisely it may be made. They are so recent as hardly to need recalling. After the sketch of Lord J. Russell's opening speech, the following remarks occur.]—TRANSL.

This scheme, which, indeed, exceeded the hopes of the one party, and the fears of the other, excited the most intense interest throughout the country; and the struggle between its opponents and supporters lasted for above a year, within and without the walls of Parliament, till at length it was decided in favour of the latter. It was my intention to make you acquainted with the whole

progress of this struggle; and, to that end, I had
drawn together all the arguments for and against,
in two long speeches; but this plan is attended
with great inconveniences; it exhibits what was
gradually evolved, and arose historically out of
various opposing arguments, as simultaneous. It
changes the dialogic and dramatic into the epic,
and leaves no trace of the individuality of the
speakers, which was here so remarkably conspicuous. I only wish you may not find what I have
compressed into a few pages, from volumes of
speeches, either too dry or too fragmentary. I
must crave your indulgence if I perform my task
neither to your satisfaction nor to my own.

[Here follow the leading topics urged by members in the follow-
ing order:—Sir Robert Inglis, Mr. Twiss, Lord F. L. Gower, Mr.
Shelley, Lord Darlington, Sir John Walsh, Sir Charles Wetherell,
Mr. Bankes, Mr. Baring, Mr. Croker, Sir Robert Peel (of whose
speech a somewhat longer abstract is given than of the others),
Lord Althorp, Lord Newark, Mr. Jeffery (Lord Advocate), Mr.
Gisborne, Sir James Graham, Messrs. Harvey, Tennant, Lord
Palmerston, Mr. Macauley.]

Such were the most prominent arguments for
and against the Reform Bill. On the question,
whether it should be read a second time, there
was a majority of only one—302 for, 301 against.
The members for the universities and the threatened boroughs were in the minority. On the
22nd of March, 1831, there was also a majority.
On the 19th of April there were 299 against, 291
in support of General Gascoigne's motion, that
the number of members of Parliament be not
diminished.

This motion was closely connected with the

project of maintaining unaltered the old system of rotten boroughs; *i. e.*, of rejecting one half of the Reform Bill. In all other respects a diminution of the number of members of Parliament would have been in favour of the aristocracy and the monarchy, and the king was accordingly inclined to it: but the more immediate object of the Tory opposition was to undermine and blow up the ministry. The latter inclined more to concession than the king; but their defeat was soon turned into victory,—since, of the two alternatives, to dismiss them, or to appeal to the people, the king chose the latter. On the 21st of April, 1831, parliament was dissolved. This dissolution has been called a tyrannical and perverse exercise of royal and ministerial power: it appears to me quite otherwise.

The momentous question of parliamentary reform had been agitated with unexpected violence. It was discussed in the amplest manner, and every man had therefore every possible means of forming or correcting his judgment. The two parties were nearly equal, and a majority of two or three votes could not be received as a final and complete settling of the question. Nothing, therefore, was more natural, or more consonant with the spirit of the English constitution, than that, after these pleadings of the great cause, recourse should be had to the electors,— the jury of the nation,—in order to ascertain whether, in fact, a great majority of the people were for the measure,—as one party affirmed and the other denied. Certainly more universal and

pressing reasons existed for this dissolution of
Parliament than for that of 1835, which had
hardly any results. The debates, of which I
have given you a slight abstract, had the useful
effect of correcting errors, and of enabling the
champions of the Reform Bill to make important
alterations and improvements on their first project. On the 21st of June, 1831, the new Parliament was opened, and a great many speeches
were made, the views and the conclusions expressed in which, so nearly resembled the former
ones, that I may venture to pass them over in
silence. The speech of Sir James Mackintosh deserves, however, even in this condensed sketch,
particular mention. On this division, 367 voted
for the second reading of the bill, and 231 against
it. The majority was thus raised from 1 to 136.
In the minority, there were one hundred and
sixty persons who had an immediate interest in
the matter.

I must mention, as a very important subordinate
debate which grew out of the main one, that on
the motion of Mr. Hume for granting a place in
the legislature to the British colonies; on the
ground that it was absurd to concede political
rights to small English towns, while they were
denied to millions of subjects of the empire. The
motion was rejected on various grounds; such as
the impossibility of an adequate representation
of such remote countries, and the like. On the
21st of September, 1831, the Reform Bill passed
by a majority of one hundred and nine; and on
the 22nd was solemnly carried up to the Peers by
Lord John Russell.

The objections which I have already quoted were there brought forward anew.

[Here follows an abstract of some of the speeches of the Lords.]

Without going into any detailed inquiry as to the possibility of amending the bill, it was thrown out by a majority of forty-one, on the 7th of October, 1831. Only two of the bishops—Norwich and Chichester—voted for it; a fact which excited great disgust. The Commons lamented the fate of the bill in the Upper House, professed their firm attachment to the principles of it, and their unaltered confidence in the integrity, perseverance, and talents of ministers, who had merited their thanks by the introduction of a bill so important to the weightiest interests of the country. The Duke of Wellington and the Tories saw the impossibility of forming a new ministry, and after the prorogation had expired in December, 1831, the debates began a third time. That ministers had altered several not unimportant points in the bill, was cited by their friends as a proof of readiness to receive suggestions, and a desire to carry the measure; by their enemies, as a proof of precipitation and levity. The problem was to hold an equal way between obstinacy and weakness.

[Here follows a brief account of the further discussions.]

When the bill was sent up to the Peers this time, they did not reject the entire principle of the bill, but allowed it to be read a second time, and proceeded to an examination of its details.

On the 2nd of May, 1832, they decided that
the question should first be debated, to what
places new franchises should be granted; by
which the entire direction of the discussion
would have fallen into the hands of the Tories,
and the disfranchisement of the rotten boroughs
have become impossible.   Although the King
was reminded that, in the last fifty years, Tories
had almost exclusively been raised to the peerage,
and that therefore it was necessary to restore the
balance by an addition to the Whig peers, he
would not consent to a numerous creation, and
ministers consequently resigned.

I can neither blame the King for refusing to
create a number of peers, nor for accepting the
resignation of ministers.   Undoubtedly he lost
his popularity for the moment by the latter step,
but he adhered to the constitutional course, and
rendered a permanent service to his people.   As
public opinion had been sufficiently tested by the
dissolution of parliament, no other means remained for accurately testing the strength of
the Tory opposition, and for bringing this party
to a knowledge of itself and its own position,
but by encouraging its leaders to take the reins
of government, and, if experience should demonstrate to them the impracticability of the experiment, to adapt themselves to circumstances which
they could not control.

The next day the (unreformed) House of Commons sent a petition to the King, praying him to
confide the government to men who were determined to carry through all the material provisions
of the bill.

Neither Wellington nor Peel were able to form a ministry; and the ministers who had gone out took office again, under the tacit condition that if the Peers offered a continued stubborn resistance, it was to be met by new creations. Under these circumstances the Tories withdrew their opposition; the bill passed the Lords on the 4th of June, 1832, by a majority of one hundred and six to twenty-two; and after some few alterations, which however did not affect the main principles, formally passed the Commons.

[Here follows a statement of some few well-known statistical provisions of the Bill.]

LETTER XXIV.

Remarks on the Reform Bill—English attachment to Forms—
England and France Constitutional States: meaning of those
words—National Bigotries—History, Principles with their
Consequences—Sir Robert Peel—Exclusive regard to Quantity, and neglect of Quality, in modern Political Schemes—
Edinburgh Review—Reports of Commissioners—Royal Authority—Centralization—Relation of number of Electors to
Population—Annual Parliaments—Ballot—Prospects of England.

London, 17*th May,* 1835.

I HAVE now endeavoured briefly to lay before you
a statement of the views and principles of the two
great parties, and here I might hold my historical
duties fulfilled; but I trust to your patience, if I
do not suppress some of the reflexions which the
consideration of this momentous subject has suggested to me.

Both parties were entirely persuaded of the
supreme and decisive importance of constitutional
forms; not one single individual so much as
alluded to Pope's well known and oft repeated
maxim,—

> " For forms of government let fools contest,
>   Whate'er is best administered is best."

The contest between Tories and Whigs turned
almost entirely on the goodness or the badness,
the value or the insignificance, of the old or of the

new *forms*. It is true that Pope's negative view
of the matter cannot be conclusive for any long
period of time: it may, however, be transformed
into a positive and pregnant reflexion, when,
without denying the importance attached in this
country to *forms,* we also assert the importance
of *persons ;* for nothing but the combination and
co-operation of both can produce a living government, and a well-constituted, true social body.
Instead, however, of striving after this union,
men, in different ages, have worshipped at one
time the one half, at another the other, with blind
fanaticism and credulity ; till, being disappointed
in the expectations they had conceived from their
idol, they flew to the opposite side, there to experience the same disappointment. Thus, for instance, in many of the Italian states in the middle
ages the bigoted and delusive confidence in forms
led to tyranny ; the exclusive and mistaken republicanism of England and France, to the military
despotism of Cromwell and Napoleon; and, to
this hour, the most exaggerated expectations are
entertained from what, without any accurate investigation of its details and results, is called, in
one word, a Constitution, and, therefore, extolled
as a universal political remedy.

If this word were understood as comprising the
endless variety of forms which history displays,
from the most remote to the most recent times,
it were, indeed, of the highest interest and importance ; but if this variety be utterly disregarded in favour of some darling scheme exclusively worshipped under the name of Constitution,

every deviation from which is regarded a damnable heresy,—however high be the claims to wisdom, it is certain that presumption and ignorance still reign supreme. Europe resented with great justice the insolent pretension of the French to remodel all other nations upon their own pattern. The charge brought against the French, that they acknowledged but one form of government, and attached the most one-sided and exaggerated value to it, is, however, but half true; for this *one* form underwent innumerable changes, and what was admired one day was held up to contempt the next. Even at this moment, only one party adheres firmly to the Charter, which a second wants to make more royalist, and a third more republican.

We are, say the French and the English, constitutional states: that is to say, there are, in France and in England, two chambers and a king. But, with this resemblance, what essential differences, the moment one goes the least below the surface! even in mere constitutional forms, and far more in innumerable other institutions! If then I understand by constitution (as in the human body) the sum of laws, principles, and tendencies; legislation and administration; religion, church, art and science, &c., &c., France and England, spite of their common denomination " Constitutional States," are not only different, but opposite; and, in this sense, there is no state, nor ever was, that has not had a constitution, nor could such a one ever exist.

As men of opposite or different temperaments

often find it impossible to understand each other, so nations and writers seldom understand those who differ widely from themselves. The Frenchman, for instance, assures the Prussian that he is a slave, because he has a censorship and no representative assembly, and no Paris journals; while on the other hand, the Prussian remarks, that the journalists of Paris are often thrown into prison, that the towns and provinces of France are without any principle of political life or self-government, and the public functionaries dependent on ministerial caprice, — consequently slaves, &c. The Englishman thinks a universal liability to military service tyrannical; while the Prussian is shocked at the aristocratical organization and the degrading punishments, which could not be endured in the English army, were it as equitably and nationally constituted as his own. The Prussian boasts the equal treatment of all religious sects; the English Tory sees in this the destruction of church and religion.

I will resist my inclination to argue the point, that true freedom in a state may assume very different shapes, and rest upon very different securities,—nay, that these differences are inevitable. He who contends that political institutions must be the same in all countries, has yet to learn the A B C of political science.

Hence it follows, further, that even in one and the same state, constitutional forms cannot remain unalterably the same; and that it is as dangerous as it is irrational to confound reforms with violent revolutions. The latter are almost invariably the consequence of a denial or unreasonable delay of the former. It is only necessary to recollect the Decemviri, the Gracchi, the Reformation, the Swiss Confederation, the Revolt of the Netherlands, the English and French Revolutions, &c. Persistance may be, and has been, as revolutionary as change.

All the general conclusions of this kind concerning the Reform Bill nullified each other; it was only in detail that they assumed any meaning. But even here there were errors. There is, for instance, a degree of diversity in local circumstances and usages which is agreeable and useful; there is a degree which leaves too much to chance, caprice, and injustice. To obliterate the former, were as bad policy as to maintain the latter, unconditionally. All government is, I repeat, mediation, and must be so in this instance. Many, struck with the errors and inconveniencies arising from these anomalies, want to reduce everything to one general rule, which they pretend should be decisive in all cases : it should be remembered, however, that if this is not thoroughly accurate, profound and exhaustive, the evil is only increased.

When a noble lord says, " Do justice, and care not for the consequences," this seemingly brilliant truth involves a heap of errors. Not to mention that what seems justice to him is injustice to another, the maxim involves a contradiction. The true and highest justice can have no bad consequences; and the hacknied phrase, " fiat justitia pereat mundus," has really no meaning. God has given man reason to look behind as well as before him, and it would be absurd to renounce the use of one-half of this faculty. The advantage of instruction derived from the past is, that we there see principles *with their consequences;* and whole systems once established by law and universally regarded as justice, when viewed by this double light, are now condemned as unjust;—witness slavery. This is by no means an objection to a really philosophical study of law ; but that is not worthy to be called so which rests upon mere abstractions.

I have the same fault to find with several of Peel's arguments. As, for instance, when he denounced the democratical tendency of the Reform Bill,—and yet praised the sort of back door, if I may use the expression, through which the borough system admitted (in a strange way enough) some so-called democratic elements. He asserted that the *evil* did not proceed from the form of the elective system,—and yet he wanted to derive the *good* from it : he said, that the consequences of every change were doubtful;—as if the consequences of every non-change could be distinctly foreseen to be beneficial: he said, *because* I do not choose to alter the constitution, I cannot grant the right of election to such cities as Manchester and Birmingham. Unless a man will frankly say, " stet pro ratione voluntas," this " *because* " has nothing to stand on ; it supposes an entire renunciation of the functions of a statesman in favour of some pretended private rights ; and loses sight of the important objection, that (setting aside the particular provision of the Reform Bill) the very nature and essence of the English constitution demanded the franchise of those large cities. Enough : all these assertions fall to nothing the moment you consider the other side; and only show the necessity for higher and more impartial views.

That many Tories wanted to fight out the battle on the field of private rights was quite agreeable to their interests, but not at all so to the matter in hand. A political function can never be claimed as private property. If, however, traffic in it had been sanctioned by law, compensation for the individual loss which a return to the just principles of public law would have involved, would not unreasonably have been demanded. But in this respect the borough-mongers were less fortunate than the slave-holders; the slave trade having been hitherto sanctioned by law, whereas the trade in boroughs and votes, and indeed all influence of the Lords on the choice of the Commons, being illegal;—a fact of which they were reminded at the opening of every parliament, when the law was read aloud.

These, however, are mere matters of detail.

There remained one general objection.—The reproach that the reformers had reduced all political science to a sum in arithmetic is unfounded : in every formula *quantity* necessarily occupies a prominent station. Yet the question remains, whether this might not have been combined to a greater extent with *quality*. The development of modern political science, rests almost entirely on this opposition between the Quantitative and the Qualitative. The revolutionary school, since 1789, have thought they could effect everything with the former; we find nothing but numbers of electors, numbers of representatives, duration of public offices; as qualifications for voting, amount of property, amount of taxes, and so on; nothing but quantities, to the utter disregard of qualities; such as orders, corporations, associations, examinations, attainments, &c. It is only in the most recent times that the French, by fixing their *catégories* and *notabilités,* and by the creation of their peers, have returned to the consideration of quality; and they will return to it more distinctly in future. In short, I entertain a perfect conviction that constitutional law must remain in an imperfect state, so long as regard is not had both to quantity and to quality.

This idea, so fruitful in important corsequences, stands directly opposed to most of the political doctrines of our days. It is impossible for me to go into any full and detailed development of it here. But one example, taken from the Reform Bill, will serve, in some measure, to illustrate it. The provision which confers the right of voting on all ten-pound householders is merely quantitative; and therefore, in my opinion, a one-sided and imperfect rule. The inquiry, whether the qualification should be twenty pounds or five pounds, instead of ten, would be equally quantitative,—and equally inconclusive. Arithmetically speaking, ten is always ten, and twenty twenty : but this is only true when we reckon with unknown quantities—not with any known ones ; least of all, when these are the circumstances of human life and the powers of political society.   Ten with the sign £. is a totally different thing from ten with the sign *d.*; and ten pounds in a remote village is a very different thing from ten pounds in London.   This quality of money,—its power and significancy, as an index to the condition and circumstances of its possessor,—is not all attended to in the Reform Bill ; everything is measured by the same abstract arithmetical rule.   The same applies to the French qualifications ; it is the same for Paris and the Cevennes.   Is not this arithmetical equality the greatest inequality ? and is not this inequality unjust and unwise ?   Instances in which the Quantitative and Qualitative are happily combined, are afforded by the qualification for the Prussian Landstände, and in that for the South German elective assemblies.

But this will lead to another of my political heresies, about which I mean to write a book as soon as I have nothing else to do ; viz., that both representative legislatures, and legislatures the members of which sit in virtue of their rank, office, profession, or other class-qualification, are defective when absolutely severed or opposed ; and that it is only by a combination of both that a government can be formed, suited to the present and the future wants of society.

I return to a reform question which stands in close connexion with what I have just said.   The one party complains that the number of electors is too great; the other, that it is too small. It seems to me that the fitness of the electoral body does not depend on its numerical size, but on its character; and what, with reference to this, may be too great in one place, may be too small in another. For the benefit of those who are opposed to all participation of the people in public affairs, I quote a passage from the ' Edinburgh Review.'

" There is scarcely a prospect in the world more curious than that of England during a general election. The congregations of people; the interests called into operation; the passions roused; the principles appealed to; the printed and spoken addresses; the eminent men who appear; the guarantees demanded and given; the fluctuations of the poll; the exultation of the victorious party—it is a scene in which there is much to attract the eyes and ears, but more to fix the mind. A person who understands the bustle before him, and thinks what it implies, sees in it the whole practical working of the constitution. He sees the majority of public opinion; the responsibility of representatives to constituents; the formation of the political virtues; the union of all classes and sorts of men in common national objects; the elevation of the popular character; the prodigious consolidation given to the whole civil fabric, by the incorporation of all parts of the state with the mass of the population; the combination of universal excitement with perfect general safety; the control of the people softened and directed by eloquence; the establishment of the broadest basis on which the happiness of a state can rest*."

So long as this picture is not entirely devoid of truth, England's sun cannot set in eternal night, whatever certain augurs of evil may say. That night will, however, be at hand, whenever the abuses and defects of elections, the cost and the corruption, come to be treated, first as inevitable, and afterwards as convenient and justifiable.

It is remarkable that in 1835 only 114 elections out of the 658, were contested: in the other 544, no opponent appeared.

It might be said that the quantitative equality of the ten-pound householders leads immediately to an inequality of their condition, and that this inequality has its good. But those who openly wanted either to extend or contract the elective franchise, pursued a much simpler and more straightforward course than those who said nothing, but rejoiced in the secret persuasion that this equality would work aristocratically in the country, and democratically in the towns. Not to mention the danger of calling forth a democratic ascendency exactly in the largest towns, where the people and the mob are the most easily united into one body;—until a sound moral education, from the lowest class upwards, is more general, political authority must often be confided to ignorant and unskilful hands.

Altogether, however, the English representa-

* Edinburgh Review, No. lii. p. 208.

tion (according to my system, the *one-half* of a complete constitution) is more equitably distributed, and more fitly established than before. But, as it is become far more conformable with the spirit and will of the people, and a much more sympathizing and faithful exponent of them, the power of the House of Commons is certainly greatly increased; and Peel was quite right when he told his city hosts that they could no longer steer the same course. So long as the borough system lasted, the Lower House sailed with a half wind; but now the wind has changed, it is of no use trying to turn the vane with their fingers, as if Æolus cared for such tricks; they must shift their sails, and make port as quickly as they can.

Expedition is not, indeed, often the property of large deliberative assemblies. The notion of some Reformers, that it would be an advantage to reduce the number of members of parliament is a perfectly just one; and nothing but the difficulties attending the execution of the project occasioned its abandonment. Every bill must be read and discussed three times in each House; not to mention the irrelevant matter which grows out of every question, and the delight with which many men hear themselves speak. How many laws are of the most urgent necessity for England, and how many years will elapse before they are passed! On the other hand, the next grand defects of all legislation—precipitation and carelessness—are not so likely to occur in this way of conducting business.

Above all, it is impossible to say enough in

praise of the profound and varied inquiries which have been conducted by the several Commissions appointed for special objects, and of the admirable reports they have laid before the government and the country. Here is a second most efficient, salutary and popular parliament, acting as pioneer and ally to the other parliament. By this means the people will attain to a perfect understanding of their own character and condition; public *opinion* rises to the dignity of public *conviction*; the for and against are placed in juxtaposition and impartially balanced, and every fact and question upon which the legislator will have to decide is clearly, appropriately, and completely placed before him. Whatever differences of opinion may exist as to particular points, these inquiries and reports, combined with the parliamentary debates and decisions founded upon them, will remain an eternal monument of the civilization, the intelligence, the clearness of mind, and strength of will—in short, of the characteristics—of Britons; a monument such as no other nation is competent to raise.

The progress of legislation in Prussia, for example, has been, in many respects, more summary, bolder, more consistent, better concatenated, more comprehensive; but it presents no monument of a people invited to deliberate with its government, and coming to a common understanding on its own affairs. The education of the people proceeded from the administration,—so often unjustly accused; but the reciprocal operation which manifests itself in these English reports and

masses of evidence, questions and answers, is
wanting in the Prussian proceedings, and occasionally lessens the unison between what was
wished and what was granted.

If the power of the House of Commons is unquestionably increased, while various expedients
for giving weight to the royal authority have
proved abortive or impracticable, the question
arises,—Are there any safe and beneficial means by
which the latter may be strengthened? It is impossible, say the croakers; we are advancing inevitably towards anarchy. To this it may be replied,
Rotten boroughs, sinecures, and such antiquated
lumber, are gone for ever; but were these the
true and solid props of the royal power? Would
not a war for such excrescences be more absurd
than that of Charles I.? And is it a loss to a just
king of England that the number of the standing
army no longer depends on him? It was natural
that, after the peace of Ryswick, William III.
should feel this restriction galling and embarrass-
ing: he was right, looking only to the day, but
those who resisted him were right for a century
to come. In the seventeenth century, most sove-
reigns held it to be not only their right, but their
duty to prescribe to their subjects what they were
to believe: has monarchy lost, or won, since this
idea can no longer by any possibility occur to
them? Elizabeth, even in her day, recurring to
feudal laws and customs, interfered in the marriages of all persons of condition. Would the
Tories, who bewail the declension of the monarchy, like to restore it to its pristine vigour in

this particular? The simple truth is this: the king can no longer treat the noble, the noble the citizen, the citizen his apprentice or his servant, the priest his parishioners, as they severally could some centuries ago. If this is a loss, it is a loss which all share. It were stupid, as well as selfish, for one to want to call back from antiquity just what seems convenient to himself, and to deny to another what, on precisely similar grounds, he would be equally entitled to demand.

I cannot persuade myself that, in the grand progress and development of the human species, nothing is perceptible but the mockeries of chance, or the consciousness of our own delusions. Faith and opinion are divided on the question how far Providence continues to manifest itself by immediate interference in particulars; but that the whole race of man is abandoned of God, and left to its own wanderings, no heathen, still less a Christian, can believe! If, however, I set up any one mode of government, state of society, or point of time,—in short, any one *form*,— as the absolutely excellent, and contemn all others, I transform Providence into a capricious patron of a section.

Emperors like Tiberius, kings like Philip II., if they were to rise from the grave and see what is going on now, would bitterly complain of the degeneracy of modern times, and would affirm that the rights and duties of rulers were no longer understood. The position of a king of England must needs appear to them poor and contemptible. In them, this madness would have method and a certain grandeur in it; but what shall we say when Tories contend that a rotten borough and a sinecure are the corner stones of the world and of civilization? Or, to mention still more miserable *mesquinéries* at home,—when persons raised from the loom to a seat in the Landstände are violently exasperated against the Prussian laws of 1810, which deprived them of the privilege of flogging their peasants and servants when they liked? They forget that, under the old laws, they would have remained *Canton pflichtig**, and would have had a few floggings themselves.

But I let my thoughts, or my pen, run on too freely. I must return to my text. In all the changes occasioned by the universal progress of society, and not by mere force, I can see no unqualified loss; not even in the present relation of the King of England to the Parliament. On the other hand, the old complaints of the dangers which threatened English liberty from the royal prerogative are now without a meaning, and, if put forward at all, are mere pretexts. The more varied and powerful is the influence and co-operation of the people, and the control of parliament, as well as of public opinion, the more vigorous an administration can the people bear,—nay, ought they to desire.

And here it seems to me more possible indirectly to strengthen the royal power, than in many other ways where it has been attempted in

---

* Under the old Prussian system, a canton was a certain district assigned to each regiment, from which it drew its recruits, and upon which probably it might, in case of need, be quartered.

vain. The centralization which (after bitter experience of the want of it) has been so beneficially introduced in the administration of the poor-laws, will perhaps become practicable and expedient for the direction of schools, corporations, &c., without falling into the French extreme. At all events, it appears to me (as I have expressed elsewhere) a thoroughly erroneous opinion, that corporations, societies, guilds, towns, colleges, endowments, or whatever they may be called, should be regarded as distinct independent bodies, inaccessible to the interference of the state. If no individual mortal member of the commonwealth can set up any such pretensions, still less should they be conceded to these great, influential, and undying organs of the social body. Their functions affect the whole, and should be in close and permanent unison with the whole; but this is incompatible with a doctrine which transforms them from living organs into lifeless parts, and contributes to the formation of isolated states within the state, in a manner which neither science nor experience can justify.

May 19*th*, 1835.

I have devoted too much space to speculations, which, however, if they please you, are not out of place. I know that though figures are generally dry and tiresome, you will like to hear what is the relation borne by the population of the most important cities and counties to the number of electors. Many conclusions may be drawn from

hence as to the wealth, the more or less democratical tendency, &c.

[Here follows a list of towns and counties, with the numbers
abovementioned annexed, which it is thought unnecessary to
insert.]

This list, which comprises the most important
towns, and the most considerable counties, shows
that the number of voters in these places, though
large, is yet very far from approaching to universal suffrage. You will see also that the population is by no means in the direct ratio, either
of the property, or of the number of voters; and
lastly, that the number of members of Parliament
is neither exactly apportioned to the population,
nor to the number of voters. If, therefore, the
English electoral system is far less based on an
aristocracy of wealth than the French, it is still
farther from being thoroughly democratical.
But by their fruits ye shall know them. What
has the reformed House (according to the Duke
of Wellington, a democratical assembly of the
worst kind) proposed to do, and what has it done?
It was in a difficult and unfortunate position, inasmuch as the most exaggerated expectations
were excited in the people; and still more critical
seems the position of the Whig ministry between
Tories and Radicals. But in spite of these disadvantages, there has been nothing of that con-
vulsion, that overthrow of all order, which many
predicted; on the contrary, much has been
effected, which, though at the time denounced as
destructive by the opposition, is now approved by
Peel and Wellington.

One of the most important, and, at the same time, most difficult problems was, the measures to be adopted with regard to Ireland. Two ministries have already been wrecked upon this rock, and more will share their fate, until a perfect civil and religious equality be established. It is indisputable that, in 1832, the government was not sufficiently strong or vigilant; and the country must have fallen back into utter barbarism, if some energetic measures had not been taken Scarcely, however, was the determination to maintain order by the severest means known, when a very general return to it was made, and it was only found necessary to put the new regulations in execution in the county of Kilkenny : with what results, the following figures will show. In January, 1832, the number of violent outrages committed there was 196; in February, 178; in March, 144 : on the 10th of April the new law was promulgated, and the number of outrages brought before the courts fell to 47, and, in May, to 15. Some excellent reforms were also introduced into the juries, the schools, and the administration of the county cess : an important law on tithes was lost by the opposition of the Tories, as I have told you elsewhere.

The new Bank charter, the abolition of the East India Company's monopoly, and of West India slavery, (all of which the adversaries of ministers either definitively opposed, or tried to postpone to an indefinite future,) are three measures not only of decisive importance for England, but beneficial, both in theory and in practice, to the whole human race. To the enlightened and liberal men composing this ministry is the country also indebted for the boldness and firmness with which they grappled with the poor-laws,—that cancer concerning which so much had been written and spoken, but which no vigorous and earnest attempt had been made to cure. Other measures, which as yet there have not been time or opportunity to bring forward, or which are only in preparation,—such as the introduction of local courts, the establishment of a regular system of registration, (which is utterly wanting in England,) the reform of the church, of corporations, and universities ; these, and other ameliorations will inevitably follow, and will in time complete the great fabric of improved institutions, which it is the appropriate business and duty of a reformed Parliament to demand and to construct. It was impossible to do everything at once ; but even if we disapprove the measures, we must admire the industry. The Parliament sat for a hundred and forty days, nine hours a-day, on an average ; and if, on the one hand, some members were absent, or irregular in their attendance, on the other, many had to work in the committees, and to prepare the matters for debate.

There are two important points which I might pass over in silence, until they assume a more decided and substantial form. But as I might be thought to shut my eyes, designedly, to impending dangers, I volunteer a mention of them : —these are, Annual Parliaments and the Ballot.

The advocates for annual parliaments very

truly assert, that this is the original form of parliament, and that in the earliest times, elections for three, much less for seven years, were not thought of. But it by no means follows that this form is suited to totally altered circumstances. On the other hand, there is just as complete an absence of all those grounds upon which was founded the extension of the duration of Parliament from three years to seven. And, in fact, as twenty-three Parliaments have been summoned since that time, the average duration has been practically reduced to five years.

It appears to me that annual parliaments and annual elections would be extremely unfavourable to the cause of good government in England, for conclusive reasons which I cannot go into here. It is, indeed, a question which it is very unimportant to discuss or to decide; since there is more reason now to complain of the shortness than the length of parliaments.

A more doubtful question, and one by no means so easily settled, is that of ballot, or secrecy of suffrage. This was discussed in Parliament in December, 1830.

[Here follows a brief abstract of the Debate.]

On the 25th of April, 1833, it was again brought before the House by Mr. Grote *.

[Another abstract of the Debate.]

Mr. Grote's motion was lost by a majority of 211 to 106. The question, however, will continue to be agitated and to be re-produced, so long as the " influence" of which Sir Robert Peel is the

* Hansard, xvii., 611.

champion is so often exercised in a tyrannical and pernicious manner. Both forms,—open suffrage and secret suffrage—have their peculiar disadvantages, nor will the remedy for these be found in form alone; the substance must be altered. On which side the evils are the lightest is a question not to be decided in general, and without reference to time and place. Certainly those who have not the courage to choose a member of an academy or a club, by open voting, have no right to call the ballot radical and revolutionary.

Still less fortunate as to comprehensiveness or freedom of intellectual vision are those who, as Cardinal Richelieu said, look at the world through the mouth of a glass bottle and predict its ruin because all looks dark within. To sages of this sort—(have you not a few in Berlin ?)—Great Britain is an abomination, a poisonous abyss, ruined, impotent, without influence, a blank spot in the map of Europe.

I, on the contrary, see this great nation resolutely bent on ridding herself of all her imperfections. The wasteful expenditure of her government,—the corrupting influence of her poor-laws,—the stain of slavery,—the restrictions on commerce,—the intolerance of her church,—the narrowness, the prejudice, the bigotry of her schools and universities: nay, even were she to fall once more into the violence and disorder of the times between 1640 and 1660, yet those times were not without fruit, or without a principle of new and better life; neither would these be so.   There is

nothing in the elements before us which affords
any certain prognostic of inevitable decay.

I live, therefore, in the hope that England
will not want skilful steersmen to pilot her
through this rocky channel; whence she will come
forth greater and mightier than ever; to the
wonder of those who now understand her not,
and to the salvation of the continent from the
dangers of the East and of the West.

END OF VOL. I.

LONDON: Printed by WILLIAM CLOWES and SONS, Stamford Street.